D0803475

D

# SECRETS OF THE
# CAVE OF LETTERS

Cave of Letters in the cliffs above. (G. Brubacher/COL Project)

# SECRETS OF THE
# CAVE OF LETTERS

Rediscovering a
Dead Sea Mystery

## RICHARD A. FREUND

Director, Maurice Greenberg Center for Judaic Studies
University of Hartford

## Humanity
## Books

an imprint of Prometheus Books
59 John Glenn Drive, Amherst, New York 14228-2197

Published 2004 by Humanity Books, an imprint of Prometheus Books

Inquiries should be addressed to
Humanity Books
59 John Glenn Drive
Amherst, New York 14228–2197
VOICE: 716–691–0133, ext. 207
FAX: 716–564–2711

08 07 06 05 04   5 4 3 2 1

Library of Congress Cataloging-in-Publication Data

Freund, Richard A.
    Secrets of the Cave of Letters : rediscovering a Dead Sea mystery / by Richard A. Freund.
        p. cm.
    Includes bibliographical references and index.
    ISBN 1–59102–205–3
    1. Letters, Cave of the (Israel). 2. Copper scroll. 3. Bar Kokhba, d. 135.
4. Jews—History—168 B.C.–135 A.D. 5. Excavations (Archaeology)—Israel.
6. Excavations (Archaeology)—Judea, Wilderness of 7. Israel—Antiquities.
8. Judaea, Wilderness of—Antiquities. I. Title.

DS110.L37F74 2004
956.94'02—dc22

2004001119

Printed in the United States of America on acid-free paper

To my wife and life-partner,
*Eliane Goldgaber Freund,*
who inspired me to go to the Cave of Letters
and is my modern-day Babatha

# Contents

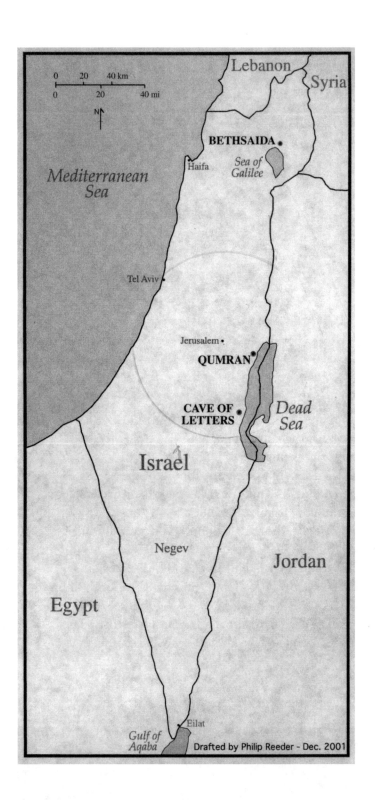

# Preface

T his is a book about archaeology, but it is also a book about discovery. It is a book for beginners in archaeology and the history of the region. While it does not require you to be an expert in ancient history, it is important to keep in mind a few time periods, so I will provide short synopses of the history or history of ideas of a period and some short definitions of information contained in each chapter. To begin with, archaeology is the science of excavating (literally: "digging") for the past (hence: archaeo- = ancient and logos = study of). Today archaeology is done by taking each layer of accumulated debris off, inch by inch (centimeter by centimeter), and establishing the stratigraphy or historical layer at which an identifiable object (pottery, metal, vessel, etc.) is found. Most people wonder how we can date a particular layer or stratum. This is generally done in three different ways. The first way is through an absolute date on an object (some of the letters that were found in the Cave of Letters, for example, were dated!). Coins have dates as well (coinage began only some 2,500 years ago, but after that it becomes relevant). The second way to date a stratum is the comparative manner. This is also the most common. Certain other sites have been dated and certain objects were found at a site that is dated, so any of the objects at that level are considered to be part of that same period. Pottery styles in antiquity, like hair and dress styles today, do not change very quickly and therefore are an excellent source for dating and very common. We can generally tell a lot from the common pottery, the "pots and pans" approach to dating archaeology. Finally, there is the modern scientific analysis known as carbon 14 that you will read about in this book. It is a reliable way to date organic matter. Since carbon is one of the elements that has a well known and trackable decomposition rate, a test was developed about fifty years ago for analyzing the carbon in organic remains found at a specific archaeological stratum. It is not a perfect test, since it generally has a broad + or – factor, but the more you know about a site, the specific elements of a layer and the use of all three dating techniques together makes the C-14 test (as it is known) more accurate.

Archaeology is done by actually digging and finding objects in the ground and analyzing them, but it is also done in laboratories and libraries by a wide variety of specialists who are employed in the pursuit of analyzing the place and the objects using a set of archaeological methods that have been pioneered in the past century and a half. Most of these methods have been revolutionized in the past half century, but one of the newest innovations has been the integration of other disciplines that were seemingly asking distinct questions about other bodies of information. In this book you will learn that all of this information is interrelated and these other disciplines can be used in the service of archaeology to clarify the field of study known as the archaeological site.

Geology, geography, and especially geophysics are subspecialties you will read about in the first chapter. Geology is the study of the earth (Geo- = earth and logos = study of). In reality geology is the study of the way the earth is formed. Geoscientists, similar to archaeologists, are analyzing a specific site and how it has been affected by the forces (both natural and human/cultural) exerted upon the earth. Geography, specifically the mapping of all of the elements present in an environment, is crucial to the long-term tracking and under-standing of any archaeological or physical site. If archaeologists tell us what a site is (and was in antiquity), a geologist tells us how it came to be what it is and a geographer insures that we have a precise notion of where exactly that place is. A geophysicist, a subspecialty of geology, asks theoretical questions about the forces that created the site and attempts to answer those questions with modeling of different kinds. In this chapter we will present a "secret" about using allied sciences together to solve questions about archaeology. Geologists, geogra-phers, and geophysicists have worked together in archaeological exca-vations before our project. This is not new. Our "secret" was that these allied sciences were used first (before excavation) and they were used to help discover the archaeology, and we were constantly con-sulting them not simply to understand the geological history of the site but to ask new and previously unimagined questions about gath-ering information at the site. Since we began our work in the Cave of Letters we have employed our "secret" at six other sites in the Israel with amazing success. Each site has provided new insights into how the future of archaeology will look when we integrate the vast array of other specialists into a totally integrated archaeology.

Archaeology, geology, geophysics, and geography are all sciences and therefore make use of logic, critical thinking, inference, hypoth-esis, and all other parts of the modern scientific method that has been around since the time of Descartes. This method is extremely impor-tant in the study of biblical archaeology and archaeology linked to bib-lically and religiously associated literatures. Before the modern period, all science was dependent upon divinely revealed information that, in an earlier age, was science. Most of the "truths" about the world were revealed in this manner to divinely inspired individuals or religious officials who often were the only repository of information about the world. The modern scientific method changed all that, and the type of biblical archaeology that is in this book deals with this change. By care-fully employing this scientific methodology it is possible to discern new understandings about the Bible and other religious literatures through the integration of archaeology at sites associated with the lit-erature. That is one of the most intriguing parts of this book and is one of the "secrets" of the Cave of Letters, precisely because this cave is associated with parts of the religious and biblical past.

New scientific technologies have been pioneered in the past quarter century that are now used by archaeology to analyze the place (called "the site") and objects (called "artifacts"), but the purpose of archaeology has always been the same: to reconstruct the original cultural, religious, and socioeconomic environment (called "the setting") in which the objects were found and to create the setting from a careful analysis of the objects. When available, written histories of the time are important. The interpretation of a site and the reinterpretation of the literature must proceed parallel to each other.

In chapter 1 you will begin to understand how science begins to uncover part of a story in one place and finds itself drawn to another. It is also a story about people and how even scientists are people who are drawn to one particular story over another, and about how even though the scientific method is objective, its application is subjective. One famous idea is that somehow the stones and artifacts of an archaeological site speak for themselves. In fact, the interpretation of stones, architecture, textiles, coins, and other artifacts requires people creating hypotheses and each subjectively defending his or her point of view because it makes more sense than other competing views of these artifacts. This is one of the "secrets" of archaeology, and especially of this cave. The artifacts and site do not speak for themselves; they require interpretation.

One of the biggest "secrets" of chapter 1 is how one begins an excavation. We began the Cave of Letters differently than we began other excavations. One reason for beginning an excavation is curiosity. We have in surface archaeology (as opposed to cave archaeology) an archaeological site, sometimes called by the Arabic and Hebrew word *Tel* (literally "mound") that is a solitary feature on the landscape that does not fit in with the natural geological features of the area. The Tel does not blend in with the rest of the natural landscape and is therefore obviously artificial. This is the result of human habitation. People choose to live at a certain site because there are basic needs that are fulfilled at that site. Natural roads and walking paths for trade and travel, drinking water, and some type of livelihood or places for grazing and/or subsistence farming. For villages and cities this all makes sense. Every generation may decide to build or rebuild over the top of another existing layer with a new architectural feature and reuse the same buildings and site multiple times. Sometimes this is simply part of the life of a village or the growth of a city, but sometimes it is because a site becomes abandoned at a certain point, and later another group comes and reuses the site because it still has the basic elements for human habitation. At a certain point people may decide to abandon a site because of natural disasters like fire, famine, floods, and earthquakes, human disasters like war, or because water and/or livelihood have been disturbed or have become outmoded. All of this creates new stratigraphic layers one on top of another, and often the building materials will be used for thousands of years, making for complicated interpretation. People did not create their cities or habitation sites for archaeologists to dig up. They created them in order to facilitate their lifestyles. These lifestyles are unpredictable; that factor makes it more difficult to interpret the site.

We began in the north of Israel at a site known as Bethsaida with a group of colleagues excavating a city on the Sea of Galilee. After seventeen years of excavations at the city of Bethsaida, we think we know how the six different historical layers or strata happened. We were drawn to a cave in the south of Israel with our specialists excavating a site in the Judean Desert near the Dead Sea because of something that we discovered at Bethsaida. When in doubt as to the locations, refer to the map in the front of the book. Each of these sites has common historical elements, so it is necessary to know something about the history that connects them.

Although this is not a history text book there are few historical markers that are key to understanding the archaeology. Israel is a small country (the size of New Jersey) with different regions that possess different characteristics but are all associated with most of biblical history. It was a bridge between the great kingdoms of antiquity, Mesopotamia and Egypt. The north of Israel, Galilee, has a biblical history that stretches from the time of King David, approximately 1000 BCE (known by archaeologists as the Iron Age), through the well-known period of the New Testament in the first century CE (in this book we will use BCE = *Before the Common Era* for the designation BC/Before Christ and CE = *Common Era* for AD/Anno Domini). This period parallels part of the foundational history of both Judaism and Christianity. In Galilee the Apostles and Jesus met in the Roman period and formulated the beginnings of their movement. The main history of this book takes place during just over one hundred years of the Roman period, approximately 25–135 CE. It encapsulates the rise of the Jesus movement and the Apostles in Galilee, the First Rebellion (or First Revolt) against the Romans and the destruction of Jerusalem (66–70 CE), and the Second Rebellion against the Romans (or Second Revolt, 132–135 CE). Galilee was a place of great religious foment from the ancient period and was where the beginnings of the movements for national and spiritual revolution were sown.

A word about the terminology of the chronology or time line is necessary. Archaeologists and geoscientists use different sorts of chronological terminology. Archaeologists prefer to use a combination of historical and cultural designations together with technological advances. For example, archaeologists generally use the designations Chalcolithic Period (4500–3200 BCE), Bronze Age (3200–1200 BCE), and Iron Age (1200–586 BCE), but these divisions are sometimes based upon technological advancements (and other times upon conventions) in the use of new materials combined with major events in the region. It is generally thought that the Israelites moved from Egypt around 1200 BCE, and that the Temple of Jerusalem was destroyed by the Babylonians in 586 BCE. These periods are followed by the Persian period (536–332 BCE), the Greek period (333–63 BCE), the Roman period (63 BCE–325 BCE), the Byzantine period (325–638 CE), the first Muslim period (638–1096), the Crusades (1096–1200 CE) and so on. Geologists generally use a much more general term for the most recent period of human history (the last five thousand years) and have developed terminology for the tens of thousands and hundreds of thousands of years that came before our human history. I have placed a simple chronology in the front of the book to help keep things straight. My point here is that the periods are based upon the combination of historical guidepoints and technological advancements. Much of the history relates to Jewish, Christian, and

Muslim events in the Middle East. This is appropriate because this is part of the problem of Israeli archaeology.

Israel is a country unlike any other in the Middle East, not only because of the events that have occurred there, but also because archaeology has been employed there on so many sites that it is possible to go back and compare and contrast the work of several generations of archaeologists. We can look at the work of one excavator in one period, who employed a series of methods and hypotheses, and learn why he or she reached a particular conclusion. This is what we shall do in this book. We will compare and contrast the results of the most famous archaeologists of Israel, Yohanan Aharoni (d. 1976) and Yigael Yadin (d. 1984), who did the first excavations at the Cave of Letters in the 1950s and 1960s respectively. The rare opportunity that we have in this book is to recognize the work of others and to see how work can be redone with new and startling results. We expect that the same will be done someday with our own work. You will learn how one site can be excavated multiple times with different results.

In chapter 1 I will tell you how I began to unravel the "secrets" of the Cave of Letters by starting at the beginning, how I came to excavate there. I think that people are interested in why one site is chosen for excavation over another and why one particular site holds so much promise. The "secrets" we discovered were as much about what we discovered about ourselves and the people who had been there before us as they were about what was found inside the cave.

# Acknowledgments

I am first and foremost indebted to Yigael Yadin and Yohanan Aharoni for the concept of this book. This book is intended for the nonspecialist in archaeology and history and is not intended to be in place of the more common, academic tome that we are working to produce in the coming years. Any errors that have occurred in the reporting of the data in this book are my responsibility alone and I hope will be ably corrected in the course of the publication of our scholarly research volumes. The results presented here, however, are the data that these scholars have collected and was reported to me either orally or in writing through interim reports, lectures, and conferences in geology, geography, religion, history, and archaeology. Scholars have heard most of these lectures in international, national, and regional conferences, but we all felt that the information and what we learned was valuable for the public to read about.

The research volumes on the Cave of Letters that we are working on include highly technical articles by the scholars who did the work themselves, and their work will be presented for serious scrutiny in due course.

This volume follows a precedent that was started by Yohanan Aharoni in Hebrew and followed later by Yigael Yadin in Hebrew and in English. They both created popular books for the general public to enjoy about their excavations before the publication of the scholarly results, and it was Yadin especially who established himself with an English language public.

Yohanan Aharoni, who with Beno Rothenberg wrote the book entitled *In the Footsteps of Kings and Rebels* ([Hebrew] Tel Aviv: Masadah Press, 1960), set the pattern. This book was an immediate best-seller in Israel and created a way for nonspecialists to read about the discoveries and enjoy the contributions archaeology is making to the understanding of the history of ancient Israel. It was followed by Yigael Yadin's popular book in English about the excavations at Masada entitled *Masada: Herod's Fortress and the Zealot's Last Stand* (New York: Random House, 1966 and subsequently into a variety of languages), later by *Bar Kokhba* (London: Weidenfeld and Nicolson, 1971) and even later by *Hazor: The Rediscovery of a Great Citadel of the Bible* (New York: Random House, 1975). There were, of course, other popular books in Hebrew and other languages, but here were the top archaeologists of Israel writing popular books for the general public. The books were directed toward both Israel and the English reading world, in order to raise the understanding of archaeology and the history of ancient and modern Israel for the general and Israeli public.

Yadin and Aharoni wrote popular books and articles about their excavations, and then the research volumes on these sites were finished much later. Yadin's popular book on the Cave of Letters inspired hundreds of thousands of readers worldwide, including me, when I read it as a student over thirty years ago.

In the case of the academic research volumes on the Cave of Letters a bibliography is provided at the end of the book, but the reader is encouraged to purchase the scholarly three-volume set *The Finds from the Bar Kokhba Period in the Cave of Letters*, published by the Israel Exploration Society, that was only completed in 2002, over forty years after the excavations conducted by Yadin were completed. Similarly, the findings of the Yadin excavations at Masada that were conducted in 1963–65 were published in a popular volume authored by Yadin, and the scholarly publications of the finds of Masada are ongoing.

Over the seventeen years since the excavations at Bethsaida began, I knew that we were engaged in an important enterprise. It has been an education for all of us involved in the Bethsaida Excavations Project Consortium housed at the University of Nebraska at Omaha (UNO) and our teacher on this educational journey has been from the beginning, Dr. Rami Arav. Rami is the rare hands-on archaeologist who teaches by "doing" in the field. He is an archaeologist created in the image of Yadin and Aharoni, and has honed his pedagogical skills over the years to make him a master educator as well as a field archaeologist. He has not only educated a generation of students (over five thousand and counting) in the hundreds of groups who have participated in the excavations, but also inspired an entire generation of textual scholars and historians who have participated with us in the field. Rami is happiest in the field, but he is equally at ease in the library researching a topic. He has been my collaborator in the excavations at Bethsaida and at the Cave of Letters, and he has given me the confidence to pursue other excavation projects around Israel with other collaborators. I have consulted with him on issues related to Qumran, Nazareth, and Yavne, and his wisdom has allowed many of the experts to go to the field with a renewed sense of purpose. In all the other archaeological projects our staff worked on in Israel, we all came to appreciate more and more the unique qualities of Dr. Arav. Working in Israel as a foreigner is not easy even for those of us who speak Hebrew well. In the case of Bethsaida and the Cave of Letters, to have a foreign university (especially ones in Nebraska and Hartford, CT) completely administrate, excavate, and publish the results of excavations in some of the most important locations of Israel is rare. We have done it in near record time in a variety of media, from lectures at national and international conferences, articles in the popular and more scholarly publications, to books, CDs, Web sites, and documentaries. The difficulties of creating a project ex nihilo at Bethsaida and continuing year after year to build it into a tourist and historical site of importance to Jews and Christians worldwide needs vision. Rami has a vision of Israeli archaeology that allowed him not to be afraid to redo the work of one of his idols, Yigael Yadin. I want to thank Rami both for these years of service to the Bethsaida Excavations Project and the Cave of Letters Project, and for his vision of archaeology that has benefited Israeli archaeology in ways too numerous to name.

I would also like to acknowledge the role of Wendi Chiarbos, coordinator of the Bethsaida Excavations Project, who helped coordinate the preparations for the excavations in the Cave of Letters. Wendi began as a student at UNO and became a colleague. Wendi coordinated many of the details for filming the first television documentary on the Cave of Letters, *Return to the Cave of Letters*, a project done by UNO TV. When I moved to the University of Hartford, the University embraced the excavations projects as a natural extension of the Maurice Greenberg Center for Judaic Studies. The president, Walter Harrison, and the chair of the Regents, Arnold Greenberg, made sure that we had the funding and the administrative support we needed. The administrative assistant, Susan Gottlieb, made sure that the work of Bethsaida and the Cave of Letters were immediately integrated into the Center, and she is credited with much of the general editing of this work. In addition, I need to fully acknowledge the early editing of this book by Julia McCord, an excellent religion reporter in Omaha, Nebraska, who understands (much better than I do!) how the general public reads about religion. Others have read parts of the text as well, but Julia helped me correct the original "academic" style into a more authentic voice. At Humanity Books, I would like to thank editors Ann O'Hear and Mary A. Read for encouraging me to give more general information, bibliographies, and the reference guide. Thank you also to Nicholas A. Read, who copyedited my book and provided some important insights into the way to best express some of the more complex elements in the book.

This book is more than just a book. It is a book that accompanies filmed versions of all our work. The first television documentary made about our work was filmed by UNO TV and was aired on Nebraska ETV in 2000. This original film was a collaboration between the University of Nebraska at Omaha and the University of Hartford's Maurice Greenberg Center for Judaic Studies. The innovative nature of UNO TV is a part of the collaborations between our archaeological staff and the this excellent television staff. We have done four projects together in Israel and the Middle East, *The Lost City of Bethsaida*, *The Shrine and the Scrolls*, *Return to the Cave of Letters*, and most recently, *The Road to Morocco*. All these documentaries have won prizes in national competitions and were exciting and innovative. Filming in a foreign country is not easy. Filming an archaeological site and resolving difficult historical and archaeological questions in a fifty-six-minute production requires skill and a more than rudimentary grasp of multiple cultural and religious histories, textual traditions, and archaeology. UNO TV has dedicated individuals who were willing to take enormous risks to film these movies in extremely difficult conditions in Israel over the years. I thank the manager of UNO TV, Debra Aliano, assistant manager Jim Adams, and the producers who made these productions possible: Gary Repair, David Rotterman, camera work by Cecilia Barton and Carl Milone, Mark Dale, and soundman Steve O'Gorman. The Israel Museum's Adolfo Roitman, Amalyah Keshet, and the director of the Israel Museum, James Snyder, for allowing us to film at the Shrine of the Book made the backdrop of the Cave of Letters exhibit accessible.

For those who would like more information, please see the Web sites of the Bethsaida Excavations Project, Nebraska ETV, the Shrine of the Book, and the University of Hartford's Greenberg Center. The Web site of the Cave of Letters, developed by Chris Morton, at www.uwec.edu/col will give the reader all of the information on the daily work of the excavations in 2000.

The Greenberg Center is responsible for helping find donors to underwrite some of the costs of making the UNO TV production of *Return to the Cave of Letters*. In particular I want to thank Stanley and Sylvia Leven of West Hartford, who provided the final funding for this film project. Stanley, a longtime board member of the Greenberg Center, was a real aficionado of biblical archaeology and met every major Israeli archaeologist over the years. He passed away in 2001 and his memory continues to be maintained by scholarships for students who study archaeology on our programs during the summer.

Another acknowledgment is necessary for the University of

Nebraska at Omaha's International Studies and Programs and its dean, Thomas Gouttierre, who through thick and thin has helped the archaeology projects continue at UNO. Gouttierre, who is better known for his work in Afghanistan, never lost sight of the importance of our archaeology programs and helped us achieve the successes of Bethsaida and the Cave of Letters. Chancellors Nancy Belck and Del Weber at UNO, the president of the University of Nebraska, Dennis Smith, and our "special" Regent and unofficial cheerleader, Nancy O'Brien, also deserve high praise in allowing these excavations to go forward. Special thanks are also due for Margie Scribante for her help on the Bethsaida Project and indirectly on the original Cave of Letters project. The original project was aided by utilizing the human resources of the Bethsaida Excavations Project, its artist, Dreanna Hadash, its restoration specialist, Charleen Green, and our photographers, including Ophir Palmon. The photographer for the 2000 John and Carol Merrill Excavations was Andrew Liakos, whose photographs are a unique part of the scientific research. Many companies were instrumental in helping us with equipment. Peter Annan Sensors & Software, Ltd., provided us with state-of-the-art high-frequency ground penetrating radar equipment, Onset computers for the equipment for our climatic study of the cave (that will appear in our scientific volume) and especially Robert Randhare at Olympus Industrial need to be mentioned. Olympus provided us with state-of-the-art industrial fiberscoping equipment for the excavations, which was a huge improvement over the medical colonoscope we used in the 1999 excavations!

The 2000 and 2001 John and Carol Merrill Excavations have the Merrills and Hershel Shanks to thank. Most of the work that you see here was meticulously recorded day after day by my assistant and colleague, Carl Savage of Drew University, and a digital record was kept by our computer specialist and geography assistant, Chris Morton. I especially want to acknowledge the work that Carl Savage contributed to the overall book, because he helped me recall nearly every detail at night and in the field. The entire staff includes many people who worked tirelessly in the cave with us and did not receive specific mention in the book, including the students of Professor Gordon Brubacher from Doane College, Laura and Denise Kraus and Karen Weatherman. Our team included a variety of experts, including classical historian Mark Smith of Albertson College; Jim Webster from the University of Georgia, who was assistant to Phil Reeder's geography team; Walter (Chip) Bouzard of Wartburg; Shachar Argov, who ran our hydraulic splitter in the 2001 excavations; and Paul Bauman's company, Komex International Ltd., provided him with an assistant, Matt Schuett, to help in the day-to-day work. We need to also thank the others who came during the course of the excavations and helped us, school age and experienced climbers, and archaeologists from all around Israel. The Parks and Nature Reserve Authority rangers provided all of the invited guests with help in negotiating the difficult turns from place to place.

A few words must be added to the acknowledgments about Baruch Safrai and Pinchas Porat in the book. They are mentioned frequently in the book, so I do not feel I need to retell their roles, but Baruch Safrai is the person who really encouraged Rami and me to do the excavations. I think we would have been happy to just rework the already existing findings of Yadin and Aharoni without reexcavating. Safrai encouraged us to do more. To him I offer my personal thanks. Pinchas Porat, who worked with us at Bethsaida for years, is also one of the great motivators of the reexcavations in the Cave of Letters after we discovered the incense shovel at Bethsaida in 1996 and were looking for an archaeological parallel. This is standard operating procedure in identifying and dating your finds. It was Porat who said he knew where we could find a good parallel. It turned out that this was key to our entire research. He personally had found a similar incense shovel in the Cave of Letters Excavations of Yadin and right there on the spot even gave us the references! We had the book on the shelf and he immediately flipped to the page, and it was a single moment that I will never forget. The photograph in Yadin's book looked exactly like the artifact we had found, and he had been the person who had discovered it thirty-five years before! Pinchas was a humble man, whose work in the cave was caught on film in the 1960s and again by our team in the 1990s. Despite being seriously ill at the time, he climbed to the Cave of Letters to participate in a day of excavations in July 2000. He passed away in 2002, and I know that I speak for many in saying that he will be missed.

Mostly these acknowledgments are for the people who do not receive mention in the book. Amir Drori, former director general of the Antiquities Authority of Israel, encouraged us to return to the Cave. Drori, who had himself excavated in the Cave of Letters with Yadin, intimately understood the importance of our work and we are indebted to him for his consultations. The present director general of the Israel Antiquities Authority, Shuka Dorfman, encouraged this work as well, because he has the vision to realize that the technological advances that we used in the Cave of Letters could be used in many other archaeological contexts. I would also like to acknowledge the input of Uzi Dahari, Hava Katz, Gidon Avni, Baruch Brandl, David Amit, Orit Shamir, Peninah Shor, and Donald Ariel, all of the Israel Antiquity Authority, for a variety of research, permits, insights, and consultations that they provided in the course of the excavations. These are the unsung heroes of Israeli archaeology because they toil daily to insure that the work is done well and systematically. I would like to thank the different officials of the Parks and Nature Reserves Authority of Israel and its director of science in 2000, Dr. Avi Pervolotsky, the head of archaeology, Dr. Zvika Zuk, and the Parks and Nature Reserves officials who helped us in the field and who are mentioned throughout. The Parks and Nature Reserves of Israel protect and preserve enormous properties (and the flora and fauna inside them) that stretch from one end of the country to the other and especially large desert reserves that often appear to people to be devoid of riches. These natural resources of the desert are so unique and so fragile that they need our constant protection and deserve our admiration for the work they do. The longer we spent in this famous Judean desert, the more I came to understand why my ancestors were drawn to the desert so often throughout our history, but I also came to respect the work of this Authority in Israel.

※　　　※　　　※

In 2000, Gary Hochman of Nebraska ETV proposed to do a television documentary that would actually showcase the scientific contribution of our work in the Cave of Letters and tell the story of the Second Rebellion. That television production by the *NOVA* science series is what motivated me to write this book. During the course of the filming of the two weeks of excavations in 2000 and three days in 2001, and then subsequently at follow-up sessions that they filmed, I was forced to continually refine my understanding of what we were doing. Many of us came together for a special conference in February 2002 to discuss these issues in sessions open to the public. It was an exciting conference chaired by Dr. Larry Schiffman and did much to further public debate on what the Cave of Letters could still reveal. The conference, held at New York University and sponsored by the Skirball Center and the Greenberg Center of the University of Hartford, also was filmed and became a part of the *NOVA* documentary.

The television documentary forced us to think about the implications of the finds from the Cave of Letters in ways that scholars are rarely asked to do in the midst of doing the work. I have to thank them for forcing us to do this on camera. This self-reflective process allows us to make scholarship more accessible for a larger audience. I applaud their efforts and hope that this book will supplement their documentary for the interested viewer.

Finally, I need to acknowledge Drs. Steven I. Firshein, Michael T. Lawlor, and Robert J. Soiffer and the nurses of Hartford Hospital and the Dana-Farber Cancer Institute without whose work and care during these past six months this book would not have been completed.

# Chronology

| | |
|---|---|
| 5500–4500 BCE: | The Neolithic (Stone) Age; pottery was introduced |
| 4500–3200 BCE: | 1. The Chalcolithic (Copper) Age; copper and flint used<br>2. Writing developed in Mesopotamia |
| 3200–1200 BCE | Bronze Age (Early, Middle and Late) |
| 1200–586 BCE | Iron Age (From the Exodus from Egypt until the destruction of the First Temple by the Babylonians in 586 BCE) |
| 586–539 BCE | Babylonian Exile |
| 546–333 BCE | Persian Period |
| 333–63 BCE | Greek Period |
| 63 BCE–325 CE | Roman Period |
| 325–638 CE | Byzantine Period |
| 638–1096 CE | Early Muslim Period |
| 1100–1200 CE | Crusader Period |
| 1200–1517 CE | Later Muslim Period (Mamluk) |
| 1517–1917 CE | Ottoman Empire Period |

1917–1948 CE    British Mandate Period
1948–Present    Modern Israel Period

## THE HISTORY OF ANCIENT, MEDIEVAL, AND MODERN ISRAEL

1800–1500 BCE:    1. Matriarchs and Patriarchs
    2. Abraham in Mesopotamia

1300–1200 BCE:    1. Exodus from Egypt, Moses, Conquest of Canaan
    2. Saul, First King of Israel (1020–1000)

1000–922 BCE:    1. United Monarchy of David and Solomon; 12 tribes and building of the First Temple by Solomon; after the death of Solomon, Israel is divided into two parts: Northern Kingdom of ten tribes and two tribes in the Southern Kingdom (including Jerusalem)
    2. Rehoboam, King of Judah (Southern Kingdom) and Jeroboam I, King of Israel (Northern Kingdom)

600–500 BCE:    1. Fall of Jerusalem; destruction of First (Solomonic) Temple by Babylonian King Nebuchadnezzar; Babylonian Exile of the Judeans (587/6 BCE)
    2. Cyrus the Great—Persian Conquest of Babylon (539 BCE) and Return of some exiles from Babylon
    3. Rebuilding of Temple completed 515 BCE

500–400 BCE:    1. Ezra arrives in Israel from Persia to oversee return 445 CE
    2. Editing of Hebrew Bible

400–323 BCE:     1. Alexander the Great's (Greek) conquests (333–323 BCE)

2. After Alexander the Great's death: Ptolemy I Greek King of South (Egypt) and Seleucus, Greek King at Babylon

323 BCE–70 CE:    1. Hellenistic/Greco-Roman Period

2. Septuagint: Greek translation of the Hebrew Bible (250 BCE)

3. The Maccabean Revolt against the Seleucid Greek King, Antiochus Epiphanes IV (164 BCE)

4. Hasmonean Jewish Rulers: Judah Maccabee (166–160 BCE)

5. John Hyrcanus I (135–104)

6. Alexandra Salome, Queen of Judea (76–67 BCE). In 63 BCE, Pompey, a general of the Roman army, marches into Jerusalem and establishes Roman hegemony in Judea.

7. Herod the Great (37–4 BCE). The four sects of the Jews: Pharisees, Sadducees, Essenes, and Zealots contend for authority in Judaism. Essenes are associated with the site of Qumran on the Dead Sea. Zealots later become the nationalist, military party that urges freedom from the Romans.

8. Herod's Kingdom divided among his sons, Archeleus in Judea (4 BCE–6 CE), Antipas in Galilee (4 BCE–39 CE), and Philip in Ituraea and Golan 4 BCE–34 CE)

9. Jesus of Nazareth (6 BCE–30 CE) and his movement.

10. Early Roman Emperors:
Caesar Augustus, 31 BCE–14 CE
Tiberius, 14–37
Caligula, 37–41

Claudius, 41–54
Nero, 54–68
year of the four emperors, 69
Vespasian, 69–79
Titus, 79–81
Domitian, 81–96
Nerva, 96–98
Trajan, 98–117
Hadrian, 117–138

11. Procurators ruling Judea 6–41 CE: Pontius Pilate (26–36 CE)
12. Paul's travels and death (50–early 60s CE)
13. The First Jewish Revolt against Rome begins in Galilee (66–73 CE). Ends with capture of Masada
14. Qumran is destroyed by Romans as they proceed to Jerusalem (68 CE). The Dead Sea Scrolls are placed in the caves around Qumran
15. Destruction of Second Temple of Jerusalem (70 CE)
16. Written accounts of Jesus' life and teachings and the writing of the New Testament
17. Rise of Rabbinic Judaism
18. Writings of Philo of Alexander (Egypt) and Josephus Flavius (Rome)

100–200 CE:

1. Rise of Christianity
2. The Sanhedrin and the rabbinic academy meets in Yavne, Usha, Shefaram, then to Bet Shearim in Galilee after the Bar Kokhba Rebellion (70–180 CE)
3. Trajan (Emperor 98–117 CE) conquers the Nabateans. Jewish Revolt in Babylon and Judea put down by Trajan's General Lusius Quietus (115 CE)

4. The Second Revolt against Rome: The Bar Kokhba Rebellion (132–135 CE) during the reign of Hadrian (117–138)
5. Beruriah, famous rabbinic wife of Rabbi Meir
6. Babatha's documents are deposited in the Cave of Letters (135 CE)
7. The Temple Mount of Jerusalem is converted into a Roman temple and the name of Jerusalem changed to Aelia Capitolina; the name of Judea and Israel, in general, is changed to Palestine by Rome

200–300 CE:
1. Earliest rabbinic texts are edited by Rabbi Judah HaNasi at Sepphoris in Galilee at San-hearin there
2. Political status given to Jews and Christians in parts of the Roman Empire (212 CE: Edict of Caracalla)
3. Rabbinic texts: Mishnah, Tosefta, Midrashei-Halachah: (Tannaim) redacted
4. Rabbinic Academy established in Babylon (Nehardea)

300–400 CE:
1. Roman Emperor Constantine becomes Christian
2. Church Council of Nicaea (325)
3. Earliest documentation of settlements of Jews in Europe
4. Palestine: The Sanhedrin and Rabbinic Academy is moved to Tiberias. In Babylon, Rabbinical Academies flourish (or are built) in Nehardea, Sura, Pumbedita, Netzivim (Amoraim)

400–500 CE:
1. Jerusalem Talmud (sometimes called the Palestinian Talmud or PT) is completed in

> Tiberias and the Tiberias Academy closed by Rome
> 2. The Sack of Rome by the Visigoths (410) and the Vandals (455)

500–600 CE:  1. Babylonian Talmud (BT) is completed
2. The birth of Muhammad (570 CE)

638–1096:  1. Spread of Islam to Persia, Syria, Palestine, Egypt, North Africa, Asia Minor, and Spain
2. Jewish academies and synagogues in Babylon, North Africa, western and eastern Europe
3. Two mosques, the Dome of the Rock and the Al-Aqsa Mosque, built on the Temple Mount in Jerusalem

1096–1200 CE:  1. The European Crusades (11th–12th centuries) Godfrey de Bouillon conquers Jerusalem in 1099; Latin Kingdom of Jerusalem established
2. The Jerusalem Temple Mount was converted into Templum Domini and the Dome of the Rock converted into a church with a cross on the Dome by Crusaders
3. Saladin (Salah al-Din) conquers Jerusalem (1187) and Islamic rule in Israel continues

1250–1517  1. Mamluk Muslims rule Egypt, Libya, Syria, Israel, and western Arabia
2. The Reconquest of Spain by Christianity results in the expulsion from Spain of hundreds of thousands of Muslims and Jews (1492)

1517–1917 CE:  1. Ottoman Muslims rule the region from Constantinople

2. Jerusalem is rewalled. It had been unwalled since 1219
Suleiman I (the Magnificent) builds the present walls of the city (1537–1541 CE)

1917–2003 CE:

1. 1917: Establishment of the British Mandate in Middle East and Israel
2. 1947: Discovery of the first Dead Sea Scrolls near Qumran
3. 1948: Establishment of the State of Israel
4. The five Qumran excavations conducted by Fr. Roland De Vaux (1951–1956)
5. 1952: Cave of Letters is investigated by Yohanan Aharoni; Copper Scroll is discovered in Cave #3 near Qumran
6. 1960–1961: Cave of Letters is excavated by Yigael Yadin
7. 1963–65: Masada excavated by Yadin
8. 1967: Six Day War—Israel takes the Golan, West Bank of Jordan River, Sinai, and East Jerusalem
9. 1987: Excavations at Bethsaida, Israel begun
10. 1999–2001: John and Carol Merrill Cave of Letters Project begun by R. Freund and R. Arav
11. 2001–2002: John and Carol Merrill Qumran excavations
12. 2002: Announcement of the final publication of the Dead Sea Scrolls

# 1

# Secrets of the Cave of Letters

## RETURN TO A CAVE ALMOST AS FAMOUS AS THE QUMRAN CAVES

Archaeologists return to a previously excavated site for various reasons. We returned to the Cave of Letters to test a number of hypotheses and to learn more about the man who made the cave famous, Dr. Yigael Yadin, the best-known Israeli archaeologist of the twentieth century. The Cave of Letters became the single most fruitful cave for both artifacts and writings in the history of Israeli archaeology when it was excavated by Yadin in 1960 and 1961. The John and Carol Merrill Expedition to the Cave of Letters that I planned and executed with a large bevy of scholars was conducted during 2000 and 2001 and showed that Yadin was both right—and wrong—about the cave. In these two summers we discovered much about the most famous cave ever investigated in the Judean desert and about the most well-known archaeologist of the century, how he wove what had been thought to be myth into archaeological fact, and how the cave made him into a legend.

Before Yadin there had been Yohanan Aharoni, another famous archaeologist of Israel, who had originally excavated the unknown cave in 1953. When Aharoni excavated the yet unnamed cave it was assumed that this large cave in Nahal Hever (25 miles south of Qumran) was part of the same Dead Sea Scrolls discovery story that had begun in 1947 at Qumran. The Essenes who had occupied Qumran and the Zealots who had occupied Masada (both groups from the first century CE) were assumed to have occupied other caves similar to this cave in Nahal Hever. It had all begun with Qumran and the first Dead Sea Scrolls in 1947, and discoveries had continued in many other caves along the Dead Sea and Judean Desert. The assumption of a Dead Sea Scrolls/Qumran/Essenes connection changed in the Cave of Letters with the discovery of Bar Kokhba-era (second century CE) documents by the most well-known Israeli archaeologist of the century, Yigael Yadin, in 1960. Our research has revealed that the Cave of Letters is connected to Qumran and the rest of the Dead Sea Scrolls story. It is connected to both the First Rebellion against the Romans (in the first century CE—as are Qumran and the Scrolls) and the Second Rebellion against the Romans (led by Bar Kokhba in the second century CE, some sixty years later).

Although there were many finds made in the Cave of Letters excavations of 1960–61, they were all made without the benefit of many new technological advances, under extremely difficult conditions, and basically using the same archaeological techniques which had been developed a century earlier. We introduced a new method in cave research. While Yadin had to use scores of volunteers for their brute strength and individual excavating abilities, we had very few nonspecialists and used brute strength and excavating only when we knew that we had a lead on a discovery. While Yadin's efforts were centered on places where it was easiest to excavate (in the corners, where there was the least roof debris, etc.) our efforts were centered on the places which were the most difficult to excavate and where we had to depend on the technology to give us a pinpoint designation for a discovery. For the first time scholars realized that it was possible to redo the work of former excavations anywhere (but especially in caves) using technology which had been used almost exclusively in gas and oil exploration—and in the case of one of our innovations, we used a technology which has saved thousands of lives in medicine.

Our understanding of the social histories surrounding the Bar Kokhba Rebellion has changed in the forty years since Yadin's excavations. In Yadin's time the understanding of the relationship between Judaism, Christianity, and Roman religions in the first and second centuries was colored by the anti-Semitism of the premodern and modern periods. The discoveries of the Dead Sea Scrolls and discoveries in the Judean desert were only beginning to shed new light on the reinvestigation of the two rebellions and the relationship between them. Finally, the slow progress of the translation and interpretation of the Dead Sea Scrolls through the 1960s and 1970s affected the ability of other scholars to develop their own understandings of the very complex nature of Judaism's religious diversity in these early centuries of the common era. Here was the richest source for our understanding of ancient Judaism and, for the most part, most scholars did not have a comprehensive understanding of the contents of the scrolls. By the time we began our reinvestigation in the late 1990s, this entire picture had changed. In the 1990s the Dead Sea Scrolls information was being released to the public with greater frequency, and a clearer picture of the life and times of the caves along the Dead Sea was starting to emerge. By the time we began our first excavation in 1999, new theories about the caves along the Dead Sea, the First Rebellion, and the period of the Bar Kokhba Rebellion had emerged. Even more importantly, the Cave of Letters was now located in a very sensitive environmental location and allowed only small expeditions with strategic goals. We were the right-sized team at the right time with the right goals, returning to the Cave of Letters at a time when the technologies to do what we needed to do existed and the social histories of the rebellions demanded new answers. We returned to the Cave of Letters to recover what we knew was still left in the cave and to reconnect it to the rest of the history of the Dead Sea Caves.

As many people know, perhaps the most daring and famous excavations of the century were conducted by Yigael Yadin. He excavated the Cave of Letters in 1960 and 1961, and then conducted the monumental excavations at Masada. Masada, located on top of a small mountain on the Dead Sea, required thousands of volunteers working almost nonstop for two years in 1963–65. It was without doubt one of the most herculean excavation efforts ever recorded in modern archaeology. Yadin's efforts were also rewarded in an unprecedented way in the State of Israel. His discoveries from the Cave of Letters were included together with the Dead Sea Scrolls in a specially constructed building, the Shrine of the Book, at the Israel Museum, which was dedicated in 1965. The Shrine is exactly that, a quasi-religious building located in the middle of new Jerusalem, which millions of Jews and Christians flock to as a place of contemplation and reflection upon the history of ancient Israel and the shared heritage of the Bible. The Shrine became the symbol for the renewal of the new State of Israel, and Yadin's discoveries were at the center of the Shrine. It was, in fact, Yadin's excavation that gave this cave its name, the Cave of Letters.

## YADIN'S PRINCIPAL DISCOVERIES AT THE CAVE OF LETTERS: BAR KOKHBA AND BABATHA

The most remarkable part of Yadin's excavations was the discovery of letters from Shimon Bar Kokhba (the leader of the Second Jewish Rebellion against the Romans, 132–135 CE). Before this discovery, Bar Kokhba was as mythical as any other biblical figure from Abraham through Jesus. As with almost all major biblical figures, literary accounts were all we possessed. Here, for the first time, were signed documents from a literary figure. The fact that signed documents from one literary "myth" were found pointed for most people to the possibility that other biblical, mythical, and legendary figures really existed.

Yadin's expedition also discovered the correspondence and documents of a woman named Babatha, daughter of Shimon and Miriam, the second wife of a man named Yehudah, who owned some real estate in Ein Gedi in the early second century CE. Her documents suddenly recreated, in miniature, a unique Jewish presence in Israel unlike anything else ever discovered. A Jewish businesswoman with property and responsibility extending from Petra (in modern Jordan) to Ein Gedi (in modern Israel). An international Jewish woman from ancient times with knowledge and business connections that revolutionized the way that we think about Jewish women in antiquity.

These two discoveries did more than the previous hundred years of excavations to further the interests of Jewish identity and the coalescing of Israeli identity and archaeology. Here was irrefutable proof that a legendary Jewish figure (known before only from literary accounts in rabbinic, Church, and Roman literature), Bar Kokhba, existed. The subliminal argument present in this discovery was not only that Bar Kokbha existed, but that if Bar Kokhba could be rediscovered, then other literary figures of biblical proportions might also be found. It gave new legitimacy to other Jewish legendary figures and to the renewed State of Israel in general. Babatha, like the new image of Israeli women who participated in Israeli society, a "Golda Meir" of antiquity, legitimated the image of the new woman in a new society, again lending support to the nascent State of Israel's claim to legitimacy in the new council of nations.

What we know about Babatha is, by most ancient standards of evidence, enormous. One might argue that by an accident of history, she became the most famous Jewish woman of all time and that therefore she is an anomaly. One might also argue that she is only the tip of the proverbial iceberg and that perhaps we have stumbled upon one of the secrets of Jewish survival in antiquity—the Jewish woman.

Who was Babatha? A woman born at about the end of the Nabatean era near the famous site of Petra (in modern-day Jordan), at the southern end of the eastern side of the Dead Sea at Zoar. She had many of her most precious personal correspondence and documents with her when she went to the Cave of Letters in the fateful year of 132 CE, in which the Second Rebellion began. These letters and documents, papyri and leather scrolls bring to life one of the most dramatic and critical times in Jewish history. Some see this as the last major rebellion by an autonomous Jewish army in Israel before the modern period. The people who participated in this rebellion stand as examples of courage. They are also enigmas. When Yadin's excavations were completed in March 1961, it was not known whether another excavation would ever return or whether one would be necessary. He knew that he had taken out an enormous amount of materials, taken almost exclusively from the corners of the cave. Every effort to excavate under the debris in the center of the main cave had been thwarted. The technology to excavate there simply did not exist in his period. In every age archaeologists decide at a certain point that they cannot do any more given the limitations of technology, even when they know that more can be found. Through a series of unusual leaps in technology and information in the past few years, our new Cave of Letters Project has succeeded in reinvestigating this venerable cave with new and startling results.

## FROM BETHSAIDA TO THE CAVE OF LETTERS

When people ask me how I became interested in reexcavating the Cave of Letters, I tell them it began with our investigations at Bethsaida. The story of our return to the Cave of Letters begins in 1996 with the remarkable discovery of a bronze incense shovel at Bethsaida.

Since 1990, I have been associated with the Bethsaida Excavations Project on the north shore of the Sea of Galilee. In 1991 I helped found, together with my Israel counterpart, Rami Arav, the Bethsaida Excavations Project Consortium housed at the University of Nebraska at Omaha. It remains one of the largest ongoing excavations in Israel administrated entirely by an American university. The Bethsaida Excavations Project Consortium, which today numbers twenty institutions worldwide, organizes one of the largest ongoing excavations of a combined first-century and Iron Age city in Israel today. Bethsaida was a very well known city in the New Testament and is written about in Pliny, the Jewish historian Josephus Flavius, and rabbinic literature. Bethsaida (literally: The House of the Fisherman) had always been one of the missing gems of sacred geography. It was a fishing village on the shore of the Sea of Galilee where most of the apostles and Jesus met for the first time. It plays a prominent role in all of the major stories of the New Testament, but no one could find it, although pilgrims had searched for it for nearly sixteen hundred years. Rami and I began our excavations at Bethsaida with a hypothesis. Our hypothesis was and is the beginning of all good science. The hypothesis was simple. There was a large, solitary (22-acre) mound located some two miles from the north shore of the Sea of Galilee that early archaeologists had noted had architectural remains and pottery shards strewn over the top. Such mounds are scattered throughout Israel and represent villages that were used, sometimes destroyed, and oftentimes abandoned for unknown reasons. Bethsaida was a fishing village on the Sea of Galilee two thousand years ago, but presently there was no good candidate for the title of Bethsaida on the north shore of the Sea of Galilee. So we thought: Perhaps the shoreline of the Sea of Galilee had changed in two thousand years and this large, solitary, unexplored mound located two miles away from the present shoreline was on the ancient coastline of the Sea of Galilee. We have spent seventeen years proving this hypothesis and we have used geophysics, geology, geography, biology, chemistry, archaeology, history, literary analysis, and numismatics, to build our case. After seventeen years, ten books, hundreds of scholarly articles, and thousands of workers, we can safely say that we have redis-covered a missing city of ancient Israel. We discovered that it was orig-inally a city in the time of King David, connected to the history of the northern tribes of Israel, continued in the Persian and Greek periods as a major center, was a fishing village that was transformed by the son of Herod the Great, Philip Herod, into a mini-imperial city and renamed Livia-Julia after the wife of Emperor Augustus probably in the year 30 CE, and abandoned after a series of earthquakes that built up the coastline in the first four centuries of the common era.[1] Thou-sands of visitors have come to Bethsaida since it was turned into a tourist site in 1998. We have educated presidents and Pope John Paul II, world leaders and religious figures on the subject of Bethsaida. Because Bethsaida was not excavated before we began, everything we discover has to be subjected to comparisons, theorizing, and hypothe-sizing to interpret the site and its artifacts.

On May 7, 1996, a short-handled bronze incense shovel was found at Bethsaida.[2] The shovel was found under debris in close proximity to a large Iron Age Bit Hilani–style palace structure close to the city gate complex and nine meters away from of the southwest corner of a struc-

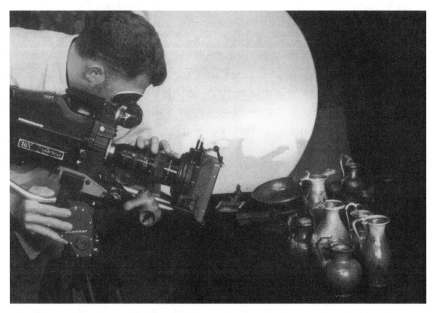

(Above and below) Filming the bronze hoard from the Cave of Letters.
(G. Hochman/COL Project)

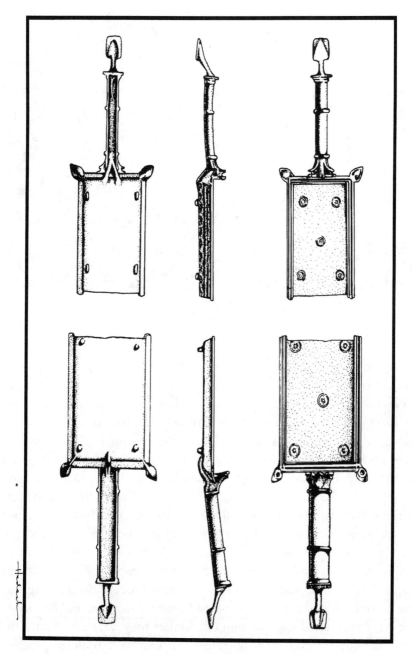

The two bronze incense shovels: Cave of Letters (upper) and Bethsaida (lower).
(D. Hadash/COL Project)

More of the bronze hoard from the Cave of Letters. (G. Hochman/COL Project)

ture, which measures twenty meters by six meters and apparently was a Roman-style temple. It's funny how one artifact changes everything. We discovered that the incense shovel bore a startling resemblance to an incense shovel found in the Cave of Letters by Yadin's excavations in 1960. The Bethsaida shovel is especially similar to the one designated by Yadin as incense shovel #5 (his illustration 6). The main reasons are its size, shape, design, decoration, and functionality suggested by the other elements. The shovels are both made out of bronze and have five small concentric circular details in the four corners of the pan and center.[3] My research[4] concluded that the incense shovels were not for burning incense but rather for carrying incense to an incense burner or altar for burning. The short handles[5] made it difficult to believe that they had ever been used for the transport of hot coals and there is no sign of burning present on these shovels. So startling was the resemblance between the Cave of Letters shovel and the Bethsaida shovel that it raised the question of whether they were cast from similar molds. In the end, it became clear that they were both the product of a similar process but were not from the same casting.

The mystery began when we concluded that the incense shovel found at Bethsaida was from the first-century CE temple there. The mystery became more pronounced when we saw that the parallels of this artifact were from other first-century temple sites! The discovery was a mystery because Yadin had identified the bronze artifacts of the Cave of Letters (including his copy of the incense shovel) as second-century CE pagan ritual items taken from a minor Roman outpost at Ein Gedi. We knew that they had to have come from a major temple setting from the first century and yet Yadin had concluded that it was from a minor military outpost. It was a confusing identification from the start. Yadin knew about all of the many parallels to these metal treasures from other first-century sites of major temple locations[6] and he even announced that this Cave of Letters hoard was "the largest collection of Roman metal vessels found to date in Palestine and the neighbouring region."[7] Yet he wanted to assign their use to "units of the Roman Legions or the Auxilia, which carried them about for ritual purposes."[8] Yadin knew that these artifacts were in use in places such as Pompeii and Herculaneum, two of the most important shrines for Roman religion of this period, and not among foot-soldiers in field operations, and yet did not think that locally they would have been a part of another Roman-period temple, such as Herod's Temple in Jerusalem? If they were clearly from a first-century temple and as impressive as he himself knew them to be, why assign them to a second-century local army group and diminish their importance?

In 1997 I delivered a paper about the incense shovel of the Cave of Letters at the Fiftieth Anniversary of the Dead Sea Scrolls international conference at the Israel Museum.[9] On the basis of a series of points which I outlined there, I concluded that similar to the Bethsaida incense shovel, the Cave of Letters artifacts represent an important first-century CE archaeological context rather than a second-century CE context as was argued by Yadin. In addition, I concluded that the artifacts were probably not from a small Roman outpost as Yadin had said, but as they were a major hoard, they were obviously from a major Roman-era temple nearby. The closest major first-century temple to the Cave of Letters was the Temple in Jerusalem. If my theory was correct, I concluded that the artifacts found in the Cave of Letters may be the only surviving artifacts from the Temple in Jerusalem.

(Above and below) The bronze incense shovel of Bethsaida. (Bethsaida Excavations Project)

As I finished my paper, there was an audible gasp from the audience. I could hear some people asking, "How could Yadin have missed what you have concluded?" I answered that I could not speak for Yadin, but I thought that the answer he came to represented the thinking of archaeologists and historians of the 1960s and I thought that he minimized their importance in order to stem the already existing atmosphere of treasure hunting going on in the Judean desert. He wanted to highlight their importance, but not so much so that it invited a search for the rest of the Temple treasures that he obviously knew might still be in this cave. It was unsettling for many sitting in the audience that day and it is still unsettling to me as I ponder our excavations in the Cave of Letters and Qumran. Was Yadin trying to protect the Cave of Letters by at once pronouncing them to be pagan military ritual objects of the second century and yet at the same time highlighting their importance? It is a strange irony that although these bronze artifacts were pagan ritual objects, Yadin was instrumental in having them placed in 1965 in the Shrine of the Book at the Israel Museum, the modern, secular "Temple" established to house the holiest objects found in the Dead Sea caves, the Dead Sea Scrolls.

I understand Yadin much better today after returning to the Cave and experiencing a little of the popular interest in the Dead Sea Scrolls and Qumran. I think that the Cave of Letters and the hoopla surrounding the Scrolls represents much more than the sum of the individual artifacts, and therefore interpreting such artifacts is much more complex than interpreting a single artifact in a single context. Today I understand that there is a whole psychology surrounding the interpretation of the facts (and artifacts), and the way that they were perceived by the scholarly and general public forty years ago is far different from the way we perceive them today.

## THE DEBATE OVER THE DATING OF THE CAVES

Present at that Fiftieth Anniversary of the Dead Sea Scrolls Conference in 1997 was Baruch Safrai, a lifetime Kibbutz resident and archaeology student who had participated in the 1953 excavations of what was later to be called the Cave of Letters. These excavations were directed by famed Tel Aviv University archaeologist, Yohanan Aharoni. When I concluded my lecture, Safrai asked me if I knew about Aharoni's 1953 dig and its results. When I said no, he told me the story of Aharoni's expedition and one unusual piece of the story recorded in the pages of *Biblical Archaeology Review* in an article entitled "More Scrolls Lie Buried."[10] The story involves finding a skeleton buried underneath a rock in the Cave of Letters in December of 1953. According to Safrai, the skeleton was dressed in a priestlike tunic. He and Aharoni concluded the body was probably that of an Essene or of a first-century priestly origin. This was part of the prevailing theory of the Dead Sea Caves in general in the early and late 1950s. Every new cave discovery was inevitably linked to the original eleven caves and the story of Qumran. The library of texts found in the caves seemed to indicate that the cave system was used almost exclusively by first-century refugees from the First Revolt against the Romans (66–73 CE). More important, the original Qumran and Scrolls research tended to focus upon the Essene sect as a proto-Christian group with little to tell us about Judaism. Why should this cave be any different? Slowly the tide began to turn in a totally new direction and the Israeli archaeologists in particular began to emphasize the Jewish aspects of the discoveries. The 1960–61 excavations of caves along the Dead Sea by Yadin, Pesah Bar Adon, and other archaeologists began to change this theory. With the discovery of letters from the Bar Kokhba Rebellion and Iron Age and Chalcolithic finds in the caves south of Qumran, the discussion began to settle upon the use of the caves as places of refuge over a long period of time, but not necessarily during the First Revolt. The Cave of the Treasure and the Cave of Letters, in particular, were shown to have clear Chalcolithic strata as well as Bar Kokhba levels. Every attempt was made to ascribe any materials from an earlier period (like the First Revolt) to the Bar Kokhba Rebellion. Mysteriously, few or no discoveries from the period of the Essenes and the First Revolt were noted in these caves. Safrai's story and the prevailing view of the caves as a first-century refuge for Essenes was systematically changed by Yadin, Pesah Bar Adon, and other Israeli archaeologists studying the period.

They have rarely been challenged, except by Baruch Safrai and scattered findings in scholarly and popular Israel literature.[11] Mr. Safrai has told his story hundreds of times to many different scholars and institutions. It generally was greeted with skepticism and sometimes outright hostility. He has researched the cave for about fifty years and feels that there is a first-century stratum linked with the Temple and many more finds to be discovered underneath the roof debris. After two hours of conversation he showed me how my view of the bronze artifacts from the Cave of Letters fit his view of the first-century stratum in the cave. If there were artifacts from the Temple in Jerusalem it would explain his story of a priestly figure buried in the cave. The priest had brought the Temple treasures with him to the cave! He told me that I should organize an expedition to return to the Cave of Letters and confirm his and now my insights. I told him as we sat there in the Israel Museum in 1997 that I would.

Truth be told, our return to the Cave of Letters in 1999, 2000, and 2001 should not have happened. Generally when a major excavation is going on, excavators do not usually receive permission to excavate another major site. Dr. Rami Arav, myself, and the other eighteen directors of the Bethsaida Excavations Project already oversee a major excavation site in northern Israel. Bethsaida is 22 acres and has been under excavation since 1987. Dr. Arav has been on-site for every session. When we petitioned the Antiquities Authority of Israel in December 1998 for two licenses—one for Bethsaida and another for the Cave of Letters—we knew that it was going to be difficult.

## IMPORTANCE OF THE CAVE OF LETTERS TO ISRAELI NATIONAL CONSCIOUSNESS

The Cave of Letters is one of the premier sites in Israel. It was the place some of the most important finds for modern Israel came from. It was the place which really made Yigael Yadin the mythological figure that he became in the consciousness of modern Israel. The site itself had become for modern Israelis the "Holy Grail" of excavations. Yadin even made sure that the finds of the Cave of Letters would be located in a central place of importance, the Shrine of the Book in the Israel Museum. Even though the Shrine is devoted to the Qumran cave texts and not to the archaeology of the Dead Sea, a special area was created below the main Shrine of the Book for the Cave of Letters finds. It resembles the Cave of Letters and has an almost holy feel to it as you walk down the stone stairs. It adds even more to the mythological quality of the cave. Yadin is so ever-present in the Shrine of the Book that he has become almost as important as the figure he elevated to real status: Bar Kokbha.[12] It is nearly impossible to visit the Cave of Letters without specialized equipment. Yadin himself had continued to publicize the Cave of Letters in the modern Israeli collective consciousness first in his archaeology show and documentary on Israeli TV in the 1960s, and next in a popular book entitled *Bar Kokhba* (which is one of the largest best-sellers in archaeology history both in Israel and abroad) published in the 1970s. He also publicized the Cave of Letters in his scientific volume entitled *The Finds from the Bar Kokhba Period in the Cave of Letters* (Jerusalem: Israel Exploration Society, 1963), which was published in near record time for archaeology of that period and which influenced an entire generation of archaeologists because of its thoroughness and large format presentation! It took nearly forty years to complete the rest of the work. The State of Israel sponsored a special funeral ceremony for the reburial of the bones he had found in the Cave of Letters and in the Cave of Horrors on May 11, 1982, on the Jewish holiday of Lag B'Omer. This holiday commemorates the deaths of Rabbi Akiva's students, presumably during the Bar Kokhba Rebellion, and is an excellent example of how Yadin continued to keep the Cave of Letters and its significance in the collective imagination of the Israeli public. Two years before his own death in 1984 he arranged for the reburial of bones he had discovered (and sent off for anthropological analysis from the Cave of Letters and Cave of Horrors) on top of a hill near the caves in Nahal Hever. People I met who were there say it was a very meaningful and moving ceremony that, like the State funeral arranged for the bones found at Masada, captured the imagination of the Israeli public in a way that few other symbolic or academic pursuits could do in this period. I tell you this to explain the enormity of the task to return to the Cave of Letters; it is a tremendous responsibility to excavate the Holy Grail of Israel's Archaeology. There are no more Yigael Yadins in Israel today, not because there are not great excavators, but because today an archaeologist is only as good as the people who he surrounds himself with and generally the others involved determine much about the work.

No one person can control all of the various subfields necessary to do a modern excavation. A good archaeologist today is someone who can manage the various experts he brings in. He needs to see the overall picture of the site, but it is seen through the lens of other people's work.

Yadin still casts a long shadow on the younger generation of excavators. First, Yadin was an Israeli army general with direct access to the prime minister and government. That allowed him to have access to more manpower and financial reserves than any archaeologist will ever have today. Very few have or will ever have again the overarching confidence and appeal of the period in which Yadin was excavating. The time right after the establishment of the State of Israel was a heady time. Yadin was the son of the premier Israeli archaeologist, who had first identified the antiquity of the Dead Sea Scrolls in Israel, Dr. Eleazar L. Sukenik. He was also a war hero and a scholar, and he had purchased by proxy the Dead Sea Scrolls for the State of Israel in 1954. His stature continued to grow after the 1967 Six Day War. But primarily it was the state of Israeli archaeology in this period that allowed him to be so authoritative on the Cave of Letters. No one could ever be Yadin again. So redoing a project which Yadin had done (apparently so masterly) was like asking for a license to remodel Versailles. If you are not sure you can build it better, you had better not try. Besides the technical problems, not being Yadin is one of the reasons no one has proposed to reexcavate the Cave of Letters again in all these forty years. In order to apply for the license we tried a new approach. We would not try to be Yadin. We would be a project headed by Arav, myself, and the other experts from the highly successful Bethsaida Excavations Project. Together, we were standing on the shoulders of a giant who came before us and we could see much further than we could as individuals.

The second problem was how we could justify doing two major excavations at the same time. We were already excavating Bethsaida, one of the premier sites of northern Israel. How could we propose to excavate a premier site of southern Israel, the Cave of Letters? We decided on a new strategy: We would not *excavate* the Cave of Letters.

## NEW TECHNOLOGIES AND A TEAM OF EXPERTS OPEN THE DOOR TO NEW INTERPRETATION

Arav and I went to the Antiquities Authority of Israel in December 1998 and proposed *not to excavate* the site in the usual way. Instead we would do a noninvasive excavation in the Cave of Letters. As we spoke about this with the Antiquities Authority, we were forced to create a new vocabulary in Hebrew to describe a noninvasive excavation. Noninvasive surgery was a well-known concept in medicine. Non-invasive excavation seemed like an oxymoron, but it really is a serious new technique for providing information in a site such as the Cave of Letters. We were proposing to do not an excavation, but a probe using proven technology on an old site in a location that might be seen to provide new information. The technology had never been used in a cave before, but it held great promise. The promise was that if this technology, which is generally used in geology to find pockets of oil and gas in sediments below the ground (ground penetrating radar/GPR and electrical resistivity tomography/ERT), and in medicine to locate tumors and other small objects in one's digestive tract (endoscope), perhaps it could locate pockets which contained artifacts and tell us exactly where they were located.

The specialists in the field, both geologists and archaeologists, told us they thought it was a waste of our time. First, to get all of the technology into the cave involved a huge risk. Even if we could get very expensive and sensitive equipment into the cave, we could have a catastrophic breakdown. More importantly, geologists warned us that the GPR (using FM waves) and ERT (using electrical current) would simply not work in a cave. The GPR works on radio signals that are reflected back from the rocks below, the ERT works on current that would simply be reflected back and not through the rocks. The smooth limestone contours of a cave would reflect and refract them around the cave and not upward, they said. They said the entire thing was a waste of time and money. Regarding the use of the endoscope, some said it was too fragile to work in the cave. They said that the endoscope was made to go inside a person's body. The endoscope can snake inside the intestines of a person. It has a camera, light, and air attachment, which allows the doctor to see and photograph what is in the field of study. But the first contact with a rock would destroy the fragile fiberscope. It simply was too fragile to work in dirt and a cave with rocks. These professional opinions were wrong. The technology proved to be more effective than we could have imagined.

Throughout the Cave of Letters expeditions in 1999, 2000, and 2001, there was always an unseen hand involved at every step. An example is how and why we came to excavate using this unusual mix of technologies and experts.

I define myself as an intellectual historian of Jewish life of the first and second centuries of the common era. As the director of the Maurice Greenberg Center for Judaic Studies at the University of Hartford and professor of Jewish History, I am surrounded by textual and intellectual historians who are very discipline-centered. The field of Jewish studies in general has tended to be an interdisciplinary academic discipline out of necessity. There are anthropologists, sociologists, textual scholars, literary historians, linguists, and a whole host of experts in Jewish studies who require constant interaction to understand something that is really the study of an entire group of people as Judaic, as the term "Jewish studies" implies. The first and second centuries are a period that is of great interest to the general public. Archaeology has reinterpreted this period in light of the discoveries of the past half century. It is the initial relationship between Rabbinic Jews and the people who became Christians that has always fascinated me. When, at what moment in history, had the rift occurred? I wrote my doctoral dissertation on the topic, have written nearly thirty articles on the topic, and I have been teaching about the relationship between Judaism and Christianity in the first and second centuries for over twenty years, and I am still not satisfied with the answers. Most of the textual sources relating to the relationship between Jews and Christians in this period have been well researched, but one emerging area that has provided most social historians with new data has come from the discoveries of field archaeologists and the interpretation of these discoveries in light of the texts. Most textual historians read about the collected archaeological data found at excavations (that they have had no hand in collecting) and are expected to rely upon the interpretations of field archaeologists, who are generally not trained text specialists or historians. Most text experts are not trained in archaeology and therefore cannot fully assess the archaeological materials. It seemed to me to be a stand-off with no real winners. But our scholars are all trained in their various disciplines and work collaboratively to assess the archaeological data together with the field archaeologists. Many of their insights have been developed from decades of field excavations. Professor John Greene of Michigan State University, for example, is trained in the Hebrew Bible, and has worked collaboratively with field archaeologists since the 1970s. His insights on the Cave of Letters and Bethsaida have been invaluable to the development of our understanding of these sites and the overall assessment of the archaeological data. I also have been involved in field excavations and archaeology for almost twenty years, and I have used the results of archaeology in my teaching for the most of these years. I always recruit and surround myself with a variety of experts to do those things they know how to do and good textual scholars and historians of different time periods. We use cartographers, photographers, geographers, metallurgists, chemists, geologists, illustrators, and other experts and develop a hypothesis in consultation with these experts and then allow them to do their work to the best of their abilities without interfering in data collection. I generally provide some of the larger ideas about what might be important to do, and then I follow up as they try to research an idea.

Sometimes people wonder where an idea comes from. I got one of the key ideas for the excavation from one of the most unlikely personal experiences. When men reach their forties (as I have), doctors recommend a checkup for prostate cancer and the like through scoping. Having a scope go through you is not an easy thing to imagine if you have not experienced it. It is both difficult and eye-opening. It reminds you how fragile life is. It reminded me how technology can be used in a variety of new and unexpected ways. I asked a doctor friend in Omaha if we could borrow an endoscope for the summer. "For what purpose?" he asked. "For excavating the insides of a cave," I answered. It could not have been more fortuitous. In September 1998 one of my students in a Hebrew course I was teaching was a doctor who was also an amateur climber and had access to an endoscope through his practice. There are, I have discovered, two different types of people who hear a new idea involving a relatively new technology. There are those who say "impossible; that is not what it was intended to do." There are others who say, "Why not?" Dr. Gordon Moshman, the Omaha doctor, is in the latter category. He is a man in his fifties with a very busy medical practice who always found time for climbing. If I had not found Dr. Moshman in my own Hebrew class, I would have had to find a person like him. This was another example of the unseen hand present in this expedition.

As Arav and I talked about who we needed to take with us on the Cave of Letters expedition, it became clear that because of the danger involved we would need to have professional staff working on the excavation and not students. On our first visit in 1997, we nearly fell down the side of the cliff as we surveyed the upper approaches. The Cave of Letters was not ravaged by treasure hunters (as other caves on the Dead Sea had been) because it was so difficult to get to. It sits on the side of a mountain with a drop into a dry riverbed below and the only way in requires specialized climbing equipment and specialized knowledge of the way in. It was so dangerous that in the first excavations in the 1950s volunteers wore parachutes in case the lines holding them as they climbed failed. Aharoni had advertised in Israeli newspapers in the 1950s and had collected a group of young volunteers who had a variety of talents but whose enthusiasm and loyalty to Aharoni was a major factor in their selection. Yadin had used army soldiers and recruits. Given the possibility that our excavation was going to produce high-profile discoveries and include a certain measure of risk, we needed to find staff members who had experience in climbing and excavating, and who could be depended on to provide not only excavating abilities but some special talent.

Parachute "security" preparations for cave work in the 1950s. (B. Rothenberg/COL Project)

Dr. Fred Strickert immediately came to mind. Dr. Strickert is from Wartburg College in Waverly, Iowa. He had been involved with the Bethsaida Excavations almost since its inception. Every year from 1988 to the present, he has organized and worked with his students on the Bethsaida excavations. He was well known by all of us as one of the hardest-working directors in our consortium. In addition, Fred had become our resident coin expert. If we found coins in the cave, we wanted to insure that someone could contextualize them as soon as possible, especially since public television was going to be filming the entire excavation story. I contacted Fred and he immediately decided to join us, despite the fact that it meant two separate excavations for him in one short time period. He usually brings his groups to Bethsaida in late April. He would then have to come to Israel again in July for the cave excavations. Fred did not mind; just to be a part of this expedition team was enough. He wanted to be a part of the new Cave of Letters excavations, and if coins were found, he could be depended on to write a larger report for us.

In the winter of 1997, as we planned for the first visit to the Cave of Letters, I had started my musings about doing the Cave of Letters with Dr. Jack Shroder, longtime chair of the Department of Geography and Geology at the University of Nebraska at Omaha and the chief geologist for the Bethsaida Excavations Project. Dr. Shroder and I had been having an ongoing discussion about how geology and

Inside the Cave of Letters: Endoscope photography below debris level.
(G. Moshman/COL Project)

geography can be used in excavations. I had visited Jack in 1990, right after I had arrived at the University of Nebraska at Omaha, to ask his professional opinion about a geological problem we had with the Bethsaida Excavations Project. Like any good natural scientist, Jack was skeptical about joining a group of scholars who are basically from the social sciences. But it is not usual for a professor of religious history to consult a professor of geology. I asked him to come and investigate our geological problem at Bethsaida. I told him about our hypothesis and told him that we would not interfere with his work, but rather would help facilitate it with workers, equipment, consultations with local geologists and geographers, and historical information. At Bethsaida the question had been whether the shoreline of the Sea of Galilee had been different than it is now. Our hypothesis was that it had been different and that the Sea of Galilee had extended another two miles to the now landlocked Bethsaida archaeological site. After four years and thousands of dollars worth of geological research, it became clear in 1994 that the hypothesis was correct. In one of the great rediscovery stories in the history of Israeli archaeology, a professor from Nebraska had proven that the venerable Sea of Galilee was in fact a changing lake affected by forces that everyone had known were there (earthquakes, uplift, sedimenting of the nearby Jordan River, and building up of the shoreline). In the process,

Shroder had provided important geological information about the area. His study is now a landmark about the importance of geology at an archaeological site, and it is significant for the study of water resources, earthquake science, and environmental studies.

So in 1997, when I sat down with Shroder to consult with him about geological problems in a cave by the Dead Sea, he was still skeptical but ready to think about the possibility. Our initial conversation revolved around problems that had been present for Yadin and every other person who considered excavating the Cave of Letters. Is it possible to excavate in a cave with a tremendous amount of roof debris without bringing down more roof debris? Is it possible to establish a geological stratigraphy of a cave? Is it possible to learn more about a cave without investing millions of dollars to excavate the entire cave? Dr. Shroder immediately told me that we needed a cave expert. We walked down the hallway to Dr. Phil Reeder's office. The University of Nebraska at Omaha is not a large, well-funded university. In fact, it is a middle-sized, metropolitan, primarily commuter, public university that constantly has to deal with the changing whims of the Nebraska legislature. To find that the university not only had a cave specialist, but one who was especially far-thinking and creative enough to introduce new technologies into cave research in Israel, was not something that I would have expected. Yet Phil Reeder was the perfect person for this expedition. Reeder, a geographer in the Department of Geography and Geology at the University of Nebraska at Omaha at the time (he is now at the University of South Florida), has been working for years in caves in Belize, South America. His work includes the mapping and environmental surveys of caves. He was aware of cutting-edge work on cave mapping and investigation. His expertise became crucial to the success of our initial and long-range projects. Could he map the Cave of Letters in six days and provide us information about locations which were not mapped in the first two expeditions by Aharoni and Yadin? He thought he could. We talked for two hours. At the end of that time, Dr. Phil Reeder was the chief geographer for the Cave of Letters Project. Reeder intended to map the cave systematically and, when I suggested that we try to use ground penetrating radar in the cave, he said he

Richard Freund at left and with (from left to right) geoscientists J. Shroder, H. Jol, and P. Reeder. (COL Project)

would try to find someone who could do it. In a matter of weeks he came up with Dr. Harry Jol from the University of Wisconsin at Eau Claire. Jol said he did not know if GPR would work in this cave, but he was willing to try. He also turned out to be the perfect choice for this type of work. As a researcher at a primarily teaching institution, Jol had established a reputation in GPR circles for being able to do things with the equipment that were not the standard geology work. Having worked on archaeological sites in North America, he also had insights into the problems of the equipment. He was willing to get the equipment from the university and bring everything possible along, just in case. So we had a geography and geology unit ready to go, if we could get the license. As we wrote the proposal for the Cave of Letters to the Antiquities Authority in December 1998, we knew we needed people who could do subprojects in the cave and in the region. We needed people who knew their way around the desert environment and climbing. Dr. Gordon Brubacher, then teaching at Doane College in Nebraska, had been working on the Bethsaida Project since 1995. His resume read like an advertisement for the Cave of Letters. His main expertise before coming to work with us on the Bethsaida Excavations Project had been guiding around the Dead Sea. In addition, he was an expert climber and worked with students who were expert climbers. He ultimately brought with him three students who proved to be invaluable as climbers and excavators in the cave. Again, it was a case of "how could we have planned/expected this?" Bethsaida is clearly not on the Dead Sea, nor is it necessary to have expertise on climbing to join us there. Brubacher is an expert on ancient Near Eastern and biblical areas which are not the main areas of research at the Bethsaida site. Yet in 1995 he fortuitously joined the Bethsaida project as a director.

In March 1998, we sent Brubacher, Shroder, a group of Israeli expert climbers, Baruch Safrai (who had excavated in the cave in 1953), and Dr. Arav to view the site and to assess the needed preparations. The trip was intended to see how difficult access would be for the expedition members and whether we could get our equipment into the cave. Brubacher got into the cave with one of the expert climbers under the most dangerous circumstances imaginable. Without specialized equipment, they faced the threat of a major flood and snowstorm raging in the Jerusalem mountains that could have killed them and almost did on their way back to Jerusalem. They sent me a fax about what they had found in their entry back into the cave. On the night they returned to Jerusalem, back in America we were preparing to premiere a new promotional video called *The Shrine and the Scrolls*, which we had produced with the Israel Museum's Shrine of the Book. On March 19, 1998, when I stepped to the podium of the University of Nebraska at Omaha's Alumni House to introduce our new promotional video for the Shrine of the Book, in the presence of the curator of the Dead Sea Scrolls, Dr. Adolfo Roitman, I knew I had more to tell the crowd than how happy we were about the making of the video. I went through the congratulations to the University of Nebraska at Omaha public television staff and to the university for supporting the efforts of archaeology to inform and educate the public about the Dead Sea Scrolls. Almost prophetically in 1997 when we filmed the video, we had introduced a small section which spoke about the possibility of future discoveries of scrolls. As I introduced Dr. Roitman to speak about the importance of the video for the Israel Museum, I knew the time was right to announce our plans. Earlier in the day I had spoken to Roitman about the possibility of another joint project with the Israel Museum. He had expressed interest, and we made an appointment to meet with the director of the Museum, Dr. James Snyder, in April 1998. The Israel Museum was now a likely partner on one project. Perhaps they would consider being a part of another project as well, I thought. The promotional video speaks about the glorious past of the Shrine of the Book, but also attempts to lay the groundwork for new projects on the Dead Sea. At the end of the promotional video, Roitman says: "We are back where it all began, here at the Caves of Qumran . . . but there are many more caves and Dead Sea Scroll research is taking place all over the world. Who knows what other discoveries will be made here in the coming years?" It was a magical evening in Omaha all around. The promotional video was a great success and won a national prize. It was done in both Spanish and English and is now used by the Israel Museum for groups of visitors. I concluded my remarks that evening by introducing Dr. Roitman and introducing the crowd to the possibility that we might be involved in another excavation besides Bethsaida. "Tonight you will see the past of the Shrine and a little about the future. I want to tell you that the future is with us tonight," I said. "This past week, we sent a group sponsored by the University of Nebraska's Bethsaida Excavations Project to Israel to explore the possibilities of excavating one of the most famous caves on the Dead Sea, the Cave of Letters. We think there is still much more to excavate in the cave based on preliminary conversations with those who excavated it in the past. I received the following in a fax from Jack Shroder today: 'We surveyed the Cave of Letters on Wednesday, March 18. It was spectacular and eminently excavatable. In fact, we found and will bring back samples for further documentation of the ceiling debris covering the opening leading to one of the unexplored areas. I suggest we make plans to excavate as soon as possible. I will see you on Friday in Omaha.'"

"My dear friends," I concluded. "We are on the cusp of possibly being involved in making the next great archaeological discovery of the new millennium. This undertaking will probably require many universities and individuals to help us over the next few years. We hope that we can count on many of you here to give us your prayers and support."

The applause was unbelievable. Even Roitman was surprised by the reaction in this midwestern town so far from Israel. The atmosphere was charged with electricity. Roitman became our all-important Israeli institutional partner in the Cave of Letters Project. Since all of the materials from Yadin's excavations are housed at the Shrine of the Book, it became imperative that the Shrine participate in our work. It was the foresight and planning of many years of work with the Israel Museum which made this possible. But we did not know about our future connection with Cave of Letters (or even later with Qumran) when we began our work in 1996 on the video *The Shrine and the Scrolls*. If Hollywood had wanted to script an event like this, it would have been impossible. That evening laid the groundwork for our Cave of Letters Excavations, which was still more than a year away. We now had a small crew of professional excavators and geologists who were eager to go with us. The most prestigious archaeological museum of Israel was assisting us. We only had to apply for the licenses and figure out the logistics. We decided to start by talking to some of the earlier excavators.

One of the main steps I wanted to take in anticipation of our excavation was to talk to people who had excavated the caves in 1953 and 1960–61. I wanted to get the rest of the story and possibly to document our excavations on film. I started making arrangements to interview three participants from each excavation and to talk to some experts on the Bar Kokhba Rebellion to see what they thought about the rebellion and the cave's place in it. I decided to interview six people: Baruch Safrai, Beno Rothenberg, and Shimon Dar from the 1953 excavations and Pinchas Porat, David Harris, and David Ussishkin from the 1960–61 excavations. I also spoke to Joseph Aviram at the Israel Exploration Society since he coordinated the excavations of all four teams sent out into the Judean Desert in 1960 and was a good friend and admirer of Yadin. Aviram, who is now in his eighties, would not consent to an on-camera interview, but he spoke at length about the problems and issues associated with the excavations. And most of all, he was excited. He thought that the idea of excavating again might raise new questions about why everything had not been finished in 1961. He said he would be willing to support our application to the Antiquities Authority. His approval was crucial. Aviram is seen as the dean of the history of archaeological excavations in Israel both by virtue of his experience and his ongoing direction at the Israel Exploration Society. He has had a hand in the editing of most of the best volumes about archaeological sites in Israel. He liked my choices for interviews but expressed sorrow that Yadin was not around to talk to us.[13]

We also included Dr. Menachem Mor of Haifa University in our interview schedule. Dr. Mor is an Israeli scholar of the Bar Kokbha Rebellion who holds that it was a small Jewish revolt, localized in second-century Judea, and that the rebellion is greatly exaggerated by historical sources and modern scholars who use it as a way of understanding how Jews (and Israelis) should live and fight for their ideals in grand conflicts. Dr. Mor represents a revisionist point of view in Israel, and a near total reversal of Yadin's view of the rebellion. From the time of Yadin, Bar Kokhba and the rebellion have been used as symbols of the modern State of Israel and its struggle with outside forces. The idea that this rebellion was a nearly apocalyptic uprising of the Jewish people in all of Israel and which involved the support of the Diaspora was part and parcel of the modern State of Israel's view of itself and its own struggles in the post-Holocaust world. Mor's view is not shared by most Bar Kokhba scholars, but he is an articulate and clear-minded spokesperson for the chronology of the rebellion and the characters involved. Mor also had spent the early 1990s in Omaha at Creighton University, down the road from my office at the University of Nebraska at Omaha, and I had spent many hours discussing the Bar Kokhba movement with him. I knew that I could trust his judgment on a variety of different questions I had with the Yadin theory of the Rebellion and the Bar Kokbha movement.

I was glad to have two Omaha residents, Ophir Palmon, a photographer from our Bethsaida excavations, and Ben Shapiro, a resident of Omaha and an expert climber, to go with us to film the initial interviews. We needed to see if there were other routes into the Nahal Hever canyon, and we could not do this during a summer excavation. The Cave of Letters was located on the stark cliff face of Nahal Hever some five miles from the main road leading along the Dead Sea along a dry riverbed. Gordon Brubacher supervised three different types of reconnaissance in and around the Nahal Hever canyon. Each day we would set up a schedule of interviews while Gordon and Ben hiked into the canyon. Their goal was to see if there could have been any other access route into the cave. Yadin concluded that there was no way in from below in 1960–61 and chose coming down a dangerous route from above. We needed to see if another route into the cave from below would be safer. In the forty years since Yadin's excavations, what was left of a one- to two-inch ledge at some places had eroded away. This left us with little room for error and even more need for secure lines along the cliff face.

Wendi Chiarbos, the coordinator of the Bethsaida project, kept our interviews and reconnaissance work on track. The interviews and negotiations with Israel Television (which holds the rights to the movie footage taken by Yadin's excavations and used in his TV program on the cave), the Israel Museum, the Antiquities Authority, and others were extremely informative. Everybody was excited about our excavating the Cave of Letters, but few were committed to helping us directly. It was all up to us to decide how to do it. In addition, I made plans to visit the cave site again with Brubacher and the professional climbers to film and see just how difficult and spectacular it would be to film this expedition. The footage convinced the University of Nebraska at Omaha television to film a documentary on the 1999 excavations called *Return to the Cave of Letters*.

As they began their planning and we began our planning, it was not even clear that we would receive our licenses. There was another layer of permission necessary to work in the Judean Desert. The Nature Reserves Authority was created to oversee the environmentally sensitive areas in Israel, such as the Judean desert, to insure that they are used properly. When we began inquiries in December 1998 it appeared that there was one problem associated with work in the Nahal Hever area. The Antiquities Authority license was contingent upon our ability to receive a license from the Nature Reserves (now Parks and Reserves) Authority. The Judean Desert is one of the great natural resources of Israel, and it is extremely environmentally sensitive. In order to receive a license from the Nature Reserves Authority we would have to meet many different criteria for our work, which we did not expect. The first was the timing of the excavations. The Nahal Hever region is home to many different types of birds whose nesting seasons are from November to June. We had wanted to excavate during winter vacation (December–January) or spring break (March), or even directly after classes were finished in April. We were told that was impossible. We were informed that the earliest we would be able to go to the cave was July 1999, and it was a very small window of opportunity. In July the baby birds have just left the nest and the new breeding season has not yet begun. It had to be July. July is generally a good month to excavate, because all of our faculty and staff are on vacation from universities. But to excavate and stay in the Judean desert in July is the equivalent of being given a sentence in purgatory. The daily temperature on the Dead Sea is approximately 110–120 degrees. However, we could do it in July and no other time. We had other very strict environmental guidelines. We could not move any rubble out of the cave. We had to move the debris around the cave from side to side as we excavated. We could leave no waste matter in the cave or environs. No major noise to disturb the fledgling birds. Our movements in and out of the cave area would be monitored. Finally, we had restricted movement in the entire region. We chose to meet all of the environmental conditions and excavate in July. These negotiations took place during March and April. In May we were informed we were now cleared for receiving our Antiquities Authority license. It was going to be close.

We received our license on July 2, 1999, for an excavation which was scheduled to begin on July 12. It was nail-biting to the end. It was difficult for Israelis to acknowledge first that the cave needed to be reinvestigated and second that the "Holy Grail" of Israeli archaeology should be reinvestigated by a group almost exclusively made up of Americans.

We went to the Cave of Letters in 1999 for a six-day probe. The probe was extremely successful and we all felt confident when we left that we had accomplished exactly what we had set out to prove. There was more to excavate in the Cave of Letters. After we finished the probe, we filmed the famous bronze artifacts from the Cave of Letters in the Shrine of the Book in Jerusalem. We then went with our television team to Jordan to film there. First, I thought it was necessary to have footage from around Petra since Babatha, whose documents were found in the Cave of Letters, was from the greater Petra area.

Second, I wanted to film the Copper Scroll. The Copper Scroll is found in the Jordanian Archaeological Museum in Amman. Since I first started working on the Cave of Letters project I had harbored a suspicion that the mysterious Copper Scroll might have a reference to the story of the Cave of Letters. The Copper Scroll is one of the great mysteries of the Dead Sea Scrolls and the caves. Found in 1952 with other leather and papyrus scrolls in Cave #3 at Qumran, it has never been adequately explained. It is a scroll etched in copper which lists treasures in 64 locations from Jerusalem to Masada and the caves along the Dead Sea. Since the Cave of Letters is the largest cave complex in the area and was known in Chalcolithic and in the Bar Kokhba period, it would have been known to whoever wrote the Copper Scroll and I always suspected it was one of the locations listed in the scroll. We interviewed Dr. Fawzi Zayadine, one of the leading archaeologists of the Antiquities Department of Jordan about the Copper Scroll; visited Mount Nebo, Petra, and Madaba; and filmed the Copper Scroll in its case. My interview with Zayadine only confirmed my own suspicions about the Copper Scroll and raised my interest in doing more work in the Cave of Letters.

When we came back to the United States at the end of July 1999, I thought we had proven everything we needed to prove and there was no reason to go back immediately to excavate the cave. We did not have any money to fund an excavation, and we had not analyzed any of the data to determine how to excavate the cave. I received my photos from the endoscope (that had been operated by Dr. Moshman) and then had some of them blown up. They showed what we had not only suspected, but actually seen through the lens of the endoscope. There were still scattered finds on the floor of the cave under thousands of pounds of roof debris. Perhaps, I thought, we would be able to go back to the cave in 2001 or 2002 to collect the finds after public awareness was raised by the documentary on our excavations. Perhaps an article in *Biblical Archaeology Review* might raise public awareness and help us find a major donor to give us the funds to go back and excavate. I put it out of my mind and resolved that in a couple of years we could return to collect the finds and finish surveying and even excavate in the cave.

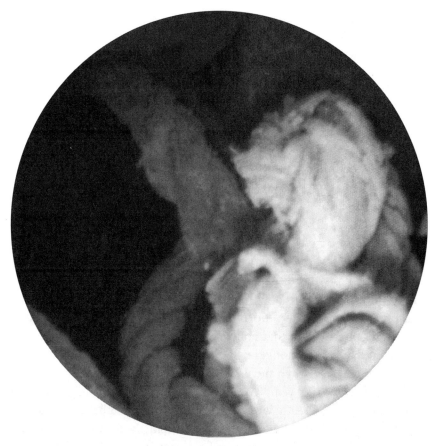

Endoscope photo of ancient sealed bags below debris. (G. Moshman/COL Project)

A single call changed my mind. I actually called Hershel Shanks, publisher of *Biblical Archaeology Review*, in August 1999 because Arav and I were in the middle of finishing an article on Bethsaida that was scheduled for publication in January 2000. Because of our work in the Cave of Letters, we had not had time to work on our Bethsaida article and we were afraid we would miss the date for the submission. Hershel Shanks is more than just the publisher of *Biblical Archaeology Review*. For more than forty years now he has been involved in archaeology not only as a reporter, but as an activist for archaeology. While others are content to stand on the sidelines and write about the news, he makes news. He has single-handedly moved archae-ology aeons ahead by forcing archaeologists to write more about what they were doing, by forcing bureaucratic administrators to release more information about archaeology, and by presenting news about archaeology in an intelligible, informative, and entertaining way, which affects the way the public sees the world. As an activist, he has made archaeology news by helping archaeologists excavate, publish, lecture, and disseminate their work. When I called Shanks in 1999 to tell him about our Bethsaida article, which had been in the works for nearly a decade, I told him that we had just come back from a probe excavation in the Cave of Letters. "Yadin's Cave of Letters?" he asked. "Yes," I replied. "And what did you find?" he asked. I was very reluctant to give out any details because they were so potentially explosive and I had not had enough time to even review our own results. But I answered simply: "We found that the floor underneath the roof debris is littered with artifacts." "Richard, you must go back and excavate it. Tell me more," he said. The Cave of Letters 2000 project was born from that conversation.

At the end of our conversation Shanks said: "Richard, I am going to do something I have never really done before. I think that you should go back next year to excavate the Cave of Letters. Do you think you could be ready with your crew by then?" There was silence on the telephone. This whole expedition had been intended to be a small part of our work in Israel and was not intended to take up our valuable staff and time. My son's bar mitzvah was planned for summer 2000 in Israel, the Bethsaida Excavations Project had planned a large Millennium conference in Israel for the summer of 2000, and I had just started a new job as Maurice Greenberg Professor of Jewish History and director of the Maurice Greenberg Center for Judaic Studies at the University of Hartford. It really seemed that it was just too much for one summer. I hesitated for a moment. But again, pushed by the unseen hand, I responded with one word: "Yes." "I know we can do it," I told Shanks; "What is the next step?" Shanks said he would call me soon and that Arav and I should plan on flying to Washington, DC, in September to meet with a donor. He told me to write up what I could from the summer's results in the Cave of Letters probe. Soon afterward Arav and I flew to Washington, DC, to meet John and Carol Merrill of Palm Beach and Virginia.

It is unusual to find donors who actually understand what you are trying to do. Over the years, I have had the opportunity to raise major sums for Bethsaida from some of the most unlikely sources. But it is rare to find people who really want to be involved in the details of the work you will do. Often, raising money for archaeological research involves explaining grand theories with little attention to substance. In the case of the Merrills, they were interested in what we hoped to find and how we were going to do it. I showed them the endoscope photos from the 1999 excavations, which clearly showed the linen bags we saw on the floor of the cave. I showed them the coins we found; wood, clay, and metal finds we discovered; and we spoke of the remarkable finds of Yadin. We spent three hours at a restaurant in Washington, DC, and we were nearly the last to leave the restaurant that night. As Arav and I left that evening with the view of the Capitol dome looming over us to the south, I remember thinking how special these types of encounters are. Arav from Israel (now living in Nebraska), the Merrills from Virginia, I now from Hartford, Shanks from Washington, DC. Here we were all discussing a single cave on the Dead Sea in full view of the nation's capitol. Except for Arav and me, we all did not really know one another before the evening began. At the end of the evening, we were all joined by a single purpose—to *return to the Cave of Letters*.

Coming back in 2000, I thought it was going to be much easier than it was in the summer of 1999. We knew the two authorities who issued licenses. We had evidence to demonstrate there was something to excavate, and we knew where we were going to excavate. We knew who we wanted to excavate with. We knew the climbing company which could get us there, and we thought we knew the equipment we would need (this would turn out to be the most difficult question!). It turned out to be much more difficult and a nail-biter right to the last moment for unexpected reasons.

# 2

# The Origins of a Cave

## INTRODUCTION

This chapter introduces you to some of the geological terminology that we will use throughout the book. Ground Penetrating
Radar (GPR) is a technique similar to radar used in the air and sea
that in the case of land-based geology involves using two paddles (that
shoot FM radio signals downward and then have the results directed
to a computer connected to the paddles). The paddles that are strategically and systematically placed along a line whose signal can be
tracked back to the computer direct the radar between two points
placed one to two meters apart to detect the different layers in the
cave without excavating. Two other short definitions of techniques are
provided here:

- *Magnetometry* assesses the different types of magnetic signatures of the different types of rocks.

- *Electrical Resistivity Tomography* (ERT) transmits electrical current through lines set up above the surface (and attached to a computer) to pass through the different formations below the surface and reveal the different types of rocks and materials below the surface.

Together these techniques can "see" below the surface and assess the subsurface without lifting any rocks. It is based upon simple ideas. Different types of materials (even different types of rocks: basalt, limestone, shale, and the like), sand, fill, wood, metal, etc., will have different signatures that can be interpreted by a careful reading of the signals by a trained geophysicist. The geophysicist can assess computer printouts of the subsurface daily and make a pronouncement about what is below the surface and direct excavations. Different types of subsurface materials have different "resistivities" (geologically speaking) and the results are color coded by the computer to show the different materials. GPR and ERT together give a complete cross-section of the archaeological strata without excavating.

The caves along the Dead Sea are unique. Since they are located in a corridor between Africa and Asia and at the lowest elevation on Earth, the low humidity of the stable desert environment allows for unsurpassed preservation of human remains.

Though there are caves in many parts of the world, the limestone Dead Sea region caves are in a desert environment that preserved the Dead Sea Scrolls for over two thousand years! Learning how to unlock the secret of this unique environment meant learning about the Dead Sea, a landlocked body of water fifty miles long that separates Israel from Jordan (the border is actually in the middle of the Dead Sea). The Dead Sea Scrolls found in eleven caves along the northern edge of the Dead Sea are actually nearly a thousand texts that were placed in the caves to preserve them. All of these scrolls are written on leather or papyrus, except for one; the one that is crucial to the entire story of the Cave of Letters is written on copper. No one has been able to convincingly unravel the reasons for writing a scroll on a material as difficult to work with as copper. Hebrew/Aramaic text was etched with a hard stylus into the copper with painstaking accuracy. It is clear that the copper scroll was created to last for a very long time and according to the scroll itself, it was not the only copy of its content. The Copper Scroll sits today in the Jordanian Archaeological Museum in Amman and unlike the other scrolls found in caves that were either biblical, religious texts, receipts, or letters, this is a list—apparently a list of the Temple treasures from Jerusalem. The other Dead Sea Scrolls tell us about the religious life of the first century; this one also tells us about the religious life of the first century. The Copper Scroll, however, unlike the rest of the Dead Sea Scrolls (written on papyri and leather) was written on copper to preserve it for a very long time. This text, found in Cave 3 near the ancient site of Qumran, is the key to the mystery of the Cave of Letters.

There are a few unusual archaeological sites along the Dead Sea. Qumran, the closest to the place where the Dead Sea Scrolls were found, Ein Gedi to the south, and Masada even further to the south are surface sites. They were sites that were originally created for different reasons, but all became refuge sites for a certain time in the ancient period.

Caves provide protection from the sun, places to live, places to store goods for future recovery, and in some cases refuge from one's enemies in periods of distress. The caves of the Dead Sea region are located along the lowest point on Earth, the Dead Sea Transform. It is sometimes called the Syrian-African Rift of Rift Valley, and it is the same Rift Valley along which human beings have been traversing for hundreds of thousands of years from Africa to Asia. As humans sought routes for travel and migration, the dry desert seasonal riverbeds of the Syrian-African Rift provided a natural route and the numerous caves along the Dead Sea must have been seen as natural places for storing goods and seeking shelter from the sun.

These caves were used for thousands of years of recorded history from the Chalcolithic period through the modern period. Geologically speaking, this same natural highway, the Syrian-African Rift, sits astride one of the more active tectonic plates on Earth, frequently shaking and making access to the caves precarious. This is one of the secrets of why so much was preserved in the Cave of Letters and perhaps in the other caves along the Dead Sea. Access to the thousands of caves was not always easy and the hot, dry climate remarkably preserved the contents within.

The Israelites in the Hebrew Bible (in this book we will use the designations Hebrew Bible and New Testament to designate the more common Old Testament and New Testament) write about these caves, the dry riverbeds of this Judean Desert, the problem of water, but they extol the virtue of shade and refuge they provide—but also the power of the earthquakes experienced there. The young David hiding from King Saul, the first king of ancient Israel, used the caves. Ultimately these caves were close to the major political and spiritual capital city of Jerusalem (one day's journey on foot), and as the population base of the Jewish people lived in the province of Judea, the Judean desert was an easy journey for anyone to undertake.

Later in the Roman period, as the agriculture and commerce of the Roman Empire spread, these places along the Dead Sea were outposts that became fortresses, transit points, tax revenue booths, and the site of year-round agriculture in the form of palm dates and other warm weather fruits and vegetables. Commerce between what is today Jordan and Israel took place on land and on the Dead Sea, and people moved freely across to the kingdom of Nabatea on the eastern side of the Dead Sea and along the major routes north and south. The Romans originally entered this region as guests in the late first century BCE, but ended up conquering the entire region for their own welfare. As in the rest of the empire they ruled, the resident population did not enjoy full political or spiritual freedom but rather were subject to the will of Rome. Different groups reacted differently to the situation. Some populations in the Roman Empire (which extended from today's Britain in the north and west to Syria in the east and North Africa in the south) accepted the Romans and continued to prosper, others prepared for rebellion, while still others created an inward life separate from the outward concerns of the Romans. All of this is recorded in writings preserved in the New Testament, the Rabbinic writings, the historian Josephus Flavius, and other Roman period writers.

Even the name of this country is a political issue affected by the Romans. What was the ancient kingdom of Israel (according to the Bible only united under King David in 1000 BCE) had even earlier been an amalgam of different smaller peoples and minor kingdoms with a variety of names. Some of the names are mentioned in the Bible and in cognate literatures of the period. The minor kingdoms and peoples were known as Philistines on the coast, the Canaanites in the middle highlands, the Geshurites in the area toward modern Syria, the Jebusites in the Jerusalem area, the Ammonites to the east and north of Jerusalem, and the Moabites in the south and east toward modern Jordan (among many others). A rift caused the division of the Kingdom of David into two parts, the kingdom of Israel in the north and the kingdom of Judah in the south, after the death of King Solomon in the late tenth century. After the destruction of the northern Kingdom of Israel in the eighth century BCE, all that remained of the glory of the biblical land was Judah/Judea. The population of the historical land of Israel by the Roman period contained a number of different subpopulations. Some had adopted some of the Judean religious and social characteristics, while others had not. The inhabitants of what was first called Israel, then Judea were ethnically diverse and extremely proficient in the languages of the region (Hebrew, Aramaic, Nabatean, and Greek— Latin being used primarily in the western part of the Empire). Judeans (Jews) of this region attempted to throw off the yoke of the Romans twice. The political/religious party that advocated the violent overthrow of Roman rule, usually known as Zealots, forced the rebellion upon the Judeans. In 66–70 CE, an unsuccessful First Rebellion against the Romans took place. In the end, tens of thousands were killed, the biblical religion of the Jews, centered at the Temple in Jerusalem, was brutally destroyed, and the Temple treasures were apparently sent off to Rome and melted down. The destruction of the political and spiritual capital of Jerusalem and the exile of most leaders in 70 CE continued with the hunting down of the rebels into the Judean desert. The rebels found refuge in the towns, villages, and caves that dotted the desert. The ruthless policy of the Romans that hunted down the rebels may have indirectly spawned a Second Rebellion, more familiarly known as the Bar Kokhba Rebellion, some sixty years later in 132–135 CE. The final irony of the Bar Kokhba Rebellion was that after the disastrous second attempt to supplant the Romans, the Romans decided to eliminate any memory of the land from the remaining Judeans by changing the name of the country to one that at once hinted at its antiquity and yet disconnected the Judeans from the land. They changed the name from Judea to P(h)listina (after the tribe of Philistines that had earlier ruled the coast), writing it as Palestine. This change would have important long-term implications for the history of the region.

## THE SCIENCE AND TECHNOLOGY OF THE EXCAVATION: GEOLOGY, GROUND PENETRATING RADAR, MAGNETOMETRY, AND FIBER-OPTIC SCOPES

Geologists, geophysicists, and geographers are extremely interested in the Dead Sea area, not only because it is the lowest point on earth, but because of the invaluable earthquake information that can be collected from this small study area along the Syrian-African Rift. Using three-dimensional ground penetrating radar (GPR) to locate the floor(s) of the caves beneath multiple layers of roof debris, along with magnetometry equipment, metal detectors, fiber-optic scopes (called fiberscopes) hooked up to video and 35mm cameras, and systematic and detailed cave-mapping techniques, our group was positioned to perform a state-of-the-art study of the caves and demonstrate that prior excavations had shown only a small part of the potential for discovery in the caves. These excavation techniques are well known in the commercial world in the search for new sources of gas and oil and in geological surveys, but are not usually put to use in archaeological surveys, and most had never been used in this area. We were told by respected geologists that GPR would not work in the Dead Sea limestone caves, especially the Cave of Letters, because the FM radio signals which are sent out by the GPR transmitter would simply be reflected from the cave walls to the receiver without an image. Thus, they said, the whole enterprise was a waste of time, since no reliable data could be collected. I could not understand why they were discouraging us from pioneering a possibly invaluable new method of excavation that could literally revolutionize the world of archaeology. I felt the same sense of frustration that must have been experienced by others who were pioneering new ways of doing old tasks, such as Alexander Graham Bell, Thomas Edison, and the Wright Brothers, who were also told that their innovations would not work or were a waste of time. They persisted as did we, and I knew that if our form of noninvasive archaeology would work as it was intended, it would not only show us where to excavate, but open up the opportunity for archaeologists to do a new form of pinpoint archaeology, which was very different from the archaeological method which has been used for more than a century. Our new technique was intended to show where the different archaeological strata began and ended and also reveal pockets of anomalies in the rock strata where artifacts might be buried. One last innovation (also one not previously used in archaeology), the fiberscope, also helped us fine tune the excavation choices.

Fiberscopes, which are commonly used to search for survivors and bodies buried in buildings destroyed by earthquakes, seemed like a perfect tool for the roof debris that has accumulated on the floor of the Dead Sea caves and thus a good candidate for using these scopes in searching for artifacts. At the frequency we used, the GPR reaches down only two meters below this debris. Using other techniques and frequencies, GPR could see down to bedrock and into the bedrock. The ERT equipment then can "see" down as far as six meters and distinguish the different types of rocks and materials below the surface. If all of the technologies functioned we could "see" down to the bedrock where the cave began and trace its history backward and forward to our own time. That at least was the theory.

The Cave of Letters was created some fifty million years ago by a west-flowing river system during the middle to late Tertiary period, when it was several hundred meters above the present-day gorge bottom. Approximately twenty million years ago, as the Syrian-African rift deepened in the late Cenozoic period, the gorge of Nahal Hever where the Cave of Letters sits was eroded downward and breached the cave roof, producing fluvial infillings and fans. Continued downcutting ultimately left the cave exposed high in the gorge wall, as it is today. The cave of today was a river millions upon millions of years ago. Although the Cave of Letters is now situated approximately 100 meters below the upper surface of the Judean Desert and some 200 meters above the floor of the present-day gorge, it was originally part of a river system which flowed toward the Mediterranean

Sea. This cave was probably difficult to get to tens of thousands of years ago, but already in Chalcolithic times (4500–3200 BCE) it provided a place of refuge for some wily hunters and gatherers.

Our chief geologist, Dr. Jack Shroder, provided us with a complete history of the origins of the cave during his three trips there in 1998, 1999, and 2000. He found that the cliff face at the Cave of Letters exposes approximately 11 meters of rock-fall debris and infillings of travertine, lacustrine, and fluvial sediment below the modern cave opening. He originally pointed out one strange geological anomaly associated with the creation of the Cave of Letters that most people miss but which he noticed on his first trip there and which we surveyed with a land survey into Nahal Hever in January 1999. The eleven meters of infillings and rock debris have created what looks like a natural "column" rising some eleven meters to the bottom of the cave floor from the ledge below and which sits just below one of the two entrances to the Cave of Letters. It was a geological anomaly which may have made the cave identifiable to travelers and refuge seekers for thousands of years from miles away and later formed an important part in our unraveling of the cave's history. It is this attention to the details of the creation of the cave which no other team had done. If Jack had not identified this geological anomaly first in 1998 and if we had not gone to the trouble of doing a ground survey from the dry gorge below we would have missed the reasons why the Cave of Letters was identified and chosen so many times as a place of refuge. It was an ancient geological signpost which had been placed there probably tens of thousands of years ago and which identified it.

The proximity (about 3 kilometers) of the Cave of Letters to the active Dead Sea-Jordan Valley tectonic fault system which periodically seismically generated roof fall has over time raised the cave opening these eleven meters above the original floor of the ancient riverbed. Eleven meters below the present cave opening is a rock ledge which we used to set up our aluminum ladder for climbing up into the cave. The two openings were originally nearly completely blocked with the uppermost fluvial infilling. Early visitors, probably in the Chalcolithic period when cave access was apparently highly prized in this area for religious and strategic reasons, had to excavate a crawl space some twenty meters long to secure access to the inner chambers of the cave. Jack showed me that the crawl space in the opening of Entrance #1 had signs of having been artificially dug out in antiquity using primitive tools. He surmised that this was done to create a larger space for air to circulate in the cave.

Our GPR measurements were made inside a cave littered with roof-fall boulders and small rocks. The larger boulders weighed 3–4 tons while the smaller boulders weighed 1–2 tons. Smaller rocks in the two- to three-hundred-pound range were movable, but even this was not a simple process. Our license specifically forbade throwing debris from the cave, and moving two- to three-hundred-pound rocks from one side of the cave to the other was difficult, especially when one did not know where the places for excavation would be. Conventional excavation was nearly impossible unless we knew exactly where we needed to excavate. That is where the GPR and magnetometry came in.

## THE GOALS OF THE EXPEDITION

We had five goals:

1. locate the different archaeological strata where evidence of habitation from earlier periods might still be found;
2. map buried, unexcavatable, but previously occupied floors;
3. map buried, excavatable, previously occupied floors;
4. limit the area for possible excavation to exact locations where unidentified anomalies between the rocks could be viewed by fiberscoping; and
5. continue the GPR measurements to pinpoint (as much as possible) the location for excavation.

Dr. Harry Jol's GPR equipment included various antennae frequencies that had different abilities to read the substratum. The 200 megahertz antennae proved the most effective in balancing our need for the depth of penetration under the rock debris against our need to

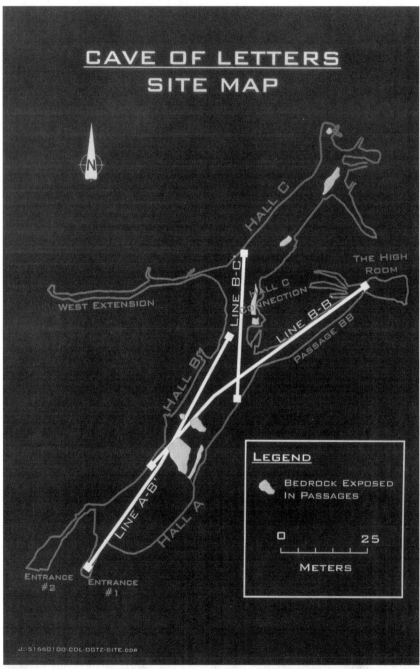

Electrical Resistivity Tomagraphy (ERT) lines. (P. Bauman/COL Project)

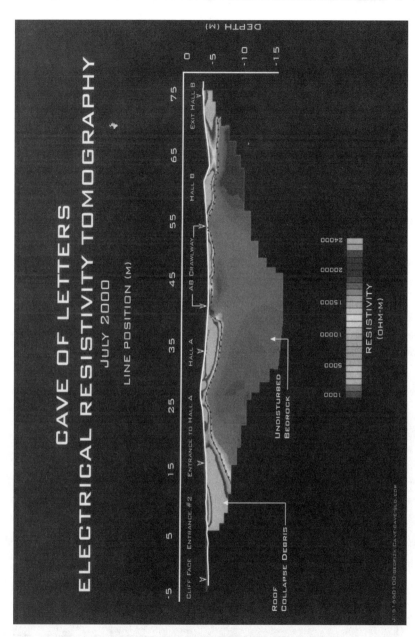

Side view of ERT line from cliff face to Hall B. (P. Bauman/COL Project)

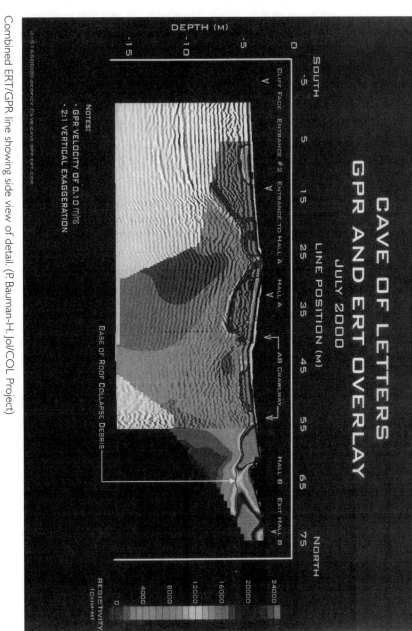

Combined ERT/GPR line showing side view of detail. (P. Bauman-H. Jol/COL Project)

have clear resolution and intelligible detail on our images. The different FM waves (measured in megahertz) gave us increased or decreased resolution. The higher frequency antennae made it more difficult to make out the anomalies we were looking for in the rock strata. The GPR images identified the cave floor and two layers which appeared to be different living floors in Chambers B and C. Since Yadin had expended so much time and effort in Chamber A, and because it was so disturbed (he literally turned over most of the surface rocks), we decided to concentrate on Chamber B, where the 1960–61 excavations made no discoveries, and in reconstructing the rather complex situation in Chamber C. Chamber C, which was the site of many of Yadin's major discoveries, is also the site of the most concentrated large-scale rock debris deposits. In the two living floors which we were able to establish the features were both irregular and difficult to track from Chamber B to Chamber C. In short, the roof-fall layers were not evenly distributed. The levels of the floors and the debris piles were often extremely different, but we were able to establish general guidelines for the floors.

One floor was 1.0–2.0 meters below the present rock debris; the other floor was 5–6 meters below the present rock debris. The chosen frequency antennae made Harry's GPR equipment extremely effective up to about 2 meters. Our endoscope survey of the floors was also limited by the length of the cable. Since the endoscope we used in 1999 was truly for exploration in the human body, it had only six feet (2 meters) of cable and limited our ability during our 1999 excavations. During the 2000 and 2001 excavations we had longer cables, but we found that manipulating the cable beyond six feet was difficult. The rock debris openings were always uneven and unpredictable; most of the time we discovered that the longer cable did not insure a look further into the recesses of the cave. Our initial survey of the floors revealed artifacts on the upper floor, and this is what mandated our initial excavations. We needed to see if the three-step process of GPR location, endoscopic confirmation, and finally excavation of the site could be replicated. If it could be done, we had literally stumbled on a new method for excavation.

Up until our excavation, most cave research used the same techniques that are used in open-air excavations. Unfortunately, the conditions for cave excavations are so different from open-air artificial mound excavations as to make the comparison impossible. In addition, most cave configurations limit the amount of debris that can be removed from any area. This limits excavation techniques even further.

What makes cave excavation so difficult also makes it unique: location, location, location. The Cave of Letters' location in the middle of a rock face one thousand feet from the ground would give any excavator or reexcavator nightmares. Yadin, as chief of staff of the Israeli armed forces, had access to manpower and a variety of differently trained volunteer groups which no excavation today could ever hope for. The physical locations of the different chambers of the cave were also problematic. Chamber A is separated from Chamber B by a small opening that allows an adult to crawl on his belly to reach the next chamber. The opening between Chamber B and Chamber C is better but still not as large as the main chambers themselves, which resemble small gymnasiums. Our equipment limited the number of excavatable places we could work. Even then we had to figure out a way to excavate in and around the massive boulders left by the roof fall without moving them from chamber to chamber. It was difficult to move them from one side of a chamber to the other. We had to know exactly which boulders had to be moved to which side and know that we did not want to excavate beneath the place we were placing the boulders. It was a calculation which each time required a clear knowledge of what was underneath each boulder. That was the "secret" of the pinpoint archaeology technique we were using.

Most of Yadin's finds in the Cave of Letters are indicative of the techniques of most cave research until the present period: surveyed studies with controlled, but accidental finds. In earlier periods, when finds were made in caves, a map of exactly where finds were found was not always meticulously maintained or maps were not prepared by experts until after the fact. The finds and the survey maps were systematic in that search parties with specific missions were employed and a surveyor did create the map that has been used by Yadin. Unfortunately, Yadin's map of the cave was created using techniques which would probably have been more appropriate for surface excavations and road surveys. Little or no careful stratigraphic and plotting information (even of finds) was collected (as would regularly be done outside of caves). Nor were levels and elevations taken at each discovery, so it is nearly impossible to fully assess where the finds were found and whether the finds represent a level of habitation or buried treasure randomly discovered by carefully directed individuals.

Our Cave of Letters Project was an attempt to look at the entire cave as a series of different environments stacked one upon the other. We needed to understand the general physical environment before we could excavate. Our ethno-environmental studies of the cave will be completed in the coming years. We did not just assess finds, we also figured out how life was conducted in the cave. We wanted to know how air circulated, how water might be brought in, how fires and cooking might have been done, and where living quarters might have been. We wanted to know what would have been eaten daily and how those who occupied the cave might have lived in this environment from sunup to sundown, especially since the lives of refugees were so different from the lives of surface dwellers. We wanted to know about their sleeping quarters, toilet facilities, and lighting. We conducted a regional survey around the Cave of Letters that included the investigation of the closest available water sources.

How long could people have lived in the cave? Was it a short time or a long time? Six months or six weeks? In the Cave of Horrors, which is across the gorge from the Cave of Letters, excavations showed that the people apparently died of dehydration and starvation. When it was discovered in the 1950s, it was dubbed the Cave of Horrors because of the horrific scenes of death which were present upon entrance. The dried skin on the hand of one child still clutching at some unknown object was captured on film by photographer and archaeologist Beno Rothenberg. He told me that even the most hardened soldiers were moved by the scene. Here were long-dead rebels, their ancient counterparts, captured in a cave. It reminded them, in those days just following the Holocaust, of the scenes from the concentration camps. It affected the national psyche in a way that made the Bar Kokhba rebels (more than the rebels of the First Rebellion) national symbols.

It is perhaps inevitable that national symbols and grand images obscure the analysis of the data. In our case, we wanted to insure that we knew everything about the caves. Where did the people in the Cave of Letters (and the Cave of Horrors across the gorge) get their water? Did they really die of starvation and dehydration, or was this simply a retrojection from the scenes of the Holocaust back upon the Bar Kokhba era? Water and food were crucial questions that were only partially resolved in the last part of our regional study in 2000.

## WATER SOURCES AND SURVIVAL IN THE CAVES

A major water source—a deep pool hidden away below the Cave of Letters in what we came to call Hidden Valley in Nahal Hever—and other water sources in the area were investigated on three separate occasions by our staff member Dr. Gordon Brubacher. Nahal Hever and the entire Judean desert is a different place during different times of the year. Flash floods as dangerous as any experienced in the desert Southwest of the United States occur in the dry waterbeds called *wadi*(s) (Arabic) or *nahal*(s) (Hebrew) during the winter. Gordon, accompanied by volunteer Ben Shapiro of Omaha, attempted daylong hiking trips into Nahal Hever to look for the water sources in January 1999. January is the coolest point in the year in this part of the desert, but it is still a trip filled with danger. Without specialized climbing equipment it was impossible for them to reach beyond some of the areas of the dry riverbed. They could see the Cave of Letters from the *wadi* (dry riverbed) below, but they could see no way for them to possibly reach the cave from any of their vantage points. They arrived at a dried-up waterfall below the Cave of Letters and peered up at the cave above. In July 1999, Gordon tried again with some of our own team of climbers. Even with specialized gear to climb up the rock face of the waterfall, it was a dangerous and complicated climb. Temperatures hovered around 120 degrees. It was dangerous and it was really beyond the scope of what we could do with a limited crew.

In the summer of 2000, with very specialized climbing gear, Gordon was able to get above the waterfall and found three separate

On the cliff. (G. Brubacher/COL Project)

water sources that had never before been identified in the literature. They included a very large pool just above the waterfall that was still filled, even though it had been a drought year, a second filled pool cut deep into the limestone riverbed, and a living spring at the upper end of what we began to call the Hidden Valley. (We called it that because it was hidden to us from the cave and hidden to those in the Roman camps above. It also was not easily accessible except to those who knew it was there.) Both summers Gordon returned to look carefully at the water sources and he even treated and drank the water to test for himself and collected Roman pottery which may or may not have washed down from above. This pottery may also have been an indicator (in certain areas) that people had made this trek before. Here is what we now know about the water for the two caves, Cave of Letters and Cave of Horrors, and for the Roman camps:

1. The Romans in the camp above the Cave of Letters probably went to Nahal Arugot near Ein Gedi on an irregular basis to get clean water while laying siege to the area. It is a 20–30-minute walk downhill to get there. A 45-degree angle hill makes getting back a long and arduous climb. They did it in one and a half hours (we did it as well!) with filled water skins. If the refugees had attempted to climb up and around to this water source they would have been seen by the Roman guards posted at key locations around the cliffs. So it was not feasible for the refugees to access this water source in the conventional manner.

2. There are natural limestone pools that are filled with water year-round. We found four of them filled with fairly drinkable water even in July 2000 after a drought that had lasted nearly a year. They were all a 20–30-minute hike from the Roman camp above, but even a stealthy refugee would have been visible to Roman sentries posted along the way. We found a guard tower in the middle point between the Roman camp on top of the Cave of Letters and the water pools. These sources would have been good for the Romans, but not feasible for the refugees in the caves.

3. The two water sources which Gordon identified in Nahal Hever provided the best sources for the refugees. One source is the living spring which comes right out of the rock on the side of Nahal Hever. The problem is a sheer limestone cliff that drops 200 meters

from a natural ledge just below the mouth of the Cave of Letters. No path, no access, no easy way down or up from the riverbed below. In 2000 Gordon conducted the water research survey subproject by hiking into the Nahal Hever gorge in 120 degree temperatures! He found that there is a natural buildup (fan) of earth and rocks that winds from the bottom of the gorge upward and that makes the climb between the bottom of the cave and the top of the fan of earth and rocks only 100 meters in the middle of the cliff. According to our geologists, this fan was probably created millions of years of ago and has continued to develop because of earthquakes and erosion of the cliffs. We sat one afternoon and worked out how water could have been brought to the Cave of Letters. It could have been facilitated either by other rebels helping from below or by the use of an old Bedouin trick which we learned about from our climbers. The natural fan from below extends up on a natural trail that is used today almost exclusively by wild ibex. It is possible to lower water skins on ropes from the bottom of the natural ledge below the Cave of Letters to the ibex trail, where a rebel from below could help fill them in the natural spring at the base of the gorge, and then they could be brought back up. One hundred meters is still a lot, but it's possible. It required someone from another rebel camp to hike into the gorge, know the precise time and location of the operation (perhaps by signals) to take the empty skins, fill them and then make sure they are properly brought back up. It could be done also by lowering a small child on a rope, having him/her fill the skins from the small rock pools, and then bringing him/her back up. We found ancient rope of all sizes all over the cave. We also found the burials of children and an ancient small child's sandal by the entrance to the Cave of Letters. The rope was found throughout the cave and was strong and still useful nearly two thousand years later. We always wondered why there was so much rope and this was part of our answer. The Romans would not have been able to prevent the refugees in the Cave of Letters from getting water via this method. At no time could the Romans above the Cave of Letters be in line of sight of the operation. Only from the Cave of Horrors Roman camp was any of this observable and it was nearly impossible to stop from above. It was a dangerous but not impossible means of delivering water to the cave. These were desperate times, demanding desperate answers, but not impossible solutions. It reminded me of something that I had been told by the local Bedouin. I asked one once how they ever got into places like the Cave of Letters that required us to have specialized rappelling equipment. They said that one of the ways they got into the caves along the Dead Sea without sophisticated climbing equipment was by lowering small but agile individuals down by rope and then having them set up rope ladders and the like for others to get in. So much for our sophisticated techniques! A new theory of occupation was emerging! This cave may have provided more than a short period of protection for those inside. Instead of weeks, we started to think about months of refuge in the cave.

## AIR SUPPLY VENTILATION

We used climate monitors to collect environmental data while we were in the cave and when we were gone. Using small but sophisticated computer-operated data collection devices, we collected readings first every couple of minutes, later by hours, and then later on in our excavations by days, months, and now we continue to monitor data by years. The analysis of this data is very important for our understanding of the cave's internal workings, when we are there and when we are not there. It is a microclimate that has served our finds well and it is important to understand what that microclimate is. We now understand how the cave lives and breathes. It lives and breathes differently when we were present (or others—we discovered a variety of other people have visited the cave in our absence!) and when we are gone.

When I say that the cave breathes I do not mean it figuratively. In 1999 we found what appears to be a hearth in the second chamber, Chamber B, which, on first blush, seemed to all of us an unlikely place to build a cooking facility. Archaeologists who came to see it could not believe their eyes. "Why," they asked, "would anyone ever build a hearth in the second chamber of a deep cave? Didn't they know that the smoke and fumes could kill them?" Together with hundreds of pieces of ancient wood, there it was, a large hearth in the middle of the Cave of Letters. It resembles *taboons* (ovens) found in archaeological sites around Israel and even in modern Bedouin villages. It was made from materials available to the refugees, including some binders for the clay such as organic matter (hair of an animal skin) in the grit of the thick clay used to make the oven. Carbon 14 tests on samples of the organic matter used to bind the pottery grit together provided an excellent dating opportunity. The oven was built in the period between 60 CE and (continuing statistically until) 340 CE according to our C-14 analysis. Later in this book I will tell you how we know that it was built in the first century. Unfortunately, for a variety of reasons in the testing of a small fragment of animal skin, it was impossible to get a more exact date. We were more successful with the collection of wood around the oven. Pieces of wood from the area around the oven were dated to 150–250 CE and 50 BCE–50 CE. The oldest piece of wood tested (all found in the same general area of the oven and under hundreds of pounds of rock debris) gave us an even older date: 100 BCE–50 CE. This wood is very important because it points to the use of the oven over a long period of time. Even though wood can remain for hundreds of years, it was a very rare commodity in the Judean desert and would be collected and generally immediately put to use. The oven's clay pieces, which contained the hair of an animal skin in the grit, indicated that it was repaired at a later date using binders of clay and animal hair available when it was repaired.

The question remained as to how they could cook in the second chamber of a three chamber cave. The air in the cave was heavily laden with bat guano and dust and there was rarely enough air circulation, making exertion somewhat difficult. But even without the bat guano, air circulation in the cave was—and according to our geologists must always have been—a problem. Because there is only a small opening to Chamber B from Chamber A, we could not figure out why they would have built a hearth in the second chamber. Wouldn't it asphyxiate everyone when the fire was stoked? Wasn't it impossible to have the smoke drain from Chamber B to Chamber A? Because there is even less air circulation in Chamber C, wouldn't the smoke back up to C and not drain at all? This is what experimental archaeology is all about. Creating circumstances which closely parallel an ancient occupation and seeing how the conditions solve a theoretical problem. We tried an experiment.

We used a specially designed smoke device to test the air flow. It is a modified smoke bomb and we worried all of the time that it might end our excavations on the spot if the smoke just lingered in the cave. We waited until the end of the second week of the excavations, when we were about to leave for the night, to try the experiment. And, miracle of miracles, the smoke drained immediately through cracks in the rocks between Chambers A and B, moved forward along the walls of Chamber A and directly out the two entrances of the cave without backing up into Chamber C. Once we had discovered toilet facilities in Chamber A, directly adjacent to the air flow to entrance #1 (and right above the bronze artifacts!), a hearth in Chamber B, and the letters and burials in Chamber C, an entire life of a cave began to emerge.

Other wonders followed. The microclimate data processors showed us that the barometric pressure suddenly spiked at midnight in the cave and then returned to normal at 4 AM. Seeing the data processors register this spike every morning was somewhat unnerving during the course of three weeks. Finally we realized what was happening after leaving one of the film crew in the cave overnight to film one dramatic sequence from sunset to sunrise on time lapse. The thousands of bats who lived in the recesses of the cave left, en masse, at midnight to search for food, causing the sudden spike, and returned in smaller packs until dawn. To us, this is systematic cave research. It is not as glamorous as the treasure hunting which others had done before us, but we understand the life of the refugees much better today than we did before because we started with understanding the life of the cave.

## WHO LIVED IN THESE CAVES AND WHEN? QUESTIONS ABOUT STRATIGRAPHY

No matter what the environmental, geological, and geographic problems that we resolved, the most pressing archaeological problems remained. We started with a simple archaeological hypothesis—the hypothesis I had started with since reading about the cave for the first time. It was Yadin's contention that only two occupation layers could be found in the Cave of Letters: Chalcolithic (4500–3200 BCE) and Bar Kokhba period (132–135 CE).[14] This seemed to many of us difficult to understand. Many of the caves in the area had been used in a number of different periods, especially the Hellenistic and early Roman periods; why not this cave too? Yadin's theory assumed a tremendous amount of serendipity. Somehow Bar Kokbha's rebels stumbled upon this cave and led a group of upper-middle-class refugees from their homes in Ein Gedi in the second century to an unknown cave. In fact, it would have taken an incredible effort to stock and prepare a cave of this sort, and it would have been useful in other periods from Chalcolithic times. In fact, circular reasoning and perhaps a small element of Yadin's personal predilection, developed during the decade before the discoveries of the 1960s, may have created the need to identify only two periods of occupation in the cave in light of and often in spite of the apparent dating of the finds in his own period. Yadin, for example, redated and reevaluated pottery, limestone ware and Herodian lamp fragments he found in the Cave of Letters to make them fit the second century CE.[15] In the 1960s limestone ware was clearly known to be a Judean/Jerusalem ware type from the Second Temple period (that is, before 70 CE). Two years later while excavating at Masada, Yadin found the same limestone ware and immediately assigned it to the first century. In the case of the Cave of Letters, Yadin clearly went out of his way to make sure that nothing pointed to a systematic habitation from the First Rebellion or Qumran.[16] Roman cooking pots, which are clearly linked to first-century cooking pots from Qumran (by Yadin's own admission), are called "a direct continuation of the cooking pots found in Phase II (first century A.D.)" and reassigned to the second century. It was Yadin's steadfast attempt to keep the entire Cave of Letters as basically one archaeological stratum, which is one of the weaknesses of his excavation.

We could not figure out why he might have done this except as a counterbalance to other cave research from the 1950s and 1960s which concentrated on the Qumran, Essene, and First Revolt stories, and not upon the Second Revolt. At the end of the 1950s most cave research concentrated on the impact of the Scrolls upon the understanding of early Christianity, and did not add focus upon the impact these finds had upon the self-definition of Israel, Judaism, or the life of Jews. But the finds from De Vaux's excavations of Cave 1 (cloth, wood, palm fibers, olive and date pits, sandals, combs, etc.) look very similar to the artifacts we began to uncover in the Cave of Letters—and to those which Yadin himself had found.[17] Since there were no Jews or Israelis on the Scrolls research teams, it was also a matter of national pride that drove Yadin and other scholars to find their own research agendas in the other caves. If the Qumran and Dead Sea Scrolls research centered upon the importance of these finds to Christianity, Yadin focused his attention on the Bar Kokhba caves and the importance of these finds for the history of Judaism.

It also seemed possible that Yadin's reluctance to assign the cave a first century CE designation may also have had more to do with the state of affairs in cave research in the late 1950s than it did with archaeology. By the late 1950s cave robberies were in full swing. The efforts to curb it in both Israel and Jordan had been unsuccessful, and it was in fact this fear of cave robberies which forced Israel to organize the assignment of four teams to excavate the Judean desert of Israel in 1960. The official story was that the team had been organized to stop cave robberies in Israel. The cave robbers had been frustrated somewhat by the lack of discoveries after 1956. No more major scroll finds emerged from the caves around Qumran after 1956. But there was still a steady stream of manuscripts and artifacts turning up on the black market in the late 1950s. There was, however, another motivating factor for organizing an elite team for Israeli archaeology in 1959. In 1959 the entire cave research would suddenly be turned upside down by the publishing of a scroll that had been found in 1952 and only fully understood in 1959. It was the Copper Scroll.

## THE COPPER SCROLL, TREASURE SEEKERS, AND THE INFLUENCE OF NATIONAL PRIDE

Unlike any other Dead Sea Scroll, the text of the Copper Scroll is neither a part of the Bible nor a sectarian text. It is an inventory. Because it was found near Qumran, it was immediately assumed to date to before the destruction of the Temple in Jerusalem in 70 CE. The settlement of Qumran had been destroyed by the Romans in 68 CE on their way to Jerusalem, and since many of the scrolls found near Qumran were dated by paleography to before the destruction, the Copper Scroll was also assumed to be from before the destruction. Unlike the other Qumran texts written on papyrus or leather, it was written on copper. Divided into 60 sections, the text lists 64 locations where the treasures of the Temple were buried. The locations included Jerusalem, Jericho, and the Dead Sea caves! In this list are large amounts of metal treasures. Some estimate that the amount of treasure was 26 tons of gold and 65 tons of silver! The Copper Scroll was discovered in Cave #3 of Qumran in 1952 and scientists only figured out how to properly unroll it in 1956. Its findings were formally introduced to the world in a series of publications beginning in 1956. Full translations became available in 1959 and 1960, and one of the reasons for the launch of four simultaneous massive excavations by the Israelis in 1960 was to insure that if the treasures listed in the Copper Scroll were in the caves on the Israeli side of the Dead Sea (they shared the sea with Jordan in the north), a scientific team (and presumably one from Israel!) needed to get there first. The Copper Scroll explicitly stated that there were enormous first-century Temple treasures to be found in the Dead Sea area and (if it were true) it would signal an open season on ravaging the caves in search of the treasure.

Although Yadin notes that the massive excavations of 1960 were motivated by sales made by Bedouins of newly found artifacts and documents on the black market in 1959, such sales had actually declined in the years preceding their excavations. The catalyst for the assigning of four separate teams led by the leading archaeologists of the period to this enterprise must be seen as the result of some specific knowledge which was circulating in 1959. Why suddenly was Israel motivated to mount the most ambitious archaeological assault ever undertaken by the State at precisely this moment?

Professors N. Avigad, P. Bar Adon, Yohanan Aharoni, and Yigael Yadin were assigned to four areas of the desert. J. Aviram, the honorary secretary of the Israel Exploration Society, coordinated the efforts. Groups were sent out from Beer Sheva to a number of prede-termined areas. When Yadin started his excavation of the cave that would become known as the Cave of Letters, it was not clear whether it was from the First Revolt or Second Revolt. The discovery of a single coin apparently changed his mind. Five days into his excava-tions a single Bar Kokhba coin was discovered at the base of their ladder outside of the cave. This is crucial since Yadin then brought in a mine detector to look for more coins in the cave and this led to the discovery of the bronze hoard of ritual vessels. Yadin had early on decided not to excavate below the top layer of debris, either because his first and only effort to break up rocks was unsuccessful or because he simply did not want to look for earlier occupations of the cave. He simply assumed, as he wrote, that "there was little sense in trying to move or break up the huge blocks of rock on the floor, for no level of habitation could lie beneath them."[18] He did try to break up the huge blocks of rock with a pneumatic drill and was unsuccessful. It may be that Yadin's desire to assign everything to one level was motivated, in part, by the pragmatic recognition that it was not going to be possible to break up the rocks and excavate underneath them. I also think that Yadin's reluctance to assign (or even look for) a first-century CE layer to the Cave of Letters was motivated in part by his desire in 1960 to keep treasure seekers from destroying the historical materials in the cave in search of the gold and silver written about in the Copper Scroll. It may also be that Yadin's nationalism motivated him to want to tell the story of the Second Revolt, rather than the First Revolt. The discoveries of the Babatha and Bar Kokhba letters later in the excavations gave him ample opportunity to interpret everything in light of these finds. He also slowly (after the discoveries in the second year of excavations) began to see the Bar Kokhba Rebellion as a symbol of Jewish courage (against all odds) for other reasons. It is to be remembered that in April 1961, just as the discoveries of the Bar Kokhba letters were being released to the press, the preparations for the trial of the infamous Adolf Eichmann were beginning in Jerusalem. The tragedy of the ancient Bar Kokhba rebellion as a back-drop for the tragedy of the modern Holocaust must have also con-tributed to the drama of the time. The Cave of Letters became a symbol of Jewish resistance and life and created an artificial line of demarcation between Bar Kokhba cave research and Qumran cave research. For forty years the cave and most of its contents were assumed to be only from the Bar Kokhba period without any connection to Qumran and Masada, which are nestled so closely nearby.

However, it is possible, in mitigation, to say that Yadin's method and hypothesis for the single stratum in a cave may also have been a product of cave research at the time, which did not provide—or even aim to provide—a clear stratigraphy.

Most people assume that it is impossible to achieve a clear stratigraphy in caves. We started with the opposite assumption, that is is possible to do so. Most people in previous periods assumed that work in caves was so unlike above ground excavations that simple ideas which apply above ground did not apply in caves. What I have learned from all of our cave researchers is this assumption is patently wrong. The idea which we started from was that we needed to establish a scientific and systematic stratigraphy for the cave or we would never be able to make sense of the findings within the cave. We did this using Electrical Resistivity Tomography (ERT) and Ground Penetrating Radar (GPR), which showed us the layers of the caves. The roof fall debris on the floors of the caves has confused all of the other excavators of caves (including the Dead Sea Scrolls caves). Yadin assumed that the roof debris in the cave was all from the same time period, that it happened before Bar Kokhba's time, and that everything on the layer he excavated was from the same period. He wrote:

> Luckily we determined after only a very short while that the large blocks of rocks must have fallen before the period of Bar-Kokhba, since many areas of the ceiling were still covered with soot, indicating that there had been no substantial changes in the structure of the cave since ancient times.[19]

We discovered otherwise. First, most of what Yadin identified as "soot" (from an unknown hearth) was associated with bat urine and is found throughout the cave. It is black but not real soot. We found one area where soot from smoke occurred, near the hearth. The hearth was some six feet (and thousands of pounds of rock layer below) below the surface. Some ancient soot was indeed present at this one location in the cave, but any other "soot" on the ceiling was usually associated with Bedouin and other modern visitors to the cave rather than ancient dwellers. The recent soot wiped off cleanly.

Second, the GPR and ERT clearly indicated multiple layers of the cave and that roof debris was obviously from different periods. So parts of the cave had more layers than others since roof fall was not consistent throughout the cave. The layers indicated differences between surface, recent, and ancient roof collapse material, the "Bar Kokhba" floor (occupation floor), the ancient roof collapse material, and the limestone bedrock (the original cave surface). Excavations later confirmed this. Each time we went back to the GPR and ERT to show us where the floor was, we determined the one thing most important to the archaeologist—the context. It is clear that the roof debris is not evenly distributed throughout the cave and that the context of the cave presents different archaeological strata in different parts of the cave. The context of the Cave of Letters is the single most important aspect of the cave.

There are actually two things we have learned from the roof debris that can be compared with the historical record. Major recorded earthquakes affected the region in 1927, 1896, 1837, 1759, 1546, 1457, 1303, 1202, 1157, 1114/5, 1033/34, 859, 756, 749, 551, 363, 306, 115, first century CE,[20] and the first century BCE.[21]

There was a roof fall after 135 CE, how long after, we do not know, but probably in the famous earthquakes of the fourth century CE. I think this is the case, since many monks and monasteries were established in the Judean desert in the fourth and fifth centuries (even at Masada, for example) and perhaps by that time the path leading to the Cave of Letters had so eroded as to make it difficult to get to it or the entrances had become partially blocked. But it is clear that the Bar Kokhba level was covered with only a small amount of debris (and not the six feet of debris encountered with the discovery of the hearth in Hall B or the hoard of bronze artifacts in Hall A).

Yadin discovered one level below the 135 CE finds level. It was a Chalcolithic level. We discovered two levels below the 135 CE finds level. Sometimes these finds were neatly laid out in different levels, other times they were at the same level of occupation. We assume that there were first-century and Chalcolithic finds on the same level at one place and second-century and Chalcolithic on the same level elsewhere. All of this leads us to the conclusion that the roof fall was not a single, evenly distributed event but rather a series of different seismic events that littered the floor in a distinctive but uneven pattern. Yadin's assumption of a single event burying everything was his first mistake (Bar Kokhba and Chalcolithic period finds). Whether he assumed this because of his nationalism, his pragmatism, his desire to keep other illegal excavations out of the cave, or because he was following the protocol of cave research in his period, it was the first step of the mistake in understanding the secrets of the Cave of Letters.

# 3

# Bar Kokhba

## The Second Coming
## of the Messiah?

## INTRODUCTION

In this chapter we will try to reconstruct some of the social history of the era that makes it hard to understand the split between Judaism and Christianity. Conventional wisdom has always held that the rift between Jews and Christians began with the messiahship of Jesus. In fact there had been many different Jewish groups with their own messiahs before Jesus and there is no reason to think that this split the Jews of the time. That there were many different sects of Jews in the first century is well known. Even the Pauline innovations of the second half of the first century that brought in gentiles with little or no commitment to the Law of Moses into the faith of Jesus would not have split the Jews from their Christian neighbors in Israel. There was a shared destiny among the people of Israel who lived in the Land of Israel in the first and second centuries of the common era. The fear and loathing of the Romans (and their common suffering under the

Romans) united them. A general commitment to the principles of Jesus' Jewish faith made both Jews and Christians seem (in at least the eyes of the Romans) like Jews. I think that the split between Judaism and Christianity occurred during the middle of the Bar Kokhba Rebellion (133–134 CE) over the definition of the messiah, the meaning of the messianic movement of the Jews and the early Christians, and especially the means they were willing to employ in this period to the end of achieving the messianic kingdom. There were no Christians in the earliest part of Christianity. There were different brands of Christians with a variety of different practices into the second and even into the third century CE. There were scores of sects of Jewish-Christians that observed a variety of different Jewish practices in this period and they were for the most part probably indistinguishable to most Roman pagans.

Jewish-Christians and probably even Gentile-Christians who held onto the promise of a messianic kingdom that had been preached by Jesus of Nazareth and who lived in Israel were part of a cultural mix of Jewish expectation of a coming redemption from the Romans. When the messianic kingdom did not emerge in the time of Jesus (30 CE?), it was held that Jesus would return ("Second Coming") and complete his mission. The Jews of this time period believed in a messiah who would, in fact, initiate a messianic kingdom, and they awaited his arrival as well. Shimon Bar Kosiba, a charismatic leader of the second century CE, was seen by some of the rabbis of this time period as the anticipated messiah. One aid for reading this chapter is an understanding of who the rabbis were and what rabbinic literature is. The rabbis are leaders who formally emerged in the first century CE as the combined juridical, political, and religious indigenous leadership of Judaism. The term occurs in a historically validated literary source for the first time in the New Testament, where Jesus himself is called a "rabbi." The term probably meant "my teacher" and is a Hebrew term that is paralleled by other Aramaic versions of the term such as "rabban" (as in Rabban Gamliel). The rabbis themselves constructed their own history and apparently used the term "rabbi" for the first time in the first century. This is found in the famous "rabbinic" pairs mentioned in the Mishnah called Pirqei-Avot, Hillel and

Shammai (who lived in the first part of the first century, in the time of Jesus). Neither Hillel nor Shammai had the title "Rabbi" attached to his name, but it is found in the next generation. The rabbis apparently came to the fore with the destruction of the Temple of Jerusalem in 70 CE, when the prophetic and priestly leaders were destroyed or exiled and the center of their power, the Temple of Jerusalem, was removed. The emerging new/old religious structure of the synagogue, the Bet Midrash (the study house), and the Sanhedrin (the Jewish court) created a new power base for the rabbis. While the rabbis themselves speak about the reestablishment of these institutions with Rabban Yohanan Ben Zakkai at a city called Yavne in the aftermath of the destruction of Jerusalem, it appears that the rabbis are relying upon an oral tradition that may stretch back much further than the first century.

The most important part of this rabbinic process was the ongoing growth of a literature that the rabbis refer to as "the oral tradition" of Judaism that was ultimately redacted by Rabbi Judah the Prince, while he lived in the Galilean city of Sepphoris. This literature that includes a collection called the Mishnah was followed by a parallel collection called the Tosefta and an entire exegetical literature referred to as the Midrash, that mined the words of the first five books of the Bible for religious insights. The Mishnah, Tosefta, and the Midrashim were followed by an ongoing process of inquiry and reinterpretation called the Talmud. The literature was redacted in Israel (usually called the Jerusalem or Palestinian Talmud—PT) in the fifth century CE and ultimately in Babylonia (usually called the Babylonian Talmud—BT) in the sixth and seventh centuries CE. The process did not end there, and rabbinic literature continued to be written into the modern period, each layer building upon an understanding of an earlier tradition. Rabbinic tradition is textually difficult to master but certainly provides ancient insights that are as worthy of assessment as the archaeological data that the tradition purports to interpret.

## THE TANGLED WEB: JEWISH SECTS, THE ORIGINS OF CHRISTIANITY, ARCHAEOLOGY, AND RABBINIC LITERATURE

This chapter reveals another secret which emerges from the Dead Sea Caves and Qumran research, the secret of putting the discoveries into the context of a social history. Many of my colleagues often laugh and say that it must be nice teaching about the ancient period. The punch line to the story usually is, "It must be easy teaching about things that happened so long ago, since nothing ever changes!" In fact much has changed in the past fifty years regarding our understanding of ancient history, thanks in part to the discoveries made in the area of the Dead Sea and Qumran. Much of what we know about this period has been revealed only in the past century through archaeological excavations and discoveries of new texts at Qumran, in the Judean Desert, and in the Dead Sea Caves, but also in the meticulous unraveling of the histories of early Christianity and rabbinic Judaism. I personally have spent the better part of the last quarter century searching for the point at which Judaism and Christianity split apart. I have always felt that if I could understand what caused the split, it would illuminate the beginnings of Christianity and rabbinic Judaism. I have now come to the conclusion that the split occurred in the midst of the Bar Kokhba Rebellion and that the ensuing disaster of that rebellion created an irreconcilable difference between Jews and Christians. The Cave of Letters became for me my window into the past to explore this moment in history.

This unraveling of the histories of Christianity and Judaism has always been present in the textual information available in rabbinic and church literatures, but when they are taken together with the new discoveries, a new understanding of the common origins of Judaism and Christianity emerges. In the next two chapters the secrets which will be revealed are ones which have been imbedded in traditional textual works which may be unfamiliar to the general public, but which have been the basis of both Church and rabbinic teachings for nearly two thousand years. These texts are considered by many Jews and Christians to be as holy as the Bible itself. I take these texts very seriously as possibly authentic reflections of information from the ancient period which needs to be taken as seriously as the archaeology. These texts contain traditions about this period which illuminate and inform us about the archaeological discoveries as much as the archaeology illuminates and informs us about these texts. Rabbinic literature is a complex web of interpretation and exegesis with a dizzying number of texts which were written down for the first time in the third century CE and continued to be written, formulated, and edited into the eleventh century CE and beyond. They come from Babylonia, Israel, North Africa, and Asia Minor, and often give insights not found anywhere else. These texts and the Church traditions, which also stretch from the second and third centuries until the early Middle Ages, inform us about life and traditions which were important to both Christians and Jews in their own centuries and in previous ones. These texts often contain traditions about the Church and Jewish life which were passed on in oral fashion and only written down much later. Are they authentic reflections of the biblical ideas and history of Jews and then Christians? It is hard to know. It is, however, important to consider what they say now, especially in light of the information which has emerged in these past fifty years.

I have often said that Bar Kokhba was for some second-century Jews what Jesus had been for some first-century Jews. This is an extremely broad generalization, which however difficult it may seem for most professing Jews in our century, seems to apply to some Jews in the ancient period.

Jews were involved both in the first-century movement that assigned messiahship to Jesus of Nazareth and in the second-century movement that assigned messiahship to Simon Bar Kokhba. The idea of Jesus as the messiah and leader of the spiritual (and perhaps political) overthrow of the Romans was a major element of the rebellion that culminated both in the First Revolt against the Romans in the years 66–73 CE and in the Second Revolt against the Romans in the years 132–135 CE.

While some early (Jewish) Christians continued to live in Israel, Gentile (Pauline) Christianity continued to grow in the late first and second centuries in the area from Rome to Asia Minor. It would be only peripherally involved in a movement such as the Second Revolt of Bar Kokhba. In Israel, however, Jewish-Christians and Pauline Christians might have been attracted to the figure of Shimon Bar Kokhba as the messiah and "Second Coming" of Jesus. Between 73 and 132 CE a second coming was seen as imminent.

There was an uprising among Jews in the Diaspora against Trajan in 115 CE. The fact that there was a major earthquake in the Middle East in this period may have been interpreted by the faithful that the Divine's will was (or was not) present in their undertaking, which was quickly put down. Divine will was either with them or against them in their attempt to free themselves from the clutches of Roman culture and government in the Middle East. During 115–117 CE, an offshoot of this rebellion spread to Judea in what rabbinic literature refers to as the War of Quietus—revealing what the rebellion was ultimately about; i.e., the freedom of Judea and Jerusalem. It made a big impression also upon the Christians in Israel and the Diaspora who still had not completely split from the Jews in this period. The fourth-century Christian writer Eusebius includes this episode in his *Ecclesiastical History*:

> While the teaching of our Saviour and the church were flourishing daily and moving on to further progress, the tragedy of the Jews was reaching the climax of successive woes. In the course of the eighteenth year of the reign of the Emperor [Trajan: 98–117 CE] a rebellion of the Jews broke out and destroyed a great multitude of them. For both in Alexandria and in the rest of Egypt and especially in Cyrene, as though they had been seized by some terrible spirit of rebellion, they rushed into sedition against their fellow Greek citizens, and increasing the scope of the rebellion in the following year started a great war while Lupus was governor of all Egypt. . . . The Emperor suspected that the Jews of Mesopotamia would also attack the inhabitants and ordered Lusius Quietus to clean them out of the province. He organized a force and murdered a great multitude of the Jews there, and for this reform was appointed governor of Judea by the Emperor.[22]

Shimon Bar Kosiba, who must have been born at the beginning of the second century CE in order to be in a position of leadership in 132, was probably in his teens during the War of Quietus in 113–115. His birthplace is not known (see below), but one can assume that he was fully familiar with Judea from his ability to direct his commanders around intricate caves and tunnels in the area. If the pattern of biblical precedent holds, it is possible that he or his parents were from the Bethlehem area and that he had a lineage connection with King David. Shimon Bar Kokhba, as he was known from non-Jewish (primarily Christian) sources, was known as Shimon Bar Kos(z)iba in Jewish sources. His life and teachings have obvious parallels with the first-century figure of Jesus.

He was called the Messiah by some Jewish followers. His name and birth (Bar Kokhba—"Son of the Star") were apparently associated with constellations, as was the birth of Jesus. He is connected with the Davidic lineage, as was Jesus.

## BAR KOKHBA AND RABBI AKIVA

Rabbi Akiva was a well-known supporter of Bar Kokhba.[23] Why was Akiva a supporter when many other rabbis were not? What did he believe that other rabbis did not? What I have found was that Rabbi Akiva represented a very different view of the world than other rabbis of the period.[24] Despite his obvious significance in the organization of rabbinic literature in general, his apocalyptic vision of the world was greeted with some skepticism by other rabbis of that time. One might ask whether Rabbi Akiva's apocalyptic vision was the result of his own personal experience or whether the Jewish apocalyptic vision was the dominant view of the rabbis of this period. Rabban Shimon Ben Gamliel and John of Gischala (a messianic leader of the First Revolt), for example, enjoyed a relationship of mutual respect (according to the historian Josephus) during the period of the First Revolt against Rome.[25] Rabban Shimon Ben Gamliel exercised influence upon Anan ben Anan and Joshua ben Gamla, the former high priests. John played a leading role in Galilee and then escaped to Jerusalem in 69 CE. He brought with him many Jews from Galilee to defend Jerusalem.[26] The near-messianic power attributed to him by the Zealots and the traditional leadership of Anan ben Anan allowed him to desecrate the inner precincts of the Temple, its wood supplies, purity laws, and according

to Josephus to bring the final destruction of the Temple.[27] His religious conviction held that ultimately God would aid his efforts. His
apocalyptic zeal was apparently respected by some of the rabbinic
leadership.[28] Rabbi Akiva, however, was living some sixty years after
the First Revolt's disastrous events which had somewhat reduced the
apocalyptic zeal. For Rabbi Akiva, however, these events were the
result of a lack of authentic leadership. Unlike some of his colleagues,
Rabbi Akiva held that miracles were an extremely profound and major
part of the Divine's work on Earth. He held that there was active and
regular divine intervention in the world, so the expectation that at any
moment the apocalypse could come was both real and palpable in his
writings. Rabbi Akiva was known for having what bordered on a "martyrdom wish" (as opposed to a "death wish"). His final torture and
death are captured in a number of versions of the same story.[29] He
thought that perhaps what was lacking among most of his contemporaries was a true commitment to the Divine kingdom, so he met his
martyrdom with an unusual sense of relish. It is also this type of commitment that was apparently found in the leadership of Bar Kokhba.
Rabbi Akiva was apparently executed before the end of the Bar
Kokhba Rebellion:

> And when Rabbi Akiva was executed in Caesarea, the news reached
> Rabbi Yehudah ben Beva and Rabbi Haninah ben Teradion. . . .
> Rabbi Akiva was executed only as an omen. . . . In a short time from
> now, no place will be found in the Land of Israel where bodies of
> slain will not have been cast. . . . Not long thereafter, it is said, war
> came and put the entire world into chaos.[30]

His apocalyptic interpretation of the biblical verse from
Deuteronomy 6.5, "You shall love the Lord your God with all your
heart, with all your soul, and with all your might,"[31] was meant to suggest that total commitment to the Divine implied the possibility of
giving of one's life for divine principles. In a period when other rabbis
were seemingly trying to limit self-sacrifice and martyrdom to very
specific cases, he was apparently expanding the definition. To him, the
commitment was one that stretched to public and private moments
and even to circumstances that might otherwise be ignored.

The rabbinic interpretation of Leviticus 18.5 shows the divide between Rabbi Akiva and his contemporaries. Leviticus 18.5 states, "You shall keep my statutes and my ordinances; by doing this a man shall live: I am the Lord." This was taken to mean that if a Jew was given the choice of survival or of observing Jewish Law, his physical survival took precedence over observing Jewish Law. So the rabbis interpreted:

> "You shall therefore keep My statutes, and My ordinances, which, if a man do, *he shall live by them.*" "He shall *live* by them," and not "*die* by them."

This is the interpretation of the other school of rabbinic interpretation from the second century CE—that of Rabbi Yishmael (the archrival of Rabbi Akiva). It is in counterdistinction to the apocalyptic standards of Rabbi Akiva.

What makes Rabbi Akiva so compelling as an apocalyptic figure is that he could not or would not wait for the end of days to be initiated by the Divine. Following in the line of other biblical and postbiblical figures, he held that the end of days would be ushered in by human beings, and then only later by a final divine intervention. Rabbi Akiva also held that ushering in the end of days was not necessarily a group action but possibly an individual action. The stark contrast between the view of Rabbi Akiva and Rabbi Yishmael is very clear. It is Rabbi Akiva who found in the Torah: "A star (*Kokhav*) shall come out of Jacob" in Numbers 24.17 and changed the word ever so slightly so that it corresponded closely to the family name of Bar Kosiba. He interpreted: "A *Koz(i)ba* shall come out of Jacob."[32] This second-century CE interpretation is an extremely provocative use of the word given what we know about another group of people who apparently had their own "Koziba." Similarly, in many of the first-century sectarian Qumran texts, one finds the designation of a leader, *Ish HaKazav* (the *Man of the Lie*) and *Matif HaKazav* (the *Spreader of the Lie*). The Damascus Document has references to *the Man of the Lie*, the opponent of the true messianic leader of the group, the *Teacher of Righteousness.*[33] Were the rabbis who were against Bar Kokhba referring to him using terminology that had been used earlier by the Jews of the Dead Sea

Scrolls? One can only speculate. It is Rabbi Yishmael who taught that revelations of the sort made by Rabbi Akiva concerning Bar Kokhba were "among the seven things that are kept from human beings until they are the day of his death . . . and the kingdom of David, when it will return and the Kingdom when it will be pulled up."[34]

Rabbi Yishmael's thinking is found in many collections of rabbinic literature.[35] In the *Derech Eretz Rabbah*, chapter 11, the view of Rabbi Yishmael is encapsulated very clearly:

He who works out the end does not have a part in the world to come.

Human beings should not be involved in speculating on (or perhaps also working on behalf of) the coming Apocalypse. Divine planning will accomplish these things in its own time.

## THE SECOND-CENTURY JEWISH COMMUNITY AND THE DEBATE OVER THE APOCALYPSE

Apart from Rabbi Akiva and Rabbi Eleazar of Modi'in, no other sages explicitly[36] mention Bar Kokhba. Rabbi Akiva's hailing of Bar Kokhba as the messiah was attacked by Rabbi Yohanan Ben Torta, who said: "Akiva! Grass will grow in your cheeks and the son of David will still not have come."[37] It was, however, this same Ben Torta who held that the Temple would be rebuilt in his own lifetime![38] The movement of the Sanhedrin to Bethar in the days of Rabbi Akiva signaled his influence. But it is nearly impossible to say if Rabbi Akiva commanded a large following of sages in the issue of Bar Kokhba's messiahship, because most of the materials about Bar Kokhba were edited after the failure of the rebellion. Many other sages, however, were arrested during the Bar Kokhba Rebellion for defying decrees associated with it.[39] Overall, the reaction of the rabbis after the Bar Kokhba Rebellion is negative both to the person of Bar Kokhba and to the principles that he advocated.

A series of enactments by late-second-century rabbis seems to confirm an attempt to cap apocalyptic speculation. Many of the elements associated with the reestablishment of the Temple (and Temple service) in Jerusalem (a major flashpoint for the rebellion) were pro-hibited by the rabbis following the Bar Kokhba Rebellion.[40] This would insure that some of the religious passions that were rampant during the rebellion would be curtailed. Despite all the changes sug-gested by post–Bar Kokbha Rebellion rabbis, the view of Rabbi Akiva permeates the writings of the rabbis. It is tempered, however, by the views of Rabbi Yishmael (and others), and the sobering political situ-ation that followed in Palestine certainly made it difficult to realize. Rabbi Yehudah HaNasi, the third-century "final" redactor of the ear-liest collection of rabbinic literature, the Mishnah, includes a specially designed section at the end of Mishnah Sotah that addresses the apoc-alyptic trend in Judaism (BT 49b):

> In the footsteps of the Messiah insolence will increase and honor dwindle. The vine will yield its fruit [abundantly] but wine will be dear. The government will turn to heresy and there will be none [to offer them] reproof; the meeting-place [of scholars] will be used for immorality; Galilee will be destroyed, the northern frontier deso-lated, and the dwellers on the frontier will go about [begging] from place to place without anyone to take pity on them. The wisdom of the learned will degenerate, fearers of sin will be despised, and the truth will be lacking. Youths will put old men to shame, the old will stand up in the presence of the young, a son will revile his father, a daughter will rise against her mother, a daughter-in-law against her mother-in-law, and a man's enemies will be the members of his household. The face of the generation will be like the face of a dog, a son will not feel ashamed before his father. So upon whom is it for us to rely? Upon our father who is in heaven.

It is an apocalyptic and catastrophic view of the end time. Perhaps as a result of the Bar Kokhba debacle, the rabbis seem to want to adopt Rabbi Yishmael's wait and see attitude but recognize that the apoca-lyptic trend gives them hope as in BT Sanhedrin 97a:

> Even as R. Zera, who, whenever he chanced upon scholars engaged thereon [i.e., in calculating the time of the Messiah's coming], would say to them: I beg of you, do not postpone it, for it has been taught: Three come unawares: Messiah, a found article, and a scorpion.

By the fourth century CE, later rabbinic figures looking back on these early centuries and events did not look back with nostalgia upon the events of the First and especially Second Revolt. Instead, they tend to minimize the importance of apocalyptic visions in Judaism:

> Ulla said; Let him [The Messiah] come, but let me not see him. Rabbah said likewise: Let him come, but let me not see him. . . . Abaye enquired of Rabbah: What is your reason [for not wishing to see him]? Shall we say, because of the birth pangs [preceding the advent] of the Messiah? But it has been taught, R. Eleazar's disciples asked him: What must a man do to be spared the pangs of the Messiah? [He answered:] Let him engage in study and benevolence; and you Master do both. He replied: [I fear] lest sin cause it, in accordance with [the teaching of] R. Jacob b. Idi, who opposed [two verses] [viz.,] it is written, And, behold, I am with you, and will guard you in all places whither you go.

This view holds that despite efforts to the contrary, the advent of the apocalypse will not benefit the lives of the people sufficiently to justify the price to be paid. There would be no second coming for Bar Kokhba, either prayed for or desired.

## JESUS AND BAR KOKHBA: VERY DIFFERENT MESSIAHS

One of the things which clearly differentiated Bar Kokhba from Jesus is the militaristic and noncompassionate stories which circulate about his life. Bar Kokhba, unlike Jesus, was a military leader. He led the Second Rebellion against Rome, which began in earnest in 132 CE. Until the discovery of the Bar Kokhba letters in the Cave of Letters, we only had rabbinic and Church writings that provided information about him. Because they were written after the failed rebellion and were intended to be warnings and polemics against future attempts, these are clearly anti–Bar Kokhba. Bar Kokhba is not seen as a particularly compassionate leader either in the rabbinic writings or in his own correspondence, which reflects upon Bar Kokhba the man. Bar

Kokhba apparently was afraid of desertions and a lack of absolute commitment to his rebellion; so he devised a number of acts of courage to distinguish his troops. It is in this period that Rabbi Akiva initiates the totally new concept of "conscientious objector," which allowed people to be exempted from military service if they "cannot endure the armies joined in battle or bear to see a drawn sword."[41] This is apparently an attempt to bring rabbinic decree in line with the dramatic "right of initiation" that the Bar Kokhba troops were asked to endure in order to fight in his army. Now Bar Kokhba could legitimately weed out troops who were unwilling to endure the severe conditions that he expected in the coming rebellion. Before this time the "conscientious objector" category was limited to a few exemptions.

Bar Kokhba introduced categories for soldiers that were totally different from anything found in any Jewish literature. According to the rabbinic text Midrash Lamentations,[42] for example, Bar Kokhba demanded that soldiers be able to uproot a cedar tree in order to make sure that they were the strongest and most able to deliver against the many Roman legions in the area. We are told that Bar Kokhba instituted an initiation test for his men which called for them to cut off their little fingers to demonstrate their courage. If we take this self-mutilation test at face value (and many other armies throughout history have had more severe tests of courage!) it means that Bar Kokhba is apparently flying in the face of biblical and rabbinic regulations that forbid self-mutilation. When Bar Kokhba (according to the rabbis) suspected that his uncle, Rabbi Eleazar of Modi'in, was willing to surrender to the Romans during the final battle at Bethar, for example, it is reported in rabbinic texts that he "kicked him with his foot and killed him."[43] In what may seem like the ultimate irony, Bar Kokhba, instead of claiming that God was fighting for him, remarked that "God will neither assist nor detract [from his campaign]."[44] In these accounts, we see the main difference between Jesus and Bar Kokhba in substance as well as style. Bar Kokhba comes across even in his letters as a demagogue. He is neither a Moses, a Joshua, nor a Hillel. He is more akin to Saul and David as these figures have emerged from critical text study. He is an extremely flawed character with great courage and ability who often resorts to violence, even against his own people. The Bar Kokhba letters do little to change this image. In one extremely telling letter to his commanders, he says they should confiscate a wealthy landowner's wheat, "and if anyone opposes you, send him to me and I shall punish him."[45] In short, Bar Kokhba was not much of a messiah when compared to the model of Jesus. Nor was he much of a leader when compared to Jewish models of rabbinic leadership. But then it is difficult to trust the rabbinic texts. Some rabbis apparently so hated him that they did a wordplay on his name: From Simon Bar Kosiba they altered it to Simon Bar Koziba, meaning "son of the lie." He was put in the same category as the Deuteronomic concept of a false prophet. Other writers in the same period picked up the theme.[46]

Simon Bar Kosiba is the name we now know from the correspondence found in the Cave of Letters by Y. Yadin, 1960–1961.[47] In these letters he calls himself *Nasi* of Israel. The term "Nasi" is a biblical term that is generally translated as "prince." In the biblical period, it meant a tribal leader, but during the Hellenistic-Roman period it came to replace the more problematic term "King" in Jewish writings. It ultimately became the preferred term of rabbinic Judaism for the recognized rabbinic authority of the time who traced his origin to David.[48]

While Bar Kokhba himself never directly claims to be from priestly[49] or Davidic stock, his major goal was political sovereignty and the restoration of the Temple cult. There is some question of how successful Bar Kokhba was in securing either one of these goals during the two and one half years of the rebellion. Although there are conflicting opinions as to whether the Emperor Hadrian (117–138 CE),[50] the Jews, Hadrian and the Jews (jointly)[51], or the Jews (alone) during the short rule of Bar Kokhba (132–135)[52] actually initiated (or completed) the restoration of the cult at Jerusalem, the facts seem to point to the existence of some form of a Temple restoration *project* at the center of the Bar Kokhba Rebellion.[53] Whether a limited building restoration was coupled with some restoration of the sacrificial cult (perhaps in limited fashion and for a short time) during this period is not known, but that they were important to the rebellion is clear from the coin evidence.[54]

The crushing defeat of the rebellion by Hadrian in 135 CE was at extreme cost to the prestige of the Empire. Historian Werner Eck demonstrates in a number of recent publications that as many as twelve legions were sent to the province of Judea to put down the rebellion. Clearly Hadrian was taking no chances that the rebellion might be a protracted and embarrassing affair. Yet, judging from the lack of the regular victory formula in the report back to Rome, the war was anything but an easy affair. Dio Cassius reports in his *Roman History* 69.14:[55]

> Many Romans, moreover, perished in this war. Therefore Hadrian in writing to the senate did not employ the opening phrase commonly affected by the emperors, "If you and your children are in health, it is well; I and the legions are in health."[56]

The Second Revolt was the most disastrous event in the history of Judaism until the Holocaust in the twentieth century. Judging from the literary references in Jewish and non-Jewish sources as well as the archaeological materials discovered in the north and the south of the country, it affected a large number of the people. In short, it would have been difficult for anyone living in Palestine and the nearby Diaspora communities at this time *not* to have been involved somewhat in the unfolding rebellion.[57]

# 4

# The Minimalists and the Maximalists of Archaeology and the Bar Kokhba Rebellion

## INTRODUCTION

In this chapter you will be introduced to a major debate in historical studies in general and archaeology in particular. It is the question of revisionism, ideology, and how they affect the rewriting of history. If it is not clear to the reader already, all history has a point a view. Even a careful and critically trained historian in the United States who writes a book about war (whether ancient war or World War II!) in the era after the Vietnam War cannot but be affected by the lessons of the Vietnam War in interpreting his subject. Ideology, often political ideology, but sometimes social, economic, or cultural ideology, has affected the writing of history in the past century to the extreme. One must be mindful that this is a possibility and be forthright in presenting in an objective manner the information that one collects, always aware that an ideology may exist in one's writing or rewriting of history.[58] Yigael Yadin was not only an archaeologist, he was, as

117

were many of his generation, a state-builder. Archaeology was for him more than just the history of ancient Israel, it was a road map to the future. Other archaeologists and historians in the present period have begun to revise the conclusions of these earlier state-builders and have become cynical of the legacy of early Israel.

Revisionism is found in all intellectual movements; it is present in all fields of history worldwide, and in every discipline from archaeology to zoology. Every generation attempts to place its stamp on the body of knowledge it was handed, and often revisionism is resorted to when scholars sense an enormous change in the social view of the audience they are writing for. American revisionist historians have rethought the entire scope of America's place in World Wars I and II in light of events that have occurred in the past few decades. Revisionist historians generally come to extremely different conclusions about the meaning and significance of well-known events despite eyewitness or contemporary historians' assessments. Contemporary economic historians have revised the assessments made by earlier economists about the significance of capitalism, supply-side economics, and Communism, and have come to different conclusions about their meaning. In the past twenty years a revisionist movement has developed in Middle Eastern history, the Bible, and archaeology which affects our understanding of the time-honored conclusions in biblical archaeology in general and the Cave of Letters in particular. The revisionism of Yadin's and earlier historians' thinking in regard to the Cave of Letters, its archaeology, and the Second Rebellion is known here as maximalism (because they hold that the Second Rebellion was very extensive—Diaspora and all Israel—in agreement with literary accounts) and minimalism (because it holds that the Second Rebellion was not extensive and relies upon some literary accounts and the archaeological data). In many ways, this book suggests another maximalist interpretation, a maximalist-minimalist approach, but it still is a revision of Yadin's thinking.

There is another form of revisionism going on among scholars as well, which has broader political and social implications at its heart, and this too is aimed at the Cave of Letters, biblical archaeology, and Y. Yadin. In Israel, the history of Zionism is in general being rewritten by revisionist Zionist thinkers who have totally rethought the origins and significance of the entire idea of the modern State of Israel. In the past twenty years this has included almost every period of history, but especially the ancient period, which was used most prominently as a raison d'être for modern Israel. The acceptance of biblical history as true and accurate in its general outlines and details was challenged by biblical revisionists and by a new generation of Israeli archaeologists who broke with the conventions of study and came to totally new conclusions about the veracity of the ancient history of the region and the interpretation of biblical history in particular. The debate is framed here as a debate between the traditionalists or maximalists, who see the biblical past as true in general and in many of its details, and the minimalists, who challenge the details and general conclusions of biblical and religious history, especially as it relates to some of the main figures and places of this past. Some of the questions they have raised are: Did Abraham, Moses, David, Jesus, and Bar Kokhba ever exist in the way that the literature portrays them? Where is the evidence? Can it be deduced from archaeology? In the absence of evidence can conclusions be reached? There are shades of the debate that place different individuals in different camps (maximalist-maximalists, minimalist-maximalists, maximalist-minimalists, etc.), but in general the debate over religious history stems from the same critical method that allows the two sides to reach different conclusions by interpreting differently the same body of information.

In the case of the Exodus from Egypt, for example, revisionists have made the massive Exodus into a small group of dissidents who marched around aimlessly (perhaps) in the Sinai desert. Similarly the revisionists have made the dramatic Conquest of the Israelites under Joshua into a gradual flow of an indistinct people into a variety of locations in Israel. In the case of the kingdom of David and the ancient Temple of Solomon, it has become for minimalist-minimalists a created legacy for the benefit of inspiration for a people in a post-exile life. Jesus has been made by revisionists into a man of great hopes and expectations and little else. In the case of Bar Kokhba, the same information from the Second Rebellion that gave Yadin, the ultimate secular maximalist, his opportunity to create the image of a David and Goliath battle of enormous proportions (as reported in the literature [Bar Kokhba as David and the Roman general as Goliath]) has now been revised to a small, insignificant blip on the radar screen of history. Yadin saw modern Israel as a bulwark against future Masada and Cave of Letters, "last stand" mentalities that were a product of the Holocaust of Europe that literally brought the modern State of Israel into being.

One historical note is important here. Masada was excavated by Yadin in 1963–1965 in one of the most massive excavations ever undertaken by a government anywhere. He had tens of thousands of volunteers working nearly nonstop during the period of the excavations and the saddest conclusion of the excavation that Yadin reached was that the account of the first-century Jewish historian Josephus Flavius about Masada was accurate in general features and detail. In Josephus's account, nearly a thousand refugees from the destruction of Jerusalem in 70 CE gathered on top of the mountain fortress of Masada only to be forced into massive suicide by a Roman siege in 73 CE. This account is similar to the one that Yadin reconstructed of the Bar Kokhba Rebellion from his excavations in the Cave of Letters, even without Josephus's literary prowess. The more than twenty bodies inside of the Cave of Letters and Cave of Horrors suggested to Yadin a similar tragic, heroic fate for the Second Rebellion followers of Bar Kokhba. In both cases Yadin took to heart the courageous but disastrous conclusions of the two rebellions as if to say, "This is the ancient Jewish courageous martyrdom. In this modern State of Israel, the State will be powerful enough to insure that this will not happen again." The military honors and graduation ceremonies on top of Masada in the time following the excavations indicate the country's willingness to allow his archaeological assessment to help direct the State's ideology. The minimalists of Israel have been affected by the disastrous conclusions of the 1973 War, the occupation in Lebanon, and the protracted intifadas of the 1980s–1990s and the present that Yadin did not fully experience during his lifetime. In short, the revisionists have been affected as much by the changing political and military changes in Israel as they have by the changing methodologies of history and archaeology.

Our excavations have allowed us to add a new wrinkle to the maximalist/minimalist debate and to show that the revising of Yadin's grandiose scheme for the rebuilding of a modern-day State of Israel (in light of his archaeological excavations at the Cave of Letters and Masada) may be a necessary exercise, but it is equally important to show why and when he was right.

# THE DEBATE OVER THE
# INTERPRETATION OF HISTORY

In the past ten years an amazing phenomenon has occurred in biblical archaeology. Revisionists seek to overturn current theories of culture, art, and history in popular and professional journals, magazines, newspapers, and conferences. Recent articles in the *New York Times* and *Wall Street Journal* have affected the entire understanding of biblical history by the general public. The crux of the issue involves how much evidence is enough to confirm long-held conclusions about the Bible, biblical history, and, most important, the individuals who appear in the Bible.

Without evidence from any independent sources (other than the texts themselves), it is impossible to confirm the historicity of figures such as Abraham, Isaac, Jacob, Moses, Joshua, Elijah, King David, and Solomon. The independent sources that are usually invoked come from the world of archaeology. Recent discussions have centered upon whether the histories of these ancient figures were all constructed hundreds of years after the fact and that there may never actually have been a real historical figure by the name found in these texts. Biblical archaeology and its discoveries rarely supply specific information about an individual or event in the Bible. Biblical archaeology only supplies general background information that is from the same historical period as an individual or event. The minimalists say that background provided by archaeology demonstrates only that: background, and that little or nothing else can be learned from the general elements present in a period such as architecture, comparative ancient literature, iconography, coins, and pottery. These elements do not demonstrate the historical existence of any of these figures, and they certainly do not validate any specific event. In fact, this general background points to the absence of exact information on these individuals as evidence that these individuals never existed. In terms of this, the minimalist might simply state: The absence of evidence (of specific events and figures) is evidence of the absence (of those events and individuals). Conversely, it is clear that the only evidence sufficient to convince a minimalist would require such specificity that it would render the scientific method nearly unworkable.

Extrapolation from logical inference is the basis for the maximalist case. The maximalist states that the existence of extensive archaeological background points to a maximalist convergence between the accuracy of literary accounts and the meaning of the material culture. To the maximalist, the background of archaeological evidence is evidence of an accurate background in the literary account. If the Bible is correct in its general outlines of biblical life, it must be accurate in terms of the details of the characters as well. If the Bible has historically validated information about simple questions of daily life, ceremonies, styles, forms of communication, law, etc., this validates all statements and information in the Bible.

Both positions are untenable in an age of scientific reason, but they have polarized our understanding of ancient history. Did Moses really exist? Did Joshua conquer Jericho as described in the Book of Joshua? Did King David really conquer the nations and areas described in the Book of Samuel and Kings? If so, why isn't there any archaeological evidence to confirm any of these literary accounts? The debate involves the Hebrew Bible in particular, but also New Testament studies. One cannot fully confirm the historical existence, let alone the meaning of the messages, of John the Baptist, Jesus, and Paul without falling back on a scant series of ancient literary references and a scant fewer archaeological artifacts. What biblical archaeology does best is its great deficit. It provides the background of a life, not a life-in-itself (to use a classic Kantian term). Only in very rare instances does it actually confirm the existence of any individual and tell us something substantive about the person. The Cave of Letters documents, however, give us specific information about a specific historical or mythical person but do nothing to clarify the nature of the rebellion he was involved in. They give us details of the time but not the answers to the larger questions of the period. We now know more about Bar Kokhba than about any other key Jewish historical figure from all of ancient Jewish history. We now know more about Babatha, the daughter of Simon, than about any other Jewish woman of the period, all because of the discoveries in the Cave of Letters.

# THE BAR KOKHBA REBELLION AND THE MINIMALIST-MAXIMALIST CONTROVERSY

The case of the Bar Kokhba Rebellion is an excellent example of how far the minimalist and maximalist interpretations can be verified. The ancient literary accounts (we have Jewish, Christian, and Roman accounts about the Bar Kokhba Rebellion) agree that the rebellion engulfed the larger Jewish population of Palestine and parts of the Diaspora. In these accounts, nearly 600,000 Jews were killed and more than nine hundred villages destroyed. They picture an extensive rebellion which either achieved its goal of reaching Jerusalem and then got pushed back or nearly achieved it. The latest revisionist view has been prompted by the archaeological picture that has emerged. Most of the Bar Kokhba finds in caves and tunnels around Judea point to an intensive campaign in this area. Little or no remains outside of this area leave some scholars such as Prof. M. Mor at Haifa University in Israel thinking that the Bar Kokhba Rebellion may not have been as extensive or even as successful as was first thought.[59] Some minimalists contend that it was a small rebellion that never even achieved its main goal; i.e., the recapturing of Jerusalem. The Temple is dramatically portrayed on some of the Bar Kokhba coins. Some Bar Kokhba coins feature the Temple and the Table of Showbread in between the columns of the Temple. They indicate the year of the "Freedom of Jerusalem." In some instances the coins list the name of the high priest Eleazar. But the minimalists ask, "So what? Does this all mean that the Temple or Jerusalem were ever really recaptured, or were these coins only propaganda and indications of aspirations?"

Ancient literary accounts tend to point to the fact that the Temple was retaken by the rebels, but archaeology is very scarce on this point. Nearly ten thousand Bar Kokhba coins (many were being restruck over Roman coins and the locations where the vast majority of these coins were found is in doubt since they were not systematically excavated but rather found and only later identified) have been found in areas around the greater Judean province area, but very few in Jerusalem and its closest suburbs. Of the 13,629 coins found in Jerusalem up until 1982, for example, only three are Bar Kokhba coins (a fourth was from Ramat

Rachel near Jerusalem). This coin information has led some historians to argue the minimalist position more intensely. P. Schaefer of Tubingen University and others, on the other hand, hold that Jerusalem was retaken and Temple worship reinstituted for a short while. This last point is important because if Jerusalem had been taken and Temple worship reinstituted, it would certainly have been an event that would have commanded the interest of the entire Jewish Diaspora and population of Palestine in this period.

Other evidence with regard to the size of the rebellion is from Roman records of another sort. W. Eck from Koln University, a military historian of the Roman Empire, has categorically proven from recently reviewed Roman legion records that as many as twelve Roman legions from as far away as Britain were sent to put down the Bar Kokhba Rebellion. He argues in his article "The Bar Kokhba Revolt: The Roman Point of View"[60] that this corroboration from an outside source may indicate the "real" presence of an extremely large Roman fighting force in second-century Palestine and may mean the Bar Kokhba Rebellion was as brutal and destructive as the literary accounts say. He carefully reviewed the Roman records of this period and came up with remarkable information that gives greater credence to the maximalists. He found that the Tenth Legion was forced to abandon Jerusalem until the reinforcements showed up. The Twenty-Second Legion was brought from Egypt, routed, and apparently wiped out. Eck found that it disappears from succeeding lists of Roman legions. The Second Trajana, the Third Cyrenaica, the Sixth Ferrata, the Third Gallica, the Fourth Scytica from Phoenicia and Syria, the Fifth Macedonica, the Tenth Gemina from Mauretania, and the Seventh Claudia are among the legions that were sent. Why were so many legions sent if the rebellion was so small and limited to the area of Judea, as minimalists insist?

What has the minimalist/maximalist debate contributed to our understanding of the Cave of Letters? It affects substantially our understanding of how desperate the people in the cave may have been and our perception of their state of mind going in. Were these people like the Masada residents of 73 CE? Were they being hunted down by the Romans and therefore desperate to hide and survive at all costs? Or are they just hiding from the Romans and intending to return to their homes in Ein Gedi and elsewhere? Were these some of the last survivors of the Bar Kokhba Rebellion, or just a group who did not want to be drawn further into the rebellion or bothered by the Roman presence?

Yadin, a maximalist, held that the Cave of Letters and the cave across the way—the Cave of Horrors—represented the desperate last effort of the revolt. He assumed that the revolt was a colossal failure throughout Israel and that these people of the caves represented, in a sense, the end of Jewish autonomy in Palestine until Yadin's own days. Yadin argues that the skulls found in a burial niche tell us of their inability to bury their own dead in a proper place. And so they end up living with their last precious possessions in the cave of the living "dead."[61]

In the post-Holocaust Israel of Yadin, the caves were a stirring symbol of the new Israel's commitment to a continuing struggle. The caves, guarded from above by the Roman camps, provided a place for them to resist and die. Bar Kokhba became the symbol of the Jewish nation even before the 1967 war. The Bar Kokhba Revolt, in a sense, did not end with the people in the cave. Artifacts found in the cave such as the single fragment of the Psalms and the nineteen bronze ritual artifacts in a basket tell us how they hated pagan religion and sought religious and political freedom from Rome. It indicated an ongoing historical war of which this was only the opening battle. Modern Israel represents the culmination of the war. On Lag B'Omer (a holiday that interrupts a period of mourning between Passover and Pentecost in the Jewish calender), May 11, 1982, the State of Israel buried in a state funeral the bones found in the burial niche of the Cave of Letters and in the Cave of Horrors. Religious and political leaders attended the ceremony.

For the minimalist, the Cave of Letters is a microcosm of the small revolt of Judeans who foolishly tried to match the might of the Roman emperor. The Judeans were part of a fringe movement that was not well supported by the Jews of Palestine or the Diaspora. Their end is another example of how fringe zealots bring destruction upon themselves and others. Their possessions and letters are indicative of a middle- and upper-class group that was fleeing from the Romans stationed in their own particular village of Ein Gedi. They stole nineteen bronze artifacts from the Roman legion stationed in Ein Gedi and hid in the cave to escape detection. They also represent a Jewish fringe group because they do not keep the standard Jewish practice of burying and placing the bones together in a burial chamber. Rather, they separated the skulls of their dead into baskets and kept them in the burial niche. All in all, a small lunatic fringe using strange and desperate means to survive, but by no means representing the will of the entire Jewish people.

These debates of the minimalists and maximalists in Israel also bear a strange resemblance to the political divisions of the Israelis in the post-Intifada, post-Lebanon world of modern Israel. Many Israelis, tired by the fifty years of bloodshed and flag-waving, have begun to reinterpret the mission of the state and their own history. Post-Zionists now readily tell a tale of Israel's need to insure that small groups of overzealous settlers will not bring another destruction upon the Jewish people. Minimalism fits their new vision of an Israel which need not rest upon the myths of the past or put itself in the position of having to flee into caves to survive. The silent majority of Israel recognizes that the will of the majority is to accommodate the "other."

# EVIDENCE FROM COINS

I personally classify myself as a "maximalist-minimalist" in most areas of biblical archaeology. Coin information in the Jerusalem area is used by both maximalists and minimalists to make a point. If the rebels did achieve their goal of retaking Jerusalem and the Temple Mount, they must have done it like the Maccabees with an initial attack on the Temple *before* Hadrian was able to call in other legions from around the Empire. The troops would be called up only after Hadrian realized that his own troops could not control the situation. Since Hadrian had been in the area in 130 CE, he may have thought that the Temple was the crux of the issue—not the Jewish Temple, but the temple which Hadrian intended to build on the Temple Mount to honor Jupiter. Did Hadrian begin building the Temple of Jupiter in 132? Did the Jews then rebel? Or did the Jews rebel because of the generally oppressive measures of Hadrian? Did Hadrian build the Temple of Jupiter on top of the Temple Mount after the war? It is hard to imagine that Hadrian would begin building a major cult site on top of what he knew to be a sensitive religious site without having a large contingent of troops on hand. Hadrian and his advisors knew the Roman accounts of the First Jewish War. They knew the problems caused by even simple displays of Roman power in the time of Pontius Pilate and the procurators.

The Bar Kokhba coins were generally restrikes of classical Roman bronze and silver coins, over the images of Roman emperors and pagan symbols. Coins were excellent sources of propaganda precisely because they were used by everyone. Hadrian decided to rename the city of Jerusalem "Aelia Capitolina" and rename Judea "Palestine" to further detach Jewish aspirations from Jerusalem and Judea. He minted Aelia Capitolina coins to commemorate this event. The discovery of two Aelia Capitolina coins together with four Bar Kokhba coins from the El Jai Cave in the Nahal Michmash area seems to indicate that the building of the Temple of Jupiter on the Temple Mount by Hadrian began before 135 CE and that the rebels were preparing to restrike the Aelia Capitolina coins as Bar Kokhba coins. Although it is possible that the coins were deposited by a casual visitor in the El Jai Cave after 135 CE, H. Eshel and especially Arieh Kindler, one of the world's leading coin specialists on the Bar Kokhba Rebellion, concluded that the Hadrian coins prove that the building of the Temple was the main cause of the rebellion. Kindler, in particular, has made a science of understanding what the Bar Kokhba coins tell us about Hadrianic forays into the Middle East in general. Kindler has studied all the Hadrianic coins and discovered that how Hadrian is depicted on the coins may tell us more about the man than was first suspected. Kindler's "psychology of coins" has important implications since his interpretations tell us that the coins of Aelia Capitolina were minted by Hadrian late in the 120s CE (128–129 CE) rather than the earlier theory of various historians that renaming the city Aelia Capitolina was done after the war. On the early Hadrian coins, Hadrian has a portrait of himself which differs from coins later in his career. The portrait on the coin, therefore, tells us when the coin was minted. The Aelia Capitolina coins have a more flat-topped, round-faced Hadrian, which is more in line with coins from the 120s than those from the 130s. Perhaps Hadrian was naive, but the reconstruction of a prized piece of real estate in Jerusalem may have seemed benevolent to him.

In addition, we know that Hadrian had been adopted into the former emperor Trajan's family. He so valued this privilege that he listed his father's name on coins during his building phase of the 120s. After the horrible Roman troop losses of the Bar Kokhba Rebellion, however, he did not list his father's name. It is as if he was embarrassed or was taking full responsibility for the results—something which matches his letters to the Senate in this period. On coins from the Rebellion, only his name is listed on the coins. During the building process, it appears that he had been trying to demonstrate the continuation of the policies of his adoptive father and to show how proud he was to build up the Roman Empire in these areas. The coins were apparently minted after the renaming of the city was accomplished. They are found together with the Bar Kokhba coins because, like the other Roman coins found in Bar Kokhba coin hoards, they were going to be restruck by Bar Kokhba to create new coins. Between Hadrian's visit in 129–130 CE and the end of the rebellion, Hadrian had renamed Jerusalem Aelia Capitolina and was in the process of perhaps making the ancient site of the Temple in Jerusalem into a temple dedicated to Jupiter. This sparked the rebellion and the rest is history.

## THE CHRONOLOGY OF THE REBELLION

I thought it would be helpful to see what I think was the chronology of the Second Rebellion that ultimately affects our understanding of the events in the Cave of Letters. Here is what I think happened:

1. Hadrian actually made two trips to Palestine. He first visited in 129 CE on his way to Egypt. His presence at Gerasa is evidenced by an inscription. On his first trip Hadrian would have seen the state of the Temple Mount and Jerusalem. He probably decided that he would undertake (as he did elsewhere in the empire) the restoration of the ancient site. He would have ordered the beginning of work on the new temple to Jupiter on

the Temple Mount and minted coins (as he did elsewhere) in honor of the event. This would have sparked the beginnings of the opposition movement which resulted in the coalescing of a rebellion. The other cause of the rebellion is apparently a growing anticircumcision movement. While Dio Cassius says the Aelia Capitolina project initiated the rebellion, the *Scriptores Historiae Augustae* says it was the prohibition against circumcision. The Aelia Capitolina coin minted in honor of the initiation of the work shows tethered oxen preparing the ground for the Aelia Capitolina. If it had been in commemoration of the completion of the work, an actual temple of Jupiter would have been more appropriate. Coins were used as commemoration devices for major events. The iconography suggests an early point in the construction. Hadrian remained in Egypt through 130 CE. In the beginning of 131 CE he returned to Palestine apparently to see the progress of the work.

2. In 131 CE he would have seen the preparations in Jerusalem for the inauguration of his Temple of Jupiter.

3. In 132 CE Bar Kokhba and his rebels seize the construction site. Bar Kokhba coins are minted in celebration of the initial victories. They, in turn, portray a hybrid temple which incorporates elements from the Hadrianic temple and the Herodian and/or an imagined Third Temple. With his initial victories, Bar Kokhba has access to coin hoards in caves around Judea and Samaria that had been gathered for Temple tithes and reconstruction since the destruction in 70 CE. These were the funds for the initial rebellion, which he could access only if he was committed to a Temple cause.

4. In 133 CE Hadrian sends for major reinforcements. Bar Kokhba rebels begin guerrilla warfare. They begin living in tunnels around Jerusalem and Judea. Restriking of coins begins. The caves that are used to store the coin hoards are the same caves that had been known from the First Revolt and which stored the Temple tithes which had continued to be collected from 70 CE onward. Temple Mount has been lost to the rebels. Coins with other symbols of redemption are chosen (grapes,

lyres, palm trees, amphorae, freedom of Israel/Jerusalem/Zion, redemption of Israel). In the early coins a Temple priest, Eleazar, is named on the coins. His name was later removed.

5. In 134 CE Bar Kokhba coin hoards around Judea and Samaria were augmented in anticipation of victory.

6. In 135 CE all Hadrianic reinforcements arrive in anticipation of major battles.

7. In August/September 135 CE, Beitar and Bar Kokhba Rebels are defeated. Some rebel groups escape to caves in the Judean desert in the hope of escaping destruction. The Roman armies decide to initiate a search and siege policy similar to the one exercised by Vespasian and Titus when they crushed the First Revolt.

8. In 136 CE Eusebius describes the ultimate transformation of Jerusalem into a full Hadrianic Aelia Capitolina after the complete destruction of the Bar Kokhba Rebellion.

If the coins tell us anything, it is that in this period dreams/hopes/ aspirations were not normally stamped on coins. Coins generally commemorate events that have happened rather than attempting to predict the future. One does not usually appoint a high priest in anticipation of the coming time when his services will be necessary. If the Bar Kokhba rebels were able to take the Temple Mount and Jerusalem for even a short time, they might have begun to issue coins only after the fact. If they were driven from Jerusalem by the end of the first year, it would stand to reason that no Bar Kokhba coins would be found in those areas. By the end of the first year of the rebellion Bar Kokhba coins were probably being issued from rebel headquarters outside Jerusalem. The rebels were clearly motivated by the real circumstances of reclaiming Jerusalem forever, and not simply exercising wishful thinking.

# 5

# Returning to the Cave

## The Road from Bethsaida
## to the Dead Sea

This chapter deals with influence, with how much outside influence Judaism accepted in the ancient period, and how certain views from later periods often impress themselves onto the earlier periods. The Bible is filled with admonishments of the Israelites for walking in the ways of the non-Israelite religious traditions and it is clear that the prophets were concerned about worshiping the idols of the other groups present in ancient Israel. This influence continues in later periods as well. Greco-Roman rulers and religion provided a different model for the Jews. The toleration of Jewish life by some of the Greco-Roman rulers (Alexander and the Ptolemians in the fourth to second centuries BCE and the early Roman rulers from Julius Caesar to Augustus) may have tipped the scales in favor of some type of veneration of the Roman emperors and their imperial religion by Jews in an official and unofficial way in ancient Israel. This religion, called in this chapter "the Roman imperial cult," may have had a very different form in Judea than it did elsewhere in the Roman Empire, but certainly it had an influence. While the Jews were exempted from worshiping the emperor in the way that Roman citizens did, the veneration and recognition of the non-Jewish leader of a country in which Jews live has a long and honorable role in Judaism. Most theories about the relationship between Jews and ancient pagans developed in the past century under the specter of modern anti-Semitism and the Holocaust. It was hard for Jewish scholars educated in European institutions in the past century to acknowledge that the relationship between Jews and their neighbors was anything but difficult. My own teacher, S. Lieberman, a brilliant, classically trained Talmudist, is indicative of this attitude. He could only imagine that the Jews (like Lieberman himself) knew and could conduct business in Greek but he was unable to understand that the Jews (not only the very assimilated Jews) could engage in a full Greco-Roman world experience on their own terms.

Before the modern period, the stormy relations between Jews and non-Jews meant that an outside influence was difficult because of fiat either from without (Jews were forbidden to practice non-Jewish arts and crafts during the Middle Ages) or from within (Jews were forbidden by the rabbis from practicing non-Jewish arts and crafts during the Byzantine and early medieval periods). A common understanding of the Decalogue that states, "Thou shalt not create any graven images . . . to worship them" was that the Jews were forbidden to practice art. In fact, what the study of archaeology has revealed is that Jews practiced art in almost every period and most found no religious problem in doing it, especially in the Roman period. Jews apparently engaged in every single form of art practiced by their neighbors from the Iron Age onward. They made small idols; they designed a variety of different stone carvings and, in the later period, mosaics. Apparently the interpretation of the biblical injunction was read in its entirety, not to create artistic renderings that were then worshiped (in place of the Israelite deity!), but they could be made and perhaps even appreciated in some extended definition of religious accommodation. Although this may seem difficult to imagine, this form of accommodation is done throughout the religious world. In India, temples filled with the statues of other religions are found, and traditionally venerated. In China, Buddhists, Taoists, and Confucianists interacted with one another's teachings interchangeably.

Rabbinic literature, however, is very clear in its prohibitions of almost any form of Greco-Roman art, but again, these pronouncements were written down only later (in the Byzantine period) and often the Babylonian tradition was the final redacting home for most of these traditions. Babylonian society was very anti-Greco-Roman art and would have encouraged these traditions of enmity to be emphasized. Some good examples of how far the literary traditions are from the reality of archaeology should be noted. The use of Zodiac mosaics (that include almost every major character of Greco-Roman religion and myth) on synagogue floors in Israel and in the Diaspora starting in the third and fourth centuries CE cannot have suddenly emerged in a vacuum ex nihilo. They must have been built from a tradition of religious art that was in play in an earlier period.

The examples indicate that the Jews had adapted the Roman art and mythological forms to their own needs. It was commonly held, however, by most scholars until quite recently that the Jews could never adapt any of the Greco-Roman art to their own purposes because it was so rooted in Greco-Roman religion. Apparently the Greco-Roman Jews of Israel found ways, especially in their own land, to adapt the Greco-Roman art forms to their own needs for two reasons. First, their benefactors expected that the peoples they ruled would in fact participate in the religion of Rome. Second, adaptation took many forms. Accepting gifts that were prominently displayed in the Temple of Jerusalem is one of the ways that Roman religion may have found an outlet, even in the most sacred realms of Judaism. In the hinterlands of Israel, far from Jerusalem, this interaction may have been more liberally applied, especially in the time of the Herodians. The imperial cult of Rome in Israel may have been an excellent way for the Jews to honor the leader of the empire that preserved their economic and social life. The Temple in Jerusalem that existed in the time of King Herod was by all accounts a place of Roman favor. The utensils used in Jewish religious practice resembled the articles of Roman religion. It would have been the equivalent of a Jewish Kiddush wine cup resembling the Roman Catholic wine chalice used in the Mass. Was a utensil such as the incense shovel we discovered at Bethsaida a part of Roman religion or the Jewish religion? It is like asking whether the Kiddush wine cup used in synagogues could also be used as part of Roman Catholic religion. The artifact was the same; perhaps made in the same fashion after a form that was aesthetically pleasing in this period. What we know is that the same kind of artifact, the bronze incense shovel, was used in centers of Roman religion like Pompeii and Herculaneum and was found in Israel as well. It is clear that the Jews were influenced by Roman religion, and Jewish religion could not but be influenced as well.

This chapter suggests one step more in this argument, that the Temple in Jerusalem was home to artifacts, either gifts or utensils fashioned by Jewish artisans, that bore the marks of Roman religion, and that some of these artifacts were spirited away to the Cave of Letters by priests in the days before the destruction of Jerusalem in 70 CE. Why? Perhaps they felt that the only way to revive the religion when they had the opportunity was to use elements from the destroyed Temple.

※　　※　　※

I tell people that the road to the Dead Sea Cave of Letters began at the city of Bethsaida in the Golan. In 1996 the discovery of a first-century imperial cult site at Bethsaida, and an incense shovel near the site, taught us that the imperial cult of Rome had a much more profound effect upon Jewish Palestine in the first century than had earlier been suspected. Bethsaida was refurbished in the first century by Herod Philip, a son of Herod the Great. His two brothers, Archaeleus and Antipas, both refurbished some of the cities they were in charge of in the earlier part of the first century, so it is not unusual to find that Herod Philip does the same thing in 30 CE. He renamed the city of Bethsaida in 30 CE after the wife of the emperor of Rome, Livia-Julia. From 30 CE onward, Bethsaida is now Bethsaida-Julias. It is easy to see how profound the effect of the imperial cult is when we have renamed cities such as Ptolemais, Tiberias, Scythopolis, Diocaesarea, Sebaste, and Diospolis all over Roman Palestine in the first century CE. It is more difficult to understand that the influence of Hellenization (better: Romanization) of Jewish religion and life was felt all the way to Jerusalem.

Jewish art and architecture reflected the impact of the imperial cult of Rome in Jewish Palestine. The Roman imperial cult had an impact in the provinces all around the Middle East, so it is not surprising that it had an impact in Israel, but the main issue has to do with the Temple in Jerusalem. Did the imperial cult extend all the way to Jerusalem and into the Temple, or was it limited to far-flung areas such as Bethsaida and Caesarea? It is important to remember that many of the improvements to the Temple in Jerusalem were done by Herod the Great. In the period following the death of Herod the Great in 4 BCE, his sons and later the Roman Procurators, the leaders of Judea appointed by the emperor, continued the process. It is easy to see why people like the Essenes lived on the Dead Sea and created their own version of Jerusalem or why John the Baptist and others railed against the situation. The effects of Roman rule in Palestine were profound. Even though the Jews modified Roman practices to suit their unique religious requirements, by the middle of the first century Roman and Roman-Jewish art and architecture may have already been living a symbiotic existence in Israel.

## THE ROMAN PERIOD INCENSE SHOVEL AND THE DATING OF THE CAVES

The Roman period incense shovel found at Bethsaida, which was used there in the first century, may have been indistinguishable from an incense shovel used in the Temple in Jerusalem in the same period. The discovery of a first-century incense shovel in the Cave of Letters and the cave's identification as a first-century refuge cave for the Zealots and other First Revolt exiles would have been perfectly acceptable until 1960. In fact, it was the prevailing interpretation of this cave until Yadin's excavations. Yohanan Aharoni had written his reports on Caves 5 and 6, and because of the small number of finds could not interpret them otherwise. He held that the small number of pottery finds (among them an ostracon, a small inscribed shard of pottery), textiles, and other artifacts could be either from the First or the Second Revolt. Archaeologist Pesah Bar Adon, for example, another contemporary of Aharoni and Yadin (and one of the four archaeologists who went into the Judean desert for the 1960 expeditions), wrote that the caves he investigated nearby "served as places of refuge for those fleeing from the sword at the time of the destruction of the Second Temple [in 70 CE]."[62] But in his 1980 final report on the *Cave of Treasure*, Bar Adon revised his earlier thinking based upon Yadin's conclusions. He suddenly wrote that the limestone vessels, oil lamps, jugs, and juglets that he had earlier assigned to "the Herodian period" and that were clearly similar to artifacts at Qumran and Masada were being reassigned to the second century CE on the basis of Yadin's assessment of the finds in the Cave of Letters. He apologetically wrote that "since then it has become clear that the Herodian vessels, on whose presence this suggestion [that the cave was used during the Second Temple period] was based, have in fact a span down to the mid–second century CE."[63] He wrote, "Only two occupation levels could be distinguished in the cave, one of the time of Bar Kokhba, and the other of the Chalcolithic period. And there were no signs of occupation, even of the most transitory nature, between the two periods."[64] He came to this conclusion because by the time he penned his final report in 1980, the conclusions of Yadin had already become the standard model of interpretation. In 1960 the Cave of Letters discovery of Bar Kokhba period documents and Yadin's interpretation of the cave changed the way everyone interpreted not only the artifacts from the Second Revolt (which we knew very little about), but also other caves in the area. Two periods of occupation became the norm for interpreting most of the Dead Sea caves that contained any Bar Kokhba artifacts. Earlier (Hellenistic and Herodian) artifacts were interpreted as being used for longer and longer periods. The Chalcolithic (4500–3200 BCE) and Bar Kokhba (132–135 CE) were seen as the major periods for caves without religious documents.[65]

In addition, the caves debate had one other, more personal, element associated with it. Yadin had more to prove than that the Cave of Letters contained artifacts only from the Bar Kokhba era. First, Yadin had a penchant for trying to demonstrate the superiority of his work over that of his other major contemporary, Y. Aharoni. Aharoni and Yadin were more than just archaeologists to most Israelis. In the 1960s and 1970s Aharoni and Yadin represented two different approaches to archaeology at two of the major institutions of higher learning in the two major cities of Israel, Tel Aviv and Jerusalem. In Israel, archaeology had become the religion of modern Israel. Archaeology was, as the modern State of Israel itself, a secular vehicle for writing and rewriting Jewish history and rediscovering a heroic (and not necessarily religious) tradition of the Jews. Yadin entered archaeology after a stellar military career as an officer in the *Haganah* (the precursor to the Israel Defense Forces in 1947) and later as chief of staff of the Israeli army in 1949. He received his doctorate in 1955, writing his dissertation on "The War Scroll of the Children of Light and the Children of Darkness," and taught in Jerusalem at the Hebrew University. In 1955–1958 he worked on Hazor, one of the largest excavations at the time supervised by the Department of Antiquities of the State of Israel.

Y. Aharoni was a soft-spoken field archaeologist who was born in Frankfurt, Germany, and only came to Israel in 1933 as a teenager. He had been a kibbutz-dweller, tracker, and guide extraordinaire, who pursued a doctorate in archaeology under Prof. Benjamin Mazar at Hebrew University in Jerusalem, writing on "Settlements in the Upper Galilee." He worked at the Department of Antiquities of the fledgling State of Israel, supervising parts of the Galilee and the work at Hazor. His interests also took him to the Negev and the Judean desert, and in 1953 he began the work in Nahal Hever which was documented in his book with Beno Rothenberg, *In the Footsteps of Kings and Rebels* ([Hebrew] Tel Aviv: Masadah Press, 1960). He supervised projects at some of the major sites of Israel, including Ramat Rachel, Arad, Lachish, and Beer Sheva, and although he began teaching in Jerusalem, he ended his career teaching at Tel Aviv University and died (much too young) in 1976, at age fifty-six. Aharoni was soft-spoken, Yadin outspoken. Yadin was an extrovert, war hero, and general. Aharoni was the reserved pedagogue and scholar. Yadin had already been involved with Aharoni at Hazor (1955–58), a major Iron Age city in northern Israel. Yadin had been the director of excavations. But it was Aharoni who was the driving archaeological theorist at the time. Aharoni was a geographer, historian, tour guide, and archaeologist. He was also a person who began to theorize about the

Yohanan Aharoni. (B. Rothenberg/COL Project)

way that sites in Israel contributed to the "big picture" of the history of ancient Israel and who contributed to the public debate by writing columns in the popular press on the significance of excavations. After Yadin's success at the Cave of Letters, Yadin returned to the excavations at Hazor (1968–69) and began to write publications that roundly contradicted the Aharoni thesis on the destruction of the city of Hazor[66] and updated many of the writings of Aharoni with his own assessments of the work at Arad, Beer Sheva, and Lachish.[67] In short, one of the possible reasons why Yadin did not consider the First Revolt theory, which had prevailed until his excavations, was that it had been proposed and continually advocated by students of Aharoni.

Second, Yadin may also have wanted to disconnect the Cave of Letters from the issue of the Copper Scroll treasures and the Dead Sea Scrolls for several reasons. He was interested in making sure that treasure hunters were not searching Israeli caves for Copper Scroll treasure, and he wanted to redirect the Dead Sea research from the scrolls in the caves around Qumran (in Jordan) to Dead Sea research in caves in Israel. In much the same way that a contemporary author such as L. Schiffman in his books *Reclaiming the Dead Sea Scrolls: The History of Judaism* and *The Background of Christianity: The Lost Library of Qumran*[68] has tried to reinterpret the importance of the Dead Sea Scrolls as Jewish documents for a new generation of Jewish scholars and readers, so too Yadin tried to redirect the Dead Sea archaeology of 1960 from the Dead Sea Scrolls research directed by a group that generally excluded Jews and Israelis (and primarily focused on the contribution of the scrolls to the development of early Christianity) to his own research in caves associated with the tragic but courageous story of the Bar Kokhba Rebellion.

Baruch Safrai championed Y. Aharoni's ideas about the Cave of Letters as a refuge for Zealots and other First Revolt refugees even after most scholars had accepted Yadin's views as "gospel." This book tries to change the monolithic interpretation of the Cave of Letters of Yadin and integrate some of the ideas that Aharoni wrote about his experience in the Cave of Letters nearly fifty years ago. My view that the incense shovel of the Cave of Letters was a first-century artifact from the Temple in Jerusalem is based upon three elements that Yadin already presented in his research:

1. The style and artistic rendering of the incense shovels and the rest of the artifacts found in the Cave of Letters resemble artifacts from other major first-century religious sites (Pompeii and Herculaneum).
2. Yadin had the incense shovels and other bronze items evaluated by a metallurgy expert who concluded that the objects may have been produced and used for almost a hundred years before the Bar Kokhba Rebellion. Yadin wrote, "Evidence of considerable wear and tear is visible on most of them—dents, soldering and other repairs—which would indicate that their date of manufacture was considerably earlier than that of their cache. As metal vessels can serve their owners infinitely longer than pottery vessels, it is possible to put the date of manufacture of these utensils in the second half of the first century or the beginning of the second half of the period between the two Jewish revolts—the period of Trajan."[69] Yadin mysteriously

rejects the view that they were manufactured *and used* in the first century although he knew that they were made much earlier than the Bar Kokhba Revolt.

3. The incense shovel was a well-known Jewish artifact. It is found in many middle Roman and later Roman and Byzantine synagogues in Israel. It is similar to the other synagogue iconographic artifacts which come from the Temple in Jerusalem. They include the menorah (the impressive candelabrum that was a part of the Temple in Jerusalem), the lulav (the palm branch, used in rituals associated with Sukkot, the fall agricultural and pilgrimage holiday to the Temple in Jerusalem), the etrog (the citron, also used for the holiday of Sukkot), the shofar (the ram's horn, associated with all major pilgrimage holidays in the Temple but most specifically the new year's celebrations of Rosh HaShanah and Yom Kippur). The incense shovel was probably a symbol of the incense service, which played a key role in the Temple service on Yom Kippur (Day of Atonement) and in the daily worship service. The Ptolemies, Augustus, and Tiberius donated certain artifacts to the Temple in Jerusalem in the Greco-Roman period. Emperor Augustus and Livia in the early first century CE had donated items that would still have been in use during the rebellion and would have been the subject of controversy given the views of the Zealots. Some of these items were presumably melted down by John of Gischala, the Jewish rebel leader who continued to fight in Jerusalem until the destruction of the Temple in August 70 CE. Josephus wrote, "When there was nothing left that John could extort from the people, he turned to sacrilege and melted down many of the offerings in the Sanctuary and many of the vessels required for services, basins, dishes, and tables, not even keeping his hands off the flagons presented by Augustus and his consort. For the Roman emperors honored and adorned the Temple at all times." According to Josephus, the smaller vessels seem to have been melted down by the Zealots. Presumably these included both the holy vessels constructed by Jewish artisans (that may have included Roman symbols) and the smaller vessels donated by Emperor Augustus.

In Yadin's time the understanding of how Roman symbols were used by Jewish institutions was different from the view developed in the past forty years of scholarship. Today it is clear that a variety of Roman motifs were used by Jews in a variety of ways in the period even before Roman iconography on synagogues became popular. Yadin believed the defacing of the bronze vessels was indicative of the rabbinic attitude against pagan symbols. He thought that it was possible to make them kosher for Jewish use by only a minor defacing of the specifically pagan iconography. But what type of Jewish use, if not in the Jerusalem Temple setting? No other type of Jewish worship was permitted in this period. But the question remains whether they were really defaced or just used for a long period of time. The fact that not all the vessels are defaced argues against a single policy.

When one looks closely at all of the vessels from the Cave of Letters and compares them with similar vessels from Pompeii and Herculaneum, the wear and tear of the Cave of Letters objects is not much greater or worse than the Pompeii and Herculaneum artifacts. Although one item in particular has a very severe scratch on the face of the handle, most mythological renderings on the other artifacts fare somewhat better than other items from the same period.

Other issues also presented themselves upon further analysis. Evaluation of the motif of Thetis and Achilles on the large *patera* (p. 142) showed that that motif was in fact in vogue in first-century Pompeii and Herculaneum *paterae*. It is found in a panel on the base of the menorah of the Temple in Jerusalem and on the Arch of Titus in Rome. While there is a controversy as to whether the base of the *patera* of the Cave of Letters is Jewish or Roman, there seems to be no debate as to whether or not it is a first-century symbol. If the Thetis rendering on the *paterae* of the Cave of Letters and the Thetis rendering on the menorah from the Arch of Titus are taken together, one might conclude that both the *patera* and the menorah were from the Temple in Jerusalem rather than simply discrete pagan renderings that happened to end up together in a very Jewish context. Yadin's conclusion, however, was that since everything in the Cave of Letters was from Bar Kokhba's time, the bronze artifacts including the *patera* must have been from that period as well. He constructed his "Roman outpost in Ein Gedi" theory to place the artifacts in a clear pagan context—but allowed for their Jewish use as well.

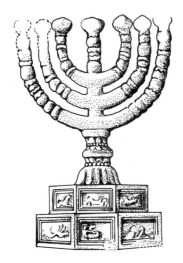

(Top left) The Arch of Titus menorah. (Top right) Thetis on the Jerusalem menorah (lower center panel enlarged). (Bottom left) *Patera* from the Cave of Letters. (Bottom right) Thetis on the Cave of Letters *patera*. (D. Hadash/ COL Project)

The *patera* from the Cave of Letters. (G. Hochman/COL Project)

The illogical nature of this conclusion is highlighted by the fact that Yadin argued that everything in the Cave of Letters was Jewish except the bronze artifacts found in the opening to the cave. The idea that these artifacts were Roman booty was further complicated by an idea that only later emerged from the study of Bar Kokhba coins. Bar Kokhba's group was in such dire need of bronze and silver for the minting of coins that he restruck Roman coins. In addition, while the state of Bar Kokhba's movement may have been popular among some Jews and Christians for a time, the need for bronze for weapons, defensive equipment, and tools must have been great. Why, then, would Bar Kokhba's troops bury bronze pagan ritual objects in the Cave of Letters? Wouldn't it have made more sense to melt them down for tools, coins, and weapons? The theory that the bronze artifacts and their iconography were pagan and from the Bar Kokhba period makes less and less sense as one considers the options that presented themselves in the Cave of Letters. In addition, other facts about the Cave of Letters documents have resulted in new questions about the possibility of a first-century occupation level in the cave.

## GRECO-ROMAN INFLUENCE ON JUDAISM

Until the 1950s and 1960s most scholars thought that Jews in antiquity did not use Roman symbols until quite late in the Roman period. Because of questions about outside influence in Jewish culture in the post–World War II era and scant archaeological evidence, the question of Roman influence on Greco-Roman Judaism was always seen as important but not profound. One of the reigning theories of Roman influence on Judaism was proposed by the longtime professor of Talmud at the Jewish Theological Seminary, Prof. Saul Lieberman, who concluded that the impact of Greece and Rome on rabbinic Judaism was profound in scope but superficial in substance, meaning that only the superficial parts of the culture would be used by Jews, often stripped of their more philosophical and religious meanings.[70] This view of Greco-Roman influence as only general beliefs, conceptions, and patterns of behavior clearly transformed biblical Judaism into a new and totally different form of Judaism. This view of the literary history of Judaism changed an age-old impression that Jews were forever cut off from the Hellenistic and Roman influences.

Although Lieberman and others were willing to allow for a modicum of Hellenistic influence upon rabbinic Judaism in conventional ways such as commerce, certain vocabulary, or even political terminology, Hellenistic influence upon rabbinic and postbiblical Judaism was, in his opinion, limited. For most of these writers, no profound philosophical or theological Hellenistic influences could be identified in rabbinic Judaism. Needless to say, it would be impossible for them to conceive of Jews using Greek and Roman art and mythology in their daily and especially their religious lives. Even as archaeology in the 1960s and 1970s continued to uncover examples of Greco-Roman art and mythology in the Rabbinic period, many text scholars continued to look for ways to reinterpret it. As Yadin himself knew, many synagogues beginning in the third and fourth centuries were decorated with Greek symbols such as naked Greek idols (Hammat Tiberias) or clothed ones (Beth Alpha). Hercules (Chorazin) and carved images of Zeus are found on Jewish graves in Beth Shearim. So the argument that Jews did not use Greco-Roman mythological images is difficult to accept. The doors of the Temple as they are rendered on the third-century Dura Europos Synagogue have mythological figures. In the Dura Europos synagogue, we find both a dolphin and a Capricorn/Thetis-like character on a number of ceiling tiles as well. In addition, among the second-century "letters" in the Cave of Letters, two small seal impressions with mythological images have been found. One has a motif of Hercules killing the Nemean lion while the other appears to be another mythological figure (mermaid?) holding a torch. While these seals may have symbolized Bar Kokhba's struggle against Rome, the use of the mythological images by Bar Kokhba suggests that they were a meaningful vehicle for communication among Jews of the second century in general. And if they were meaningful to political rebels as zealous as Bar Kokhba in the second century, one might easily infer that they were acceptable even earlier. While they are not generally held to be Jewish images, eagles are found throughout the Herodian-Roman periods in clearly Jewish/

rabbinically sanctioned contexts. Rabbinic burials in Beth Shearim as well as those of Hellenized Jews throughout Israel used the eagle despite its obvious connection to astral and immortality symbolic connotations in the Near East and its direct connect with Greek myths. Dolphins and sea creatures also appear in synagogue and other Jewish ornamentation. In short, could the bronze artifacts which were found in the Cave of Letters be first-century artifacts? Absolutely! Could they be first-century Jewish artifacts? Absolutely! Could they be first-century Jewish artifacts from the Temple in Jerusalem? Absolutely! If so, it would make this small collection of bronze artifacts located in the Israel Museum some of the most important artifacts in the world.

# 6

# The Copper Scroll
# and the
# Dead Sea Caves

On March 20, 1952, what has become known as the Copper
Scroll was discovered in Cave #3 near Qumran together with coins
dating from the Second Jewish Revolt. On April 1, 1952, the *New York
Times* reported on the discovery of the Copper Scroll(s) with the head-
line "Ancient Scrolls Found—Copper Sheets Left by Essenes are Dug
Up in Jordan." The report stated, "Coins dating from the second
Jewish revolt of 135 A.D. were discovered with the copper scrolls."
The scrolls were really two pieces of the same scroll. One is about 80
cm long and the other 160 cm long. Besides being one of the few texts
in antiquity written on the unusual metal material (almost 900 manuscripts from the 11 caves around Qumran are written on papyrus or
leather), they are also distinguished by the unusual content. It was
then and remains now one of the great enigmas of biblical archaeology. Unlike any other Dead Sea Scroll, the text is neither a part of
the Bible, nor a Sectarian text, but rather an inventory. Divided into
sixty sections, the text lists 64 locations where the treasures of the

Temple were buried. Locations from Jerusalem, Jericho, and down the Dead Sea to Masada are mentioned. But more important, the locations do not stray further than a small circle of locations in the areas from Samaria to Judea. And in this list are large amounts of gold and silver. Some estimate the amount at 26 tons of gold and 65 tons of silver. The Copper Scroll, displayed in the Jordanian Archaeological Museum in Amman, Jordan, describes the riches of the Temple, which have been distributed to a variety of locations, many of them along the Dead Sea. The original translator, J. T. Milik, suggested that the scroll was a "fairy tale created by a crank."[71] Many speculate that Milik and others created the "fiction" story to discourage "gold rush fever" from interrupting the more serious excavations at the Dead Sea.[72] Starting in the early 1950s, treasure seekers and local Bedouin had undertaken amateur and illegal excavations in many of the caves precisely because of the possibility of finding more scrolls which were being bought at an established rate per centimeter of text. In theory, therefore, it is possible that the original view of the content of the scroll as a fiction may have been promoted more to discourage others from undertaking excavations on the Dead Sea rather than for any scientific reason. Gold rush fever is palpable in the accounts written during this period. Paul Lapp, writing in *Biblical Archaeology Review* in 1978, provides graphic descriptions of the "fever" from 1962:

> Six feet down something intriguing appeared. In the dim light it looked and felt like scrolls. The digger immediately rushed it out to the light of day. It proved to be nothing but fragments of matting. Continuing below the matting, the diggers turned up bone after bone—all human bones, as they immediately recognized. Then someone spied a gold ring and the hunt was on! At this point a careful archaeologist would try to set up a foolproof surveillance while he planned a strategy for recording and recovering this piece of history; not so the Ta'amireh [Bedouin]. Seven men had not much more than a square meter apiece as they dug feverishly through the night. Breaks in the work came only when disputes arose about lines between claims and how best to keep from throwing dung in each other's faces. In their frenzy they tore ancient mats, trampled fragile ancient garments to bits with their feet, and smashed old pots to get at the gold they hoped was inside. Empty pots were smashed in dis-

gust. . . . That evening around the camp fire the bedouin discussed their strategy and traded stories about pots of gold and scrolls. . . .[73]

Coin hoards certainly existed. Qumran yielded a treasure trove of 450 coins, which, when taken together by weight, are quite substantial. In addition, although the latest coins are from the Second Revolt, a large portion are Roman coins and from the entire first century. The importance of this cannot be minimized. Coin hoards with Roman coins from the entire first century together with Bar Kokhba–era coins have been found throughout the entire area of Judea and Samaria over the past century.[74] As we began our excavations of the Cave of Letters in 1999, I was reminded of the lists of places mentioned in the Copper Scroll and I began constructing a theory about how the Cave of Letters might be one of the locations mentioned in the Copper Scroll. I also began to think about other locations associated with the Bar Kokhba Rebellion. Many of the Bar Kokhba rebels hid in caves or tunnels in the area of Judea that must have been known from the earlier Rebellion some sixty years before. These caves and tunnels allowed the rebels to hide out on the sides of roads leading in and out of the desert to Jerusalem and conduct a form of guerilla warfare. These same sites became refuge caves at the end of the war. Many of these tunnels and caves also contained coin hoards, some of them large. They included bronze and silver coins, which bankrolled the Bar Kokhba Revolt. These coin hoards have never been sufficiently explained. Where did they come from? Who brought these coins there? Were they collected over a long period of time or over the short period of the Bar Kokhba Rebellion? Temple Tax collections are one possibility. According to the rabbis, the collection of the Temple Tax continued after the destruction of the Temple in Jerusalem in 70 CE, and for the decade leading up to the rebellion and the seizure of the city by the Zealots, the Temple Tax was collected by pious Jews and held for fulfilling their future obligations. It would have been an excellent source of money for Bar Kokhba's ongoing needs, and many Jews would have seen it as a good use of the Temple Tax. The pious Jews empowered to distribute the money might have made it accessible to him because of his express desire to restore the Temple, or perhaps he made the Temple restoration a pillar of his campaign because of his need to access the money. The fact that Bar Kokhba's early coinage has symbols of the Temple on it indicates his desire to fulfill this campaign pledge.

## THE LEGACY OF THE SCROLL AND QUESTIONS OF CHRONOLOGY

Since many of the Roman coins date back to the first century and come from the region, one may infer that they were collected over a long period of time. The caves may have been well known to a limited group of Temple functionaries. According to rabbinic literature, the Temple Tax might still have been paid in coins after the destruction of the Temple with the original purpose of the donation (the biblical obligation) being maintained. The coins would be an exchange for the worth of the animal sacrifice.

Three terms are mentioned in the Copper Scroll which early on led scholars to think that it was written in the time of the Temple in Jerusalem. They are terms for offerings which were used in the time of the Temple: *Kli Dema*, *Maaser Sheni*, and *Herem*. The first term, *Kli Dema*, occurs some fourteen times in the Copper Scroll. What most scholars do not pay attention to is that although the word *Dema* appears in the Bible, the concept of *Kli Dema* is found only in rabbinic sources. *Dema* is *Terumah* (priestly share) as early as the *Mechilta de Rabbi Shimon ben Yohai* on Exodus 22.28.[75] In addition, the term *Terumah* in *Tannaitic* literature is already a general term for a type of head tax, a contribution (to the Tabernacle), a priestly share, tithe, dedicated objects, or a sacred treasure. The *House of Hakkoz*, which is a priestly family specifically mentioned in the Copper Scroll, is one of a select group of priestly families who are also mentioned in Tannaitic *baraitot* (traditions) in the Babylonian Talmud, tractate Ketubot 24b and 69b in regard to the status of Temple sacrifices and tribute. The Copper Scroll uses terms that have meaning in the Tannaitic system. But it is not using exact Tannaitic terminology. The Copper Scroll language is only *protorabbinic*. That is linguistically one stage of development before the more formalized rabbinic language. It uses words such as *Kli Dema* in an idiosyncratic way as a general concept for Temple-related offerings. It appears to be one stage before rabbinic terminology, and not simply copying rabbinic terminology itself. The rabbis, for example, use the phrase "*Bet Dema*," not "*Kli Dema*." One scholar, M. Lehmann, saw this connection. He said about the Copper Scroll, Item 4, that "there are dedicated vessels (*Klei Dema*) consisting of cups and jars with handles" and argued: "The Scroll reflects an era when various sacred items were redeemed and gathered to be transported to Jerusalem or to the Temple, but for political or Halakhic reasons this could not be done. . . . This era was between the First and Second Revolt against the Romans, and this inventory was compiled when the fortune of the war had turned against the Jews."[76]

M. Lehmann presented a similar argument to the hypothesis which we were developing. The Cave of Letters would have been one of the places mentioned in the Copper Scroll where deposits of Temple Tax could be taken and hidden, but since the names of the caves in the Copper Scroll were so different (remember: only in the 1960s did it become designated by Yadin as "the Cave of Letters"!) it would be important to link it specifically to the Copper Scroll's designations. The Copper Scroll was written before the Bar Kokhba Rebellion but after the destruction of the Temple. While M. Lehmann did not connect the Cave of Letters specifically with the Copper Scroll or the Bar Kokhba coin hoards, he raised an important issue about the number of locations, the amount of the treasure, and the need to hide it in places that were out of the way. The ongoing devotion to the Temple by Jews both in Israel and in the Diaspora, which allowed for the ongoing collection of a Temple Tax, is crucial to identifying a source of the treasure mentioned in the Copper Scroll. The other source of the treasure in the Copper Scroll was the treasury of the Temple in Jerusalem itself. As we began excavations at the cave in the summer of 2000, I thought about the sixty-four locations where items were mentioned and the nearly thirty Bar Kokhba locations which had already been discovered with large quantities of metal coins. Were these coin hoards the locations mentioned in the Copper Scroll? If they were, it would make the Copper Scroll a document that identified caves known to be locations where hoards might be placed for safekeeping. The vast majority of scholars held that the Copper Scroll was written before the end of the First Revolt. Approximately nine thousand coins were said to have been discovered in the Bar Kokhba hoards, a sizable treasure, and this is only a partial number based on anecdotal information. These coin hoards have never, nor can they ever be, scientifically studied. Almost all of the hoards were discovered by treasure hunters. Most of the information collected on the hoards is anecdotal and usually misleading. No one really knows how many more caves and tunnels were plundered over the past eighteen hundred years. The location of the Bar Kokhba hoards were known in antiquity. They probably had been used from the time of the First Revolt to the Second and beyond.

As we began our excavations in 1999, I wondered if the Cave of Letters was one of the caves mentioned in the Copper Scroll, especially in light of the major bronze finds in the 1960 Yadin excavations. If a specific reference to the Cave of Letters could be found in the Copper Scroll, it would show that the Copper Scroll not only contained information about Temple Tax treasures buried in caves from the end of the First Revolt, but also information about caves used up to and during the Bar Kokhba Rebellion. If the Copper Scroll contained a list of treasures that was buried up to the time of the Bar Kokhba Rebellion, it might also be a road map for the Cave of Letters and other Bar Kokhba caves.

In the *New York Times* article from April 1, 1952, cited above, the stratigraphy of the discovery of the Copper Scroll is said to have remained problematic. First, there is a strange indication in the story that the Copper Scroll's placement may actually be connected to the Bar Kokhba Rebellion in particular. The article mentions that "coins dating from the second Jewish revolt of 135 A.D. were discovered with the copper scrolls." Placement of objects and stratigraphy are extremely important to the determination of dating. Stratigraphy, in particular, is important in archaeology because it allows us to assess the relationship between artifacts for relative dating. One can tell whether one layer of evidence is earlier or later than another by virtue of finding it above or below another layer. Stratigraphy was only partially considered in most of the Dead Sea cave research, since it was assumed that the scrolls were all placed in the caves at the same time. In general, cave researchers knew that other, earlier settlements had used many of the caves. But since the vast majority of materials (especially near Qumran) were from one period, researchers began to assume that the entire corpus of written materials was fairly unified. In fact, the Copper Scroll was discovered in a narrow spur toward the back of the main gallery of Cave #3. A large boulder blocked the entrance to the rock spur. It is clear that roof fall blocked the entrance to the rock spur after the Copper Scroll was placed back there. Roland De Vaux, the excavator of the Copper Scroll, specifically states that a few shards were found near the scroll in this rock spur. It appears that the roof of the main gallery fell at a different time than the spur. Today the entire cave roof has fallen in, so it is nearly impossible to reassess the original placement of the items, but assumptions prevailed in 1952 that forever cast the Copper Scroll as a document from around 70 CE. The main gallery of manuscript discoveries in Cave #3 date from around 70 CE, when Qumran was destroyed. Unfortunately, the main gallery of manuscripts was assumed to be from the same time period as the Copper Scroll, which may not be the case. The entire cave may have served as a repository for manuscripts for an extended period of time. The Copper Scroll's official designation as 3Q15 tells part of the story: Cave 3Q, the third cave chronologically discovered near Qumran, and the fifteenth manuscript discovered in Cave 3. Since Cave 3 is 2 km north of Qumran, all of the finds were immediately associated together despite the fact that the Copper Scroll:

1. was found at the entrance to the cave and not in the area where other Hebrew biblical, Hebrew nonbiblical, and Aramaic, non-biblical leather and papyrii texts had been found;
2. had a totally different paleographic profile than the rest of the other scrolls;
3. had been found on top of roof debris (and not below the roof debris where the other materials had been found), suggesting that it was from a different and probably later source than the other materials in the cave.

If the Copper Scroll had been deposited in Cave 3 directly after the 115 CE earthquake, this would explain why it was on top of at least some of the roof debris. The 363 CE earthquake, which may have been the one which destroyed many cities in the area and may have destroyed many cave roofs, would also be the one which ultimately shut the Cave 3 rock spur off from the rest of the cave.

Although F. Cross dates the Copper Scroll back to the years before the destruction of the Temple of Jerusalem in 70 CE, the orthography is much more akin to that of second- and third-century Mishnah and Tosefta scripts than to the Dead Sea Scrolls and Masoretic writing. More importantly, orthographic and paleographic studies make little or no sense in the case of the Copper Scroll, because it is engraved—under difficult circumstances—and not written at all! Its letters only partially preserve the printed contours of letters from any period, let alone allow comparison of writing styles. This is the reason for the vast difference of opinion regarding the Copper Scroll among scholars. R. De Vaux, Abba Bendavid, S. Sharvit, and S. Morag all dated it to the first century despite the fact that almost everyone clearly recognized the affinity to Mishnaic Hebrew and its difference from the rest of the Qumran (Hebrew) language.[77] Because of its discovery in a Qumran cave, most were unwilling to place it in the period of the Bar Kokhba rebellion. Only Ben Zion Lurie and Ernest-Marie Laperrousaz dated the Copper Scroll to the second century and specifically to the Bar Kokhba era. Since the Copper Scroll was written in Mishnaic (second- to third-century) Hebrew and was located in a suspiciously different archaeological stratigraphy from the rest of the scrolls in Cave 3, argued Lurie and Laperrousaz, it probably was from a different period than the rest of the scrolls inside of Cave 3!

The Copper Scroll was seen as a product of the time of Bar Kokhba by Ben Zion Lurie, an Israeli scholar of Bible and rabbinic literature, in his *Megillot HaNehoshet MiMidbar Yehuda* in 1964. By 1976, only one other scholar, E. M. Laperroursaz, held the same view. M. Lehmann held that the scroll was from the end of the first century, while most scholars held that it was from before the Temple's destruction (Qumran is destroyed in this scenario before Jerusalem, in 68 CE).

What, then, is the date of the Copper Scroll and its connection to the Cave of Letters? This book offers a middle ground between most of the scholarly theories. Our theory holds that the Copper Scroll represents an authentic list of treasures collected in a post–70 CE period from Temple Tax revenues which still were collected despite the absence of the Temple. This list was originally an oral tradition which was similar to other rabbinic traditions, and finally committed to writing in light of tragic events of the second century, most notably the War of Quietus and the earthquake of 115 CE. So much treasure is listed because it was collected over a long time. The treasures were all dedicated for Temple use (including repair) and so include biblical and Temple tribute language. The language of the Copper Scroll is *protorabbinic* precisely because it represents the writing tradition of the second century, not the first century. More important, one particular series of events may have been the catalyst for the final writing and deposit.

The Copper Scroll was written in a hurried and often colloquial style. It lists some twenty locations in and around the Dead Sea. A large volume of metal treasures is mentioned. Although the terms "silver" and "gold" do not regularly appear, different metal designations are alluded to. Unless the words "gold" or "silver" are actually spelled out, they should not be used in the translation of the sections relating to the metal treasures.

Lists are not uncommon in biblical and nonbiblical literature. One finds lists in much more ancient Near Eastern literature. They are found on clay tablets and stone stelae. They include items similar to those in the Copper Scroll: in lists from lawsuits, receipts from payments, dues, sales, contracts, and deeds. Even the style of the Copper Scroll is not unique. It lists the places where the treasures will be found in a way that is similar to other documents found in the Ancient Near East. A late Babylonian rental agreement, for example, reads in a fashion similar to the descriptions found in the Copper Scroll: "The *kurubbu*-house belonging to *Nana-iddina*, which is in the district of the great grove which is in Erech, which is alongside the *kurubbu*-house of *Mushe-zibitum*, the daughter of . . . and alongside the center of the field. . . ." The documents mention specific locations that meant something to the people at the time when they were written, but that are lost on modern readers. This same type of writing is found in legal documents up to and including the period before the Bar Kokhba

Rebellion. In one of the Babatha archive documents, for example, one finds a location that was meaningful when the document was written in 130 CE but probably would be meaningless to anyone who did not live in that particular period when the document was written:

> the property of Eleazar (also known as Khthousion) son of Judah, your grandfather, a courtyard with all its rights in En Gedi and the rooms with it, everything that opens [off it] to east, north or south, every right that the aforementioned Eleazar Khthousion had in the said courtyard, abutters being, on the east, a market, on the west [property of] Maththethos(?) son of Zabbaios, on the north Aristion's land, on the south a public market.[78]

The documents were not intended to be historical documents; at the time and place they were written, they were fully understood. So too the Copper Scroll locations were understood by the writer. In Item #4 of the Copper Scroll, one reads:

> In the mound of Kahelet, there are dedicated objects consisting of flasks and jars with handles; all are of the dedicated material, plus the Sabbatical year and second tithe. Its entrance is by the mouth of the well at the edge of the canal, at a distance of six cubits from the north toward the cave of the immersion pool.

In Item #18:

> In the clay pit which is at the edge of the wood, in it are two hundred measures of silver.

While the material upon which the scroll was written suggests permanence and longevity, it is clear that the writers hoped to retrieve the materials quickly. The author was dealing with sites which he must have known would not be permanent and would be understood by only a small group of people. People in ancient times knew that topography changed. The Copper Scroll gives points of reference which were meaningful only for short-term burial. This was the first clue to when and why the Copper Scroll was written. The Copper Scroll was written by someone who had access to metal reserves to create the scroll and who apparently had knowledge of Dead Sea locations that are very similar to the locations of the Bar Kokhba coin hoards! Perhaps, we argued, the Copper Scroll treasure storage locations *are* the Bar Kokhba coin hoard storage areas!

If so, their location may tell us more about life between the first and the second rebellions than about the Second Rebellion itself. This is important because recent minimalist historians have used the location of the Bar Kokhba coin hoards of as an indicator of the farthest extents of the Second Revolt. These minimalists argue that the hoards of coins in the area around Jerusalem and in the nearby Judean desert caves (and not in the Negev, the coastline of the Mediterranean Sea, or Galilee) indicate that the Second Rebellion did not even encompass the whole land of Israel, and that is why no coins were found elsewhere. In fact, the Bar Kokhba coins were centrally minted and stored in a relatively short period of the rebellion (2.5–3.5 years) in the place the coins were being sent to. Since everyone from around the Jewish world and the rest of Israel was sending their coins to the Jerusalem area in part to fulfill their Temple Tax obligation and in part to fund the rebellion, it stands to reason this is the only place where we should find Bar Kokhba coins. We should find them only around Jerusalem and the Judean desert, and they should be coins from the period of the First Revolt until the Second Revolt—thus the coin hoards and the Copper Scroll would be both the tax and the treasure of the Temple and they needed to be located in close proximity to the Temple in Jerusalem.

But here is the paradox of the Copper Scroll. Since the style of the Scroll suggests that the writers assumed that the metal scroll would be retrieved *in the not-too-distant future*, they used site names and descriptions that were simple; assuming that these descriptions would be sufficient for easy retrieval before the terrain dramatically changed. They wrote the scroll, however, on a material that would not easily be destroyed over time if it were actually buried in the ground; on copper/bronze, because they probably were writing in a time when they did not know if the Jewish people in Israel would survive and the scroll would need to have the possibility for retrieval at some distant future date. Most important, our developing hypothesis was that the Copper Scroll must have mentioned the Cave of Letters among many other cave depositories in the area. We began to speculate that the Copper/bronze Scroll and the bronze artifacts in the Cave of Letters were directly linked. We soon found evidence that the Cave of Letters was directly mentioned in the Copper Scroll. If they were linked we assumed that the Copper Scroll (listing the location in the Cave of Letters) was written *after* the bronze artifacts were deposited in the cave. It must have been deposited after the First Rebellion that ended with the destruction of the Temple in 70 CE, but before the Bar Kokhba rebels arrived at the end of their rebellion (since they apparently did not know it was there!). The writing of the Copper Scroll suggest that it was written close to the time of the Mishnaic Hebrew of the rabbinical academies that flourished during the second century CE. The style and the placement of the Copper Scroll suggest that it had been written *after* the other scrolls in Cave 3 and deposited there at a later date than the rest of the scrolls. Had some event between the end of the First Rebellion and the beginning of the Second Rebellion sparked the writing of the Copper Scroll? We searched for historical answers.

Historians and biblical scholars have found that most ancient texts originally passed through an oral stage of transmission and were written only later during a period of upheaval and fear that the past may be forgotten. It is thought that the earliest written renderings of the Bible were sparked first by the chaos created by the Assyrian destruction of the Northern Kingdom of Israel in 722 BCE, the later renderings of the Bible by the destruction of the First Temple in Jerusalem in 586 BCE,[79] the chaos of the Maccabean period yielded new writings in the second century BCE and ultimately the desire of the rabbis to write down their oral tradition so that it would not be lost in the period following the disastrous events of the Bar Kokhba Rebellion. It is thought that the large literary production found in the caves around Qumran may have been a part of the "end of days" atmosphere that surrounded the Essene community on the Dead Sea as well as others in Israel because of the upheavals of the Herodian and later Roman procurator period leading up to the First Revolt. The question for us was: What could have sparked the writer of the

Copper Scroll to go to the trouble of producing his work? It was clearly written after the destruction of the Temple and close to the Rabbinic period. Perhaps, we thought, it was the ill-fated uprising in the Diaspora against the Roman emperor Trajan in 113–115 CE? Add to this one of the horrific natural disasters of the century; an earthquake that devastated Israel and the Middle East in 115 CE. This would have been a time of great fear in Israel and the Diaspora. At the end of the rebellion, Emperor Trajan appointed Lusius Quietus governor of Judaea. This is before Hadrian's ascension as emperor in 117 CE, but a time of great instability in the Empire. The author of the Copper Scroll may have completed his listing of the treasures collected from 70–115 CE, returned to a well-known cave near Qumran, Cave 3, and deposited his list of the Temple Tax money (and cave hoards and depositories) so future generations would have resources to rebuild the Temple in Jerusalem and reinvigorate the priestly obligations in some coming time. It is possible that the Copper Scroll was written even closer to the time of the Bar Kokhba Rebellion or even in the middle of the rebellion. The fact that Bar Kokhba coins were found with the Copper Scroll may indicate that Cave 3 was used by the rebellion. It may not be a coincidence that the Bar Kokhba rebels used a cave that was known from an earlier period or used for burying the treasure of the movement. The Bar Kokhba rebels must have known about the "large cave with the two entrances" or they would never have known to seek it out as a place of refuge at the end of the rebellion. It had to be very well known to them in advance if they were going to take the social elite of Jews from Ein Gedi (Babatha among them) who fled to the cave at the end of the rebellion. They certainly did not search out this cave for the first time at the end of the revolt! The rebels who would have accompanied the refugees must have had very good intelligence about access to these caves before they started wandering off with women and children into the Judean desert. So at the end of the Second Rebellion, as the Bar Kokhba rebels came into the cave with the two entrances (that could be seen from the dry riverbed below), they were entering a cave that was well known in local legend for at least a generation. It was well-known enough that it had been used to bury treasures for future retrieval. By the summer of 2000, our working hypothesis became, therefore, that the cave had been used before the refugees arrived at the end of the Bar Kokhba Rebellion. If this cave had been used before the Second Rebellion refugees got there (at the end of the First Rebellion in 70 CE or the Quietus War in 115 CE) there should be evidence of the earlier occupation. This evidence was there and we would uncover it in our excavations in 2000.

# 7

# The "Cave of the Column" and the Cave of the Letters

## INTRODUCTION

In this chapter I will compare and contrast some of the geology results that led us to unravel the mystery of the Copper Scroll's connection to the Cave of Letters and present the essence of my theory. I did not know there was a connection between the Cave of Letters and the Copper Scroll found in a cave at Qumran when we began working in the Cave of Letters. I had studied about the mysterious scroll and the problems but never put the two together until one fateful day when a geological reference jogged my memory. When we began our excavations I knew the following things from my research in the library:

1. In or around the Cave of Letters were found Jewish correspondence, deeds, receipts, personal documents and items of a Jewish woman, a couple of Jewish coins, a section of one psalm,

161

and commonware that indicated some Jewish habitation; therefore we knew that the Cave of Letters was a Jewish refuge.

2. The Cave of Letters had a treasure trove of bronze artifacts buried near the entrance to the cave that did not fit into the other categories of Jewish finds in the cave.

3. The treasure trove was unlike anything ever discovered in Israel in a cave or elsewhere.

4. The theory that Yadin had proposed of this being a pagan treasure that the metal-strapped Bar Kokhba rebels had stolen from a Roman garrison (and then buried without melting it down for better use such as weapons or even minting new coins!) did not make sense logically or strategically. It was an answer that did not respond to the question. I thought that the treasure trove had to be Jewish and it had to be something that someone had left a record of so that it could be retrieved.

Why would anyone bury such treasures and not mention it anywhere? While we lack many documents, and much of the treasures of the Middle East have disappeared into the treasuries of the conquerors, I hoped that someone preserved a record of this treasure. My point was based upon logic. This treasure would not have been something to safeguard if it was only pagan religious artifacts, but if this was a treasure trove of Jewish religious artifacts, it would make sense to bury it. But we wanted to know when it was buried, who buried it, and why it still remained.

How would the person who buried the treasure ever find it again if there was no map, no reference to the place where they were buried? It was a mystery. I began my search from an understanding of the geology and geography. In the Middle East and especially in the desert, where one deals with changes in landscape that can overnight be transformed by a sandstorm, an earthquake, and natural forces of the wind and water, it is important to figure out how any ancient person ever found anything they placed in the caves. I have hiked in the dry riverbeds in search of caves and in different seasons I see different contours that I had not seen before. The ancients understood this better than we do. They knew that they could not depend on simple descriptions of places to direct future generations. They needed signposts that would be nearly immovable. Oases in the desert with their trees for shade and their water sources were spoken about as nearly eternal guideposts for travelers. Having lived in Nebraska I knew that geology was a part of ancient mapmaking. Large geological features such as the Chimney Rock in western Nebraska, which directed generations of nineteenth-century settlers along the Oregon Trail, still stand to show the way to modern travelers. One day, as Jack Shroder looked up at a massive natural stone column standing under the entrance that we climbed through every morning, I knew that I had the answer: This was the signpost. A cave with a massive thirty-foot-high pillar that beckoned the eye to look upward toward the entrance; the two entrances of the cave. It had been there for hundreds of thousands of years and could be seen from the wadi below and from the cliffs around the Nahal Hever. Most important, it was so prominent that it seemed to me this must have been the signpost that the ancients remembered at countless campfires as they described to the sons and daughters the mysteries of the desert. A cave which appears to be held up by a single massive, natural, stone column with two entrances.

One small history advisory is necessary with regard to the Copper Scroll. The language of the Copper Scroll is a Hebrew/Aramaic that sounds very much like the language of the rabbis and very unlike the language of the Dead Sea Scrolls and the Hebrew Bible. It contains many abbreviations, since it was so difficult to write on the copper, and the abbreviations are unparalleled, suggesting it was written for a very limited public. It is so unique that there is really nothing to compare it to. The abbreviations have been one of the biggest problems in the unraveling of the scroll, and along with the rather idiosyncratic description of the locations of the treasure they have prompted some scholars to take radical stands on the importance of the scroll, with some scholars holding it is fantasy or myth and others saying it is not. I have always been troubled by these two radically opposed positions. If someone went to the trouble of describing in detail these locations, writing them down with so much care and difficulty, it stands to reason that it was something the writer felt was important and true. If it was created all in the name of a fantasy to bolster the reputation of the Jews and the Temple in

Jerusalem, then hiding the text in a cave may not have been the best way to publicize it. Also, the whole idea that someone had created this elaborate fiction in antiquity with such minute detail and attention to language and location in order to enhance the importance of the nonexistent Temple is untenable. A general, much less detailed list and locations would have sufficed. The most troubling problem of the Copper Scroll as fantasy was the larger implication for the rest of the scrolls in the caves around Qumran. Were all of these Dead Sea Scrolls exaggerations and unreliable reflections of the realities that the writers wanted to be so carefully preserved? If so, it would make the possibility of creating a social history of the scrolls community an impossibility. Another untenable situation. I think no Dead Sea Scrolls scholar would ever assume this. They assume that the scrolls reflect a social reality that was true for the writers of the scrolls. I think that the original reason that some early scrolls scholars declared the Copper Scroll to be a fantasy in the 1950s is tied to their desire to save whatever treasures were still in these caves from treasure hunting. I think that they really feared that by declaring the Copper Scroll to be true—that there were real treasures in the caves and not merely texts—it would have set off a treasure-hunting campaign the likes of which would have dwarfed the scrolls debacle that resulted in the destruction of many fragments of ancient texts. It is the same reason that I think that Yadin declared the treasure of the Cave of Letters to be "pagan ritual objects" and dismissed them.

Much that could have been systematically excavated and understood by archaeology in the caves has been lost to looting and amateur excavating. Perhaps a greater good was served by these scholars playing down the significance of the finds that they encountered in the name of possible future excavation. The problem is that it has misled scholarship for nearly half a century.

## FEATURES OF THE ENTRANCE TO THE CAVE OF LETTERS

One of the first things which occurred to me as I looked across to the Cave of Letters from the top of the Cave of Horrors in 1998 was how

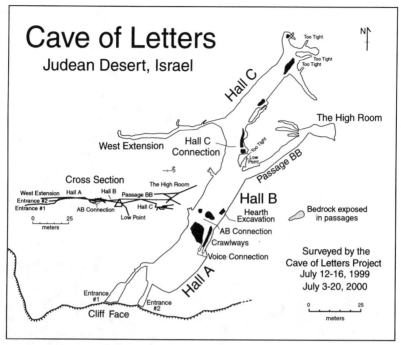

New Cave of Letters mapping. (P. Reeder/COL Project)

distinctive it was. As you look across Nahal Hever you immediately see the two entrances to the cave nearly side by side but separated by a naturally formed column of stone. It would have been visible to people walking along the bottom of the Nahal Hever dry wadi bed as they looked upward, and to those who were walking through the desert on top of the cliffs from Ein Gedi northward toward Masada. In short, the Cave of Letters and the Cave of Horrors would have been known to travelers looking for a place to stop on a long, hot afternoon. Because of the Cave of Letters' extensive size, it probably would have acquired a distinctive name. The beauty of working with geoscientists is their ability to wax almost poetic about rocks, caves, earthquakes, and deserts—in scientific terms. It is their appreciation of rock formations, their ability to assess the ancient history of a cave, and their ability to enumerate ancient features of an environment such as a cave and to trace its development and changes to our own

The natural 30-foot column below the Cave of Letters Entrance #1. (G. Brubacher/COL Project)

times. Geologists are differently trained than archaeologists, and they are often only peripherally interested in the artifacts we find. Without geoscientists, however, archaeology would be like working in the dark without making use of a flashlight. And often I have discovered archaeology that is done precisely that way. Geologists will be consulted only if there is a problem. In contrast, we wanted to know what the geologists knew before we started to excavate. It would be the geology that would be an important link in our new conclusions about the Cave of Letters.

The geoscientists immediately recognized the natural shaft of stone between the two openings of the Cave of Letters as a distinguishing feature that could help date the origins of the cave and its multiple uses. Each layer of the natural column of stone contained sediments that indicated how they had systematically collapsed one on top of the other after natural geological forces were exerted upon it. The geoscientists were able to assess how much more accessible the Cave of Letters was in antiquity, as the lip of the cliffs had eroded even in the past forty years since Yadin's excursion there. The geoscientists' assessment of the natural shaft of rock and how it had come to develop layer upon layer gave us the clue that we needed. The natural column of stone in the middle of the two openings of the Cave of Letters immediately reminded me of a passage in the Copper Scroll regarding the "Cave of the Column." It is one of the strangest descriptions of a cave in the Copper Scroll, since it suggests that there was a natural "column" visible for all to see in between the two openings of the cave. One of the places mentioned in the Copper Scroll in the midst of other unknown locations along the Dead Sea is "the Cave of the Column of Two Openings." The Copper Scroll's Item #25 states:

| | |
|---|---|
| *BaMa'arat Ha'Amud Shel Shnei* | In the Cave of the Column of two |
| *HaPetahim Tzofe Mizrah* | openings, facing east |
| *BaPetah HaTzefoni Hafur* | at the northern opening is buried |
| *Amot Shelosh Sham* Qalal | at three cubits a *receptacle* |
| *Bo Sefer Ehad Tahtav* | in it (there) is one scroll, underneath |
| *42 KK* | (are) 42 measures of treasure |
| | (my translation) |

The Cave of the Column has two entrances, which face east in varying degrees. The Copper Scroll is very specific about directions. Although the directions are not always compass points, they always lead one to important geographic features. If the cave mentioned in this ancient treasure map was to have meaning to a future generation it had to contain a prominent and distinguishing feature that would be visible to an approaching seeker. The Cave of Letters has two entrances and this natural column that is visible from above and below. What is more, when viewed from the cliffs facing the Cave of Letters, the two entrances are unique because the middle rock between the two appears from across Nahal Hever to be a naturally created column between the two entrances. It is, in fact, a naturally created column extending from 11 meters below the two entrances almost to the edge of the cave entrances as our geologists first noted. While the two entrances face the eastern rising of the sun, the cave actually has an orientation where entrance #1 is to the north. Entrance #2 is oriented to the south. This arrangement is very unusual. Most entrances should have to been lined up next to each other. The fact that one entrance is set back and oriented to the north and the other to the south makes the next line of the Copper Scroll so significant. The Copper Scroll states that the treasure is buried "at the northern opening," and in fact the major cache of bronze artifacts was discovered in the first chamber in April 1960, only ten meters from the northern-oriented entrance.

## IS THE CAVE OF LETTERS THE COPPER SCROLL'S CAVE OF THE COLUMN?

We do not know for sure. There is no sign anywhere in the cave that tells us that this is the "Cave of the Column," nor is it written on any of the finds. But the remarkable coincidences of finding a cave with these particular characteristics, with a major discovery of treasure near the northern entrance to the cave sounds strikingly close to the language of the Copper Scroll's description of the Cave of the Column. First, a *qalal* is said to be located at three cubits below the surface. J. Lefkovits, in his study of the Copper Scroll, recognizes a number of modern equivalents for the cubit in antiquity: 48 cm, 54 cm, 57 cm, 62.4 cm.[80] Using any of these measures, the artifacts were said to be buried between 1.42 meters to 1.87 meters deep (5–6 feet). This point is very important. It is clear from the Yadin excavations that the discovery of the bronze artifacts was difficult because it was located under the main level of the present cave floor. Yadin described it in very uncertain terms in his official report: "The bat droppings gave off an unbearable dust and several of the workers resorted to dust masks. After lifting a medium sized stone and removing an additional half meter of dirt, we found a basket containing a cache of metal utensils."[81]

Most of the artifact discoveries required moving some roof debris which had fallen after the last occupation. But in the case of the bronze artifacts, had it not been for the use of a metal detector, the discovery would never have been made. Other discoveries required only moving the upper rock debris. The bronze artifacts were buried under several layers of different types of debris. Even though the bronze artifacts were buried near the wall of the cave, which protected them somewhat from roof debris, they were still buried at a significant depth. Even after the metal detector indicated a metal find under the surface, it required significant excavation through a layer not only of rock debris but of ancient feces. The area apparently served as a bathroom for some of the later cave dwellers, perhaps because of its close proximity to the natural ventilation of the opening. This became a crucial clue in our dating of the bronze artifacts. It became clear that the Bar Kokhba cave dwellers were the ones who used this area as an ancient bathroom, and they may never have known about the treasure below. This natural niche in the rocks by the entrance provided ample privacy at the same time that it was well ventilated from the cave's opening. A perfect place for hiding materials in an earlier period became the best place to put latrine facilities in another period.

In 1960 the excavation of this niche was performed by volunteers who even today are still quite humbled by the experience. Mr. Pinchas Porat ( born P. Prutzky), a young volunteer in 1960, told me when we interviewed him in 1999 and again in 2000 that the digging through the many layers of feces and rock was both exciting and disgusting. "We kept hearing the metal detector going off and we did not see anything," he said. "We kept digging and digging until we arrived at some

Richard Freund (at left) and Pinchas Porat in the Cave of Letters. (COL Project)

large stones. We removed the large stones and still some dirt and the metal detector kept ringing and ringing. And then suddenly, 'a rope, a rope.' You can still see the rope. It is on display at the Shrine of the Book at the Israel Museum. It was connected to a basket and then inside of the basket, the bronze artifacts." That rope became an important clue in the final analysis of the finds.

The discovery was made some five feet below the present surface of the cave. There was debris from the ceiling that had partially blocked the top of the niche, followed by the layers of feces and finally another layer of rocks and then the bronzes. The five feet of debris that Porat had dug through in 1960 is very close to the three cubits mentioned in the Copper Scroll. For those of us who worked in this niche in 2000, it was clear that this niche was below the level of the rest of the finds made in Hall A. Whoever had originally dug out this "bathroom" niche had probably excavated an already existing depression that was in the wall and created a place for an adult to modestly use the facilities without being noticed by anyone coming in from entrance #1. It was clear to us that whoever had created this niche was probably not aware of what was buried below the rock floor. It must have seemed to the second-century residents of the cave like a natural niche for disposing of their own waste without needing to leave the cave. The Romans sat in wait in their camps above and across the wadi from it. This "bathroom" niche hid the treasure below from cave looters for nearly two thousand years.

Another small piece of information emerged during the excavations that again pointed to the Copper Scroll's association with the finds from the Cave of Letters. In the Copper Scroll it states:

| | |
|---|---|
| *Amot Shelosh Sham Qalal* | at three cubits a *qalal* (*receptacle*) |
| *Bo Sefer Ehad Tahtav* | in it (there) is one scroll, underneath |
| *42 KK* | (are) 42 measures of treasure |
| | (my translation) |

According to the scroll, at a depth of three cubits a *qalal*, a ritual limestone vessel, should be found. A *qalal* or *qalil* (vocalized in different ways) is usually a ritual limestone vessel well known in Jerusalem during the time of the Temple but apparently in use by pious Jews elsewhere as well. The *Qalil*[82]/*Qalal* appears only in the Copper Scroll and rabbinic literature and is an interesting vessel. It is generally understood to be a barrel-shaped vessel carved from limestone that was used to keep objects from becoming ritually defiled. Similar stoneware, found at Qumran[83] and Masada,[84] was especially prominent in Jerusalem and other locations close to Jerusalem during the time of the Second Temple because of the need to preserve ritual purity in the precincts of the Temple. Ritual purity was a metaphysical ideal that although biblically founded became implemented in very specific ways in the Hellenistic and Roman periods.[85] Certain materials were seen as inherently unable to contract or pass on any impurities. One such material was stone, and since limestone was readily available in the area around Jerusalem, limestone vessels became a way for the multitude of pilgrims and visitors to Jerusalem to visit the holy city without passing on their own ritual impurities. This type of *carved* stoneware found in the Cave of Letters resembles the limestone ware found in Jerusalem, Masada, and Qumran.

The discovery of a limestone vessel in the Cave of Letters is important for a variety of reasons. Limestone vessels are important to archaeologists because they tell us something about the people and their religious practices. Limestone ritual vessels are unlike pottery in that they are not very utilitarian, nor are they vessels that a group of military evacuees might bring with them, because they are so easily broken. These limestone ritual vessels were found at first-century sites such as Qumran and Masada, but they are not generally found in refugee caves exclusively associated with the Bar Kokbha rebellion. These very carefully carved limestone ware pieces are indicative only of pre–70 CE issues of ritual purity and are not generally found in other Bar Kokhba caves. In fact, nothing in the hundreds of finds made in the Cave of Letters would suggest that the Bar Kokhba rebels would need or want limestone ritual vessels. No significant Jewish religious items were found among the rest of the hundreds of Bar Kokhba era finds in the Cave of Letters. This suggests a different archaeological context. Limestone ritual vessels have the virtue of not being important to treasure seekers like the Bedouin, who ransacked these caves looking for materials to sell, so a limestone vessel would have escaped their looting (although it is so fragile it would be easily broken as someone searched for other treasures!). If a limestone ritual vessel could be found near the bronze artifacts, it would be another clue in confirming that this was indeed the Cave of the Column. During Yadin's 1960 excavation, in Hall A, adjacent to where the bronze artifacts were found, "two limestone vessels with knife shaved sides were found." As Yadin stated: "These are of a vessel-type known as measuring cups."[86] The second clue leading us to the conclusion that this was indeed the Cave of the Column was now confirmed.

So where was the "scroll" that was to be found in the *qalal* mentioned in this section of the Copper Scroll? We hypothesized that when the Bedouin who entered the cave before Yadin in 1960 found the *qalal* with the written scroll inside, they might easily have removed the scroll and broken the seemingly "unimportant" vessel. The unique language of "One *Sefer*/scroll"—*sefer ehad*—is important. Not every *sefer* in antiquity was a holy scroll, especially when it comes to the Bible. The biblical book of Esther, for example, is referred to as a (*megilla*) scroll of Esther rather than a book. In antiquity, the Book of

Psalms was specifically called a holy "book"/*Sefer* even though in this period of antiquity everything was basically a wrapped scroll. Real books or codices were innovations introduced in a later period.

In Hall A, near the place where the bronze artifacts were found, Yadin discovered one small fragment of Psalms, which had clearly been ripped from a larger section. The amount of biblical materials found in the Cave of Letters was a major question until recently. In fact, no more than a couple of small fragments of biblical materials were found in or near the cave, raising questions about whether the occupants from the Bar Kokhba Rebellion thought they would need to have documents and objects with them in the cave or just how religious this group of people actually was. The Copper Scroll constantly refers to religious documents and objects. In Item 33 of the Copper Scroll we find: *Kli Dema USefarin*, "dedicated vessels and written materials." The fact that only one small fragment of Psalms was found in the cave remained a mystery until recently.

Ada Yardeni and Hannah Cotton at Hebrew University in Israel have slowly reconstructed a trail of literary mystery and deception regarding many documents that originally came from the Cave of Letters and were purposely assigned to another cave.[87] In the 1950s, after the caves along the Dead Sea became known among Bedouin as treasure troves, many Bedouin chose not to reveal the sources of their finds. One reason the Bedouin did not reveal the location of their find was political. The second was practical. They wanted to be able to go back and retrieve other treasures at a later time and not be disturbed by the authorities. The political reason for this deception is more complicated. The Cave of Letters was within Israeli sovereignty, while other caves nearby were located in Jordanian hands and not subject to Israeli scrutiny. The Israelis did not always look as favorably upon poaching in their caves and were particularly sensitive to these issues since most of the Dead Sea caves lay in Jordanian territory. For years Bedouins and scholars trying to protect their sources of new information attributed a variety of different Psalms manuscripts to another cave in nearby *Nahal Tzeelim*.[88]

In 1960 and 1961 Yadin discovered only a few scraps of first-century biblical documents at the Cave of Letters excavations, a fragment from the Book of Numbers and a fragment from the Book of Psalms being the most famous. The Book of Psalms fragment was especially important since it was found in close proximity to the bronze artifacts in the Cave of Letters in Hall A. Since 1961, research had revealed that the two fragments, which even in the early 1960s were known to be first-century paleography, were part of larger manuscripts of the books of Numbers and Psalms and "mistakenly" assigned to another cave in *Nahal Tzeelim* by local Bedouin. This discovery meant that the Cave of Letters was the repository for texts whose history may stretch back to first-century religious manuscripts in addition to the secular second-century Babatha and Bar Kokhba letters. This would solve the mystery of the existence of other biblical texts found in Bar Kokhba caves and may explain what happened to the mysterious *qalal* with the *sefer* inside. We now know that the Bedouin who had carefully explored the Cave of Letters had taken the religious texts from the cave and broken the fragile limestone cup. Perhaps assuming it held treasure, they smashed it open and found the Psalms scroll inside. They sold part of the manuscript of Psalms and said it was from *Nahal Tzeelim* to keep people from knowing about the treasure trove of the Cave of Letters. The recovered pieces of the manuscript of Psalms have now been pieced together and analyzed by one of the people who worked with us in the Cave of Letters. Dr. Walter "Chip" Bouzard of Wartburg College is a leading scholar of the book of Psalms who not only worked in the Cave of Letters but has unraveled the mystery of the sefer/"book" from the Cave of Letters that may have been the *sefer* of the Copper Scroll. He has concluded that the scroll that came from the Cave of Letters is a unique manuscript in the history of the manuscripts of Psalms. Not only is it not like most of the Psalms manuscripts found in the Dead Sea Scrolls; it is also distinct from the canonized version of Psalms that has been traditionally passed down to us. It is different from the manuscripts that were canonized in our Bibles in a unique way: The superscriptions or titles which we take for granted in our Psalms today, those which begin with titles: "For David, a Song, " "For Moses," "For Asaf," etc., are generally missing from the manuscript found in the Cave of Letters. This would mean that this ancient copy of the Book of Psalms was from a place and time that did not need to give titles or lineage to authenticate the Psalms. It was from the hand of a scribe who may have had a different manuscript tradition of the Psalms: one that may have been in use in the Temple in Jerusalem.

Chip Bouzard concluded that the full Psalms manuscript from the Cave of Letters that has now been reconstructed some forty years later originally included as many as thirty psalms and was probably from Jerusalem and written in the early first century CE! It would have been in use in the time of the Temple's flourishing and not necessarily used by sectarians at a place like Qumran or Masada. It meant that although we had limestone ware that was similar to the limestone ware from Masada, Qumran, and Jerusalem, the text that we had was not like the texts from Masada and Qumran. It was a unique text, perhaps in use in Jerusalem by Temple priests and therefore a uniquely important link to the Temple and the artifacts in the cave. The Bedouins originally left only a small part of the ripped scroll in an area adjacent to where the metal objects were found, so in 1960 it would have been impossible for Yadin to conclude that it was an important text. He only had a couple of lines from Psalms that he saw were unusual, since they are slightly different than the Masoretic or traditional text. In addition, the Bedouin had smashed the limestone vessel (*qalal*) before Yadin's excavations, so he could not have linked the limestone vessel to the text of Psalms it had contained. All he found was a broken limestone vessel and a fragment of a Psalms scroll all within a few feet of the bronze objects. In 1961 there were not enough clues to connect all the pieces together. For us, this newly reconstructed large scroll of Psalms and the limestone vessels together after forty years was the third clue that this was the scroll of the Cave of the Column mentioned in the Copper Scroll.

The final clue is the unique abbreviations of the Copper Scroll itself. Our argument that makes the Copper Scroll's *Cave of the Column = the Cave of the Letters* centers on the bronze objects themselves found by Yadin in the Cave of Letters, the 42 "measures" of metal objects mentioned in the Copper Scroll. When one analyzes the weight of the objects mentioned in the Copper Scroll, one is forced to ask how close the weight of the objects found in Hall A is to the 42 "measures" mentioned in the Copper Scroll. Usually the "measure" is the translation of a unique abbreviation: "*kk*" translated by many scholars as the word *talent*. If it were a *talent* then the treasure of the item #25 would be hundreds of pounds of metal treasure. J. Lefkovits in his recently published 600-page landmark study of the Copper Scroll has recently shown that the abbreviation taken by a generation of scholars to mean "a Roman talent" is actually another, smaller measure of weight for metal. He holds that the "*kk*" represents the abbreviation for the words: *Kesef Karsh*; literally *silver karsh* or "*karsh* (weight)." The *karsh*, he says, is "a mere fraction of a talent."[89] He writes: "This study revises that grossly exaggerated amount to less than sixty tons of precious metal of which less than 17 percent is gold, the rest being silver and unspecified metal that could be copper and other metals."[90] He is not the first to question the interpretation of the measure or actually the abbreviation of the measure. As early as J. Allegro and Lurie's studies in the 1960s, the concept of the measure used was 1/60th of the weight of a talent.[91] It is possible that from the beginning, this entire translation of the abbreviation *kk* has been mistaken. J. Milik is the scholar who first said that the abbreviation "*kk*" meant a talent.[92] The abbreviation *kk* is found clearly thirty times in the Copper Scroll (and perhaps many more times, based upon different transcriptions of the text). Karsh is a measure of weight which is significantly less than a talent, and which, if applied throughout the text of the Copper Scroll, changes the entire meaning of the scroll. Scholars and archaeologists have been scouring the deserts of Judea since 1960 looking for tons of gold and silver. With this new understanding of the Copper Scroll they realized that they should have been looking for a much smaller equivalent of a weight of metal booty or coinage. With this change in interpretation, a number of other already discovered caves (with hordes of metal treasure = hordes of coins) presented themselves as legitimate candidates for this buried treasure mentioned in the Copper Scroll. If Lefkovits is right, the treasure may actually have been there all the time (just less of it than scholars originally imagined!).

According to Lefkovits's calculations, the 42 *Karsh* of the Copper Scroll item #25 would be equal to the weight of 420 shekels, or between 13.5 and 24 pounds of metal (depending on how we calculate the weight of the *Karsh*). If this is so, the entire weight of the 42 *karsh*/measures of treasure in the "Cave of the Two Openings" should be between 13.5–24 pounds of metal, which is extremely close to the weight of the bronze artifacts found in the palm basket near the opening of the Cave of Letters! This was the final clue linking the Cave of Letters to the Cave of the Column.

Is all of this mere coincidence, or have we finally found one of the caves listed in the Copper Scroll? Recall that the bronze artifacts were buried deep within the opening of the cave near what had been used by the Bar Kokhba rebels as a latrine. The Psalms scroll fragment and the fragment of a limestone cup were found by Yadin very near the bronze artifacts and may have originally been on top of the bronzes. This raised major questions for us:

1. Would the Bar Kokhba cave dwellers simply bury pagan bronze artifacts when they were desperately in need of bronze (they had to restrike all of their coins over Roman coins)? Wouldn't they have melted it down (as the Zealots had done in the First Revolt) and used it for metal cooking pots or coins, or made the vessels into weapons that were in great demand? Why bury it?
2. Would the Bar Kokhba cave dwellers have allowed pagan artifacts to be buried in the cave if the pagan artifacts had artistic renderings that were such an anathema that they had started to scratch out the Roman motifs (according to Yadin)?[93] If they were going to scratch out the Roman motifs on the vessels, why were only a few scratched out and the majority left intact!?
3. If the Psalms scroll and the limestone vessels were from the Bar Kokbha rebels (and not from an earlier occupation), why were they located so close to the area of ritual defilement, the latrine?
4. Why were no other religious/biblical manuscripts found elsewhere in the cave?

So all the evidence pointed to another group of people who had used the cave, especially Hall A, in an early period for different purposes. It is clear that many of the caves and tunnels used by the Bar Kokhba rebels were well known from the First Revolt. Many of the caves along the Dead Sea were used for thousands of years. Masada, built by King Herod in the first century BCE, was used by Zealots at the end of the First Rebellion. Herodion, a nearby site also built by King Herod, was used by the Bar Kokhba movement as a major military site during the early days of the Second Rebellion. Herodion had also been been used by First Revolt rebels.

The Copper Scroll reference to the Cave of Letters is important because it indicates that unlike other deposits, the treasure in the Cave of the Column was buried in the cave at a depth of three cubits. This would have placed it below whatever level would be used by occupants of the cave. In fact, the bronze hoard was down below the Bar Kokhba level of the cave settlement. If this reference in the Copper Scroll relates to our Cave of Letters, the author of the Copper Scroll already knew that the bronze items were buried at a depth below the cave surface. Since the depth mentioned in the Copper Scroll is similar to the depth that the excavators in Yadin's time had to dig through in order to arrive at the artifacts, it means that the artifacts were not at the same archaeological stratum as the rest of the artifacts that Yadin found in the Cave. In addition, since the artifacts were in the corner of the cave and not in the center, they were not covered with additional layers of even minimal roof debris that accompanied some of the other finds and that would have resulted from earthquake damage from either 115 CE or later earthquakes. The point is that the bronze artifacts were found at the same level where they had been buried by the framers of the Copper Scroll. Since the Bar Kokhba materials were found throughout the cave without major excavation (they had not been fully buried, but only covered) it meant that the Bar Kokhba refugees may never have known that these other items were in the cave.

So the evidence points to the Cave of Letters as a repository for artifacts from refugees leaving Jerusalem after 70 CE as mentioned in the Copper Scroll. The Copper Scroll must have been written after these artifacts were safely stored in the many caves and fortresses mentioned in it. Perhaps the geology will give us another clue as to when the Copper Scroll was finished and the objects stored away in the caves. As we have mentioned, one of the many major earthquakes in the area was recorded around 115 CE.[94] There had been an uprising in the Diaspora against Trajan in 115 CE, which may have caused the Jews of the Diaspora to think that a major uprising (and the need to finance it) would be the next step. In the years 115–117 CE, an offshoot of this rebellion spread to Judea. It is mentioned in rabbinic literature as the War of Quietus. This was the beginning of the ferment that would culminate in the Bar Kokhba Rebellion some fifteen years later. If the treasures mentioned in the Copper Scroll were placed in the Cave of Letters and elsewhere after the time of the destruction of the Temple in Jerusalem, it is possible that they were collected up to and during the beginning of the Diaspora Rebellion in 115 CE. As mentioned before, the Copper Scroll was found on top of some of the roof debris in Cave 3 (as opposed to below a debris level where the other scrolls of Cave 3 were found) pointing to a deposit *after* a major ancient earthquake like the 115 CE earthquake. As we have demonstrated, it is clear that the author of the Copper Scroll knew the Cave of Letters and other caves around the Judea and Samaria area. The Bar Kokhba rebels of the Cave of Letters may never have known the author of the Copper Scroll, or the exact contents of the Copper Scroll but they certainly benefited from the caves around Judea and Samaria, where they too stored their coin hordes. These caves and their coin hordes tied the rebellions of 70, 115, and 132 CE together in a way that the rebellion leaders may never have anticipated.

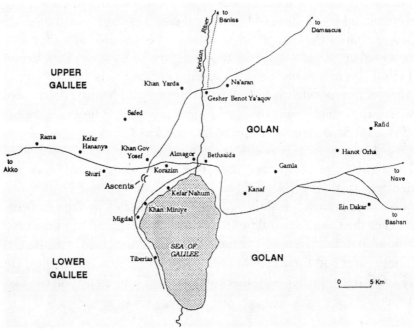

Bethsaida and ancient roads system from north to south and east to west.
(Bethsaida Excavations Project)

# 8

# X Marks the Spot
## The Rest of the Story

## INTRODUCTION

We generally say in science that if we can see further and better than our ancestors it is because we "stand on the back of giants" who have come before us. This is very true in the case of the Cave of Letters but in a different sense. Of course, we stand on the back of the work of Aharoni, Yadin, and most of the Dead Sea Scrolls community of scholars, but we also are deeply indebted to the individuals who were there with them and preserve different parts of the history of their work. Two such individuals are Baruch Safrai and Pinchas Porat. Scientists rarely consult the oral history of a site because it is generally so subjective and based upon the memory and personal reflection of individuals who are not always systematically trained and therefore possibly unreliable. I had learned from our work at Bethsaida that this is not necessarily true. Personal reflection and the oral tradition of a site must be consulted. At Bethsaida, in preparation for the writing of

Bar Kokhba coin. (COL Project)

our first book, *Bethsaida: A City by the North Shore of the Sea of Galilee*, vol. 1 (there are now three volumes on the city published by Truman State University Press, 1995, 1999, 2004) and the television documentary, *The Lost City of Bethsaida*, we had taken an oral history from a Bedouin (an indigenous Arab nomad) whose tribe had developed a connection with our site in the nineteenth and early twentieth centuries. We visited a Bedouin family that had now settled in Galilee nearby and found one ninety-year-old who remembered the site and his tribe's connection to the site. In one magical evening he recounted a history of the site that went back thousands of years. He knew history that we had only recently reconstructed through rigorous evaluation of artifacts. He told us about the different settlements at the site that he could not have known except through an oral transmission of the history from tribe member to tribe member. I learned at that moment to listen carefully to oral histories of nonscientists for clues to the way to work at an archaeological site. At the Cave of Letters we began with research—but also with an individual who been there in 1953 with Y. Aharoni and had made a remarkable discovery that was never acknowledged because it did not fit the history of the Cave that Y. Yadin had developed in the 1960s. It does fit the history that we were developing in 2000. He had waited nearly fifty years to tell his story, waiting to see if he was right or wrong. It turns out he was right.

## MYSTERY OF THE MISSING MAN

In 1997 Baruch Safrai told me about finding a priestly skeleton in the Cave of Letters in 1953. There was, however, some confusion about exactly where it was found—either in Hall B on December 10, as reported in *Biblical Archaeology Review*,[95] or in Hall C on December 12, as narrated in the book *In the Footsteps of Kings and Rebels*, by B. Rothenberg and Y. Aharoni.[96]

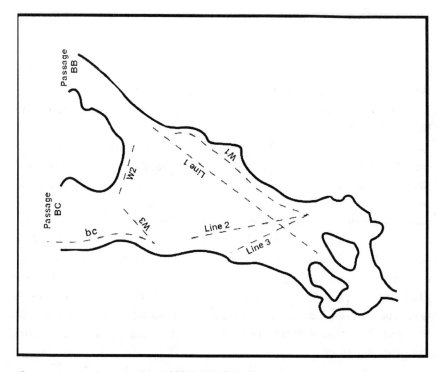

Ground penetrating radar lines 1999. (H. Jol/COL Project)

Moving debris in the Cave of Letters. (COL Project)

Under the ancient collapsed ceiling, on the western wall, were many first- and second-century items, including pottery, coins, etc. But also clearly visible under the huge deposit of the collapsed ceiling were the bones of a man wearing an ancient linen tunic with stripes of blue and a stylized belt.[97]

Baruch Safrai placed two X's on a map of the Cave of the Letters, one in a possible location in Hall C, where most people thought that the skeleton was located, and the other in a certain spot in Hall B, where he thought he remembered seeing it. The skeleton was supposed to be in one or the other of these spots.

Our work in 1999, which included using ground penetrating radar, failed to find the skeleton, but we were determined to continue the search the following summer. We utilized a three-step method. First we compiled a grid using ground penetrating radar. Then we used the endoscope in 1999 and the fiberscope in 2000 to reveal whether there was anything of particular interest in a specific area on the grid. Then we excavated.

The endoscope and the fiberscope show only a very specific and small spot; if you remove the scope and then reinsert it another day, and miss the original spot by so much as a centimeter, it is no longer recognizable. This was a problem for us because we were pushing the scope through as much as two meters of small stones and dirt which had fallen from the roof of the cave over the intervening centuries between Bar Kokhba's time and our own. Even a slight movement of some of these tiny stones or the dirt would cause the scope to arrive at a slightly different place on the floor of the cave. But the endoscope and fiberscope, if frustrating at times, were extremely useful to us. The fiberscope provided a much better view of artifacts on the cave floor than did our endoscope. Dr. Carl Savage, a biblical archaeologist and technology specialist who is a director of the Bethsaida Project at Drew University and the recorder/secretary of our daily log and operations, decided that fiberscoping was a new technique he wanted to learn how to use, so he operated the fiberscope.

## EXCAVATION IN HALL B

We began excavating at the southern end of Hall B and moved northward. Our work with the endoscope in 1999 had revealed a series of artifacts, including linen bags on the floor, which we were unable to excavate that year. In 2000 we attempted to relocate the artifacts, but found that the movement of even a few rocks made it nearly impossible to find them. We excavated to a depth of two meters below the present debris level, which revealed part of the floor in Hall B. We began excavating in the middle of the hall because Yadin had worked only at the corners. We found pieces of baskets and other remains of human habitation from the Bar Kokhba period. The area leading out to the BB passage (see the chart, p. 183) looked promising, but five-ton boulders had fallen there. Our rock-moving equipment could move no more than two tons. That area would have to wait for another expedition and different technologies.

On July 6 the *NOVA* crew stayed by me as I worked the whole day digging up two sides of an ancient basket (similar to the ones which contained artifacts like the hoard of bronze vessels found in Hall A, and to the one from the Niche of Skulls in Hall C) in the BC passage.

Unfortunately, the basket I was struggling with was pinned under a ten-ton rock which had fallen from the roof squarely in the middle of the basket; the contents were not accessible. Late in the afternoon, as I was still struggling with my basket, Carl Savage, who had been fiberscoping in Hall B near the X made by Safrai that corresponded to a GPR pocket located two meters below the debris layer, came over to me and whispered, "I think I have found him." The words took me by surprise.

"Who have you found?" I whispered back, half knowing what he meant.

"The body of Safrai's priest pinned under the rocks," he whispered, not wanting the camera-happy *NOVA* crew to overhear and start filming until he was sure.

"Who else knows about this?" I asked.

"Just us," he replied.

"Good," I said. "Until we both see it and we both confirm that it appears to have all of the signs, don't tell anyone, especially not the *NOVA* crew."

We worked our way under the rocks and probed the entire area, but were unable to finish the whole survey that afternoon. We wanted to finish it the next day, to see if there was any way that Safrai could have wiggled his way underneath this rock to get a good look at the body. Unfortunately, fifty years of rock moving by illegal excavations, as well as our own work in 1999, had pushed small rocks down the only place that could have provided Safrai the wiggle room he needed to see the body. Today we have to rely on the fiberscope; perhaps at some future time we can remove the rocks and see the place ourselves. The body was clearly pinned under a huge piece of roof debris, five or more tons of limestone, but the bones were nicely arrayed on both sides. We could see one leg on one side of the rock, the other leg on the other side; a rib cage and parts of a rope and some white textile were also visible through the scope. A small dagger appeared next to the body, a detail not noted earlier by anyone but Safrai. The body is quite close to the hearth excavation we had begun the previous year, but the body is buried by debris that is distinct from the debris found on top of the hearth; it is clearly at a different archaeological layer than the rest of the finds in Hall B.

So on the afternoon of July 7 I went to Gary Hochman, producer of the *NOVA* production, and said, "I think we have found the body that Safrai saw nearly fifty years ago, just where he said it would be. We wanted to make sure that we could find it again before we told you. We examined it on our screen twice. It is there and you can film our fiberscoping and see our small screen, and then you can have the tape from our videocamera."

They spent hours filming us filming the bones. This was the first week of our excavations; such a discovery was extremely satisfying. When you find something like this which might confirm a wholly different understanding of the cave, and a body which was seen half a century ago but never again, it is rewarding. One now had to ask whether the priestly skeleton was an Essene, a Zealot, a refugee from the Temple, or a figure from a later time. Aharoni and Safrai had assumed that this was a Temple priest from the first century. We don't really know whether he was a priest, but Safrai was right: There was a body buried where he said it would be.

## A Surprise

In the meantime, even as excavations in Hall B continued, Dr. Jim Webster was excavating underneath a boulder where the other X was on Safrai's chart, in Hall C, at the site surveyed by Aharoni December 12, 1953. The entrance underneath the rock debris was actually accessible to Dr. Webster. It was fiberscoped, and bone and fiber materials were found, which confused us somewhat since we had already found the missing bones in Hall B. Had Aharoni been right too? Were there in fact two bodies with tunics, found two days apart, in two different halls? Why not? we argued. Perhaps there was a whole other group of people whose demise was completely different from that of the people found in the Niche of Skulls. We sent this bone out for analysis as well; it turned out to date from the mid–first century CE.[98] These bodies and tunics were different from the colorful Niche of Skulls textiles, and the locations suggested a different type of death and burial than the niche.

Other finds in Hall A, Hall C, and locus 31 in the BB passage confirmed the overall theory of Y. Aharoni in 1953, that first-century refugees from the Temple in Jerusalem had made their way to the Cave of Letters as a place of refuge after the devastation of Jerusalem. These earlier refugees may have lived in the cave for longer periods, been crushed under roof debris, and died where they were. Their remains were not found by the later refugees, or they would have been gathered up in burial baskets and niches by the later inhabitants of the cave.

## THREADS OF HISTORY

Some of the exciting finds in the Cave of Letters are the tunics and textiles found by Yadin's expedition and our own. Many were remarkably well preserved. Most were made of wool and very well spun and dyed with spectacular colors—deep reds, yellows, greens, black, and orange. They had Roman elite banding or *clavi* that would have placed these people as persons of rank in Roman society. These textiles confirm that many of the biblical injunctions about textiles may have been observed during the second century CE.

Most of the textile materials our expedition discovered were from a burial niche, the so-called Niche of Skulls—locus 2 in Hall C. Only in one place was there a totally different textile: a large toga/tunic of linen that Fred Strickert and Chip Bouzard carefully recovered from underneath a rock in the back of the BB passage. The linen tunic had an area for the famous tassels/fringes or *tzitziot* mentioned in the Bible. We wondered why a nearly complete garment was so far from every other find in the cave. Yadin had discovered a burial of a man and woman in the BB passage across from our discovery in 1960, but this tunic was different from his discoveries in the same area. Again all signs pointed to different groups from different backgrounds in the cave at different times during the Greco-Roman period.

In the summer of 1999 we investigated a number of linen bags photographed by the endoscope. We also found a simple belt of cordage made from date palm fibers as we looked for the skeleton of Safrai. Natural cloth and cords do not last long in most climates; we were gratified to find so many here.

# 9

# A Tale of Two Caves

## Babatha and Her-story

## INTRODUCTION

During the filming of the television documentaries there were three moments of drama that changed my way of thinking about the discoveries. One involved the personal interviews of Pinchas Porat, who had been with Y. Yadin in the 1960s and who discovered the Niche of Skulls and the bronze horde in the cave. We enticed him to come back to the cave in 2000 to reexperience it and to talk about the discovery and the interview with Baruch Safrai, who had been there with Y. Aharoni in 1953. Their personal accounts of discovery were moving for all of us who heard them. The second moment was the actual rediscovery of places that had been worked on by Aharoni and Yadin and that we found again, and where we were able to find more artifacts in the same places. I was happy with the discoveries we made, especially those that seemed to confirm our hypothesis of a first-century CE use of the cave, but it was reconnecting with the past excava-

189

(Left to right) L. Schiffman, H. Eshel, and R. Freund on the cliff face of the Cave of Letters. (COL Project)

tions that gave me a sense of the enormous history that we were a part of. The third and perhaps most meaningful moment was the interview in the cave with one of the world's leading experts on ancient Roman documents, Prof. Hannah Cotton of Hebrew University. Professor Cotton is an athletic, middle-aged faculty member of enormous personality who I knew physically could make the climb to the Cave of Letters to speak about one of her favorite subjects of research, Babatha. Cotton gave an analysis of what she knew about Babatha at precisely the place where Babatha's documents were found. As she sat in the near darkness of the cave and recounted Babatha's life in the second century we almost felt Babatha's presence among us.

Professor Cotton was near tears herself as she told us about a woman who had died nearly nineteen hundred years ago, but who was as real for us sitting in the cave as if we were talking to Babatha herself rather than a twenty-first-century textual scholar. I realized that this is the power of a good social historian—to bring the past to life in order to give us insights not only into the past but also into ourselves. When studying women in history one is usually faced either by ideologues who are not textual scholars or by textual scholars who are unable to see the implications of their work in the broader society. Cotton has indirectly and perhaps unintentionally enlightened us more about the status of women in antiquity than any other scholar I know, and at the same time she has unintentionally created an enormous challenge to so-called feminist scholars who often are not versed in the details of antiquity.

Why Babatha was in the cave remains a mystery, since she apparently had much to lose from her association with the rebels. It is conjectured that she was there because of her family connections, or because she was in Ein Gedi at an inopportune moment in the history of the rebellion, or perhaps because of a personal connection to one of the commanders of the region. Whatever the reason, her presence in that cave at that moment in history and the time capsule of her life has unlocked a history of Jewish women in the middle Roman period that is so different from the picture that emerges only from literary texts such as the New Testament and the rabbinic literature that it demonstrates well what archaeology and social history can do when properly engaged together.

Cotton brought along another of the world's leading experts on the Bar Kokhba Rebellion, Prof. Werner Eck, to see an actual refuge cave of the rebels that connected so centrally to his own work as well. During the course of our excavations we invited many of the leading scholars who I felt could make the journey to visit the cave. Some, like Prof. Lawrence Schiffman of New York University, rarely can visit all of the archaeological sites that they assess. Textual scholars are generally content with analyzing documents in a library or in archives. Schiffman's visit to the cave was memorable for both him and the crew as he gave his historical insights on our trip out, while we were climbing in, and during our work in the cave. It was a difficult climb into the cave and he and others were not exactly prepared for the difficulty, but they realized the importance of experiencing the actual site themselves.

Other archaeologists and geologists were invited to understand the method we were developing firsthand: Amos Frumkin, perhaps the most well known cave geologist; Zvika Zuk, then the archaeologist for the Parks and Nature Reserves Authority; Adolfo Roitman, curator of the Dead Sea Scrolls at the Shrine of the Book of the Israel Museum; Hanan Eshel of Bar Ilan University; Uzi Dahari and David Amit of the Israel Antiquities Authority (IAA); even specialists such as Orit Shamir of the IAA and Elisabetta Boaretto, Steven Weiner, and Michal Kaufmann from the Weizmann Institute. It was Steve Weiner who would connect his graduate student Michal Kaufmann to our project for the DNA analysis of the bones found in the Niche of Skulls. This DNA analysis will be groundbreaking because it appears that the state of preservation in the Niche of Skulls was remarkable by any ancient standards. Ancient DNA analysis is in its infancy and we are pleased that the Weizmann Institute worked with us from the start since the collection of the samples is the key to its success. Also, as a footnote, we carefully replaced the bones back into the Niche of Skulls in 2001. These people were buried in the niche some two thousand years ago, and according to Jewish tradition it is important for all of a person's bones to be placed with them in their burial. In the past this is one of the reasons why religious figures have railed against scientists: because they do not seem to have the religious sensitivity to restore the bones (after necessary analysis) to their original resting place. We made sure that the bones were returned to the cave after sufficient DNA for analysis was extracted. The tests could take years to analyze properly and need careful comparison and analysis, but they may yet tell us much more about who these people were, how these people lived, and how they died. For the moment we know much more about when they lived. The most important and by far the most excited visitors to the Cave of Letters were John and Carol Merrill, our donors. John was featured on the cover of *Biblical Archaeology Review* in January/February 2001 on his way to the cave and I know that he was as excited to visit the cave as we were to have him visit. You could see the fear and the excitement on his face. I know that this experience will be one he will never forget. I wish that every donor had the ability to see the investment in interpreting the world that funding can make. At Bethsaida we have had many opportunities to take visitors on a simple walking tour of the site, explain to them the history, and have them enjoy the fruits of their investments. The Cave of Letters is different. Although we made it safer to visit, it still was scary getting there. But then there truly is no substitute to being there!

# HALLS A, B, AND C: TALES THEY TELL

Buried in Hall A under nearly five feet of debris and excrement were found bronze artifacts, limestone vessels, and fragments of Psalms scrolls. Some Chalcolithic finds were also found there. Very little from the daily life of the rebels is linked to this part of the cave. The finds discovered there from the Roman period—bronze artifacts, limestone vessels, the Psalms texts, etc.—were clearly religious objects. The first-century finds were apparently placed in Hall A for safekeeping and do not indicate that people used Hall A for anything but the storing of religious articles and—for the second-century rebels—a latrine. For the most part, Hall A is the story of a cave that was a "Fort Knox" of antiquity. Buried in Hall B six feet down and below thousands of pounds of roof debris was a primitive hearth, furniture, firewood, and cooking pots. This area was connected with the daily life of the cave in every period it was used. We found Chalcolithic finds as well as a makeshift oven that could have been in use in the first and the second centuries. The daily life of the cave was conducted in Halls B and Hall C.

Hall A suggests a spiritual refuge and vault; Hall C suggests a political, social, and economic refuge. In Hall C were the not very well hidden artifacts of Babatha, the letters of Bar Kokhba, and a burial niche. The artifacts tell us a story of two different caves and cave lives.

# THE NICHE OF SKULLS IN HALL C

In Hall C, during Yadin's excavations and during our excavations in 2000 and 2001, we encountered one of the most horrific and problematic parts of the excavations. It was a burial niche, which became known as the Niche of Skulls. The burial niche in Hall C contained many artifacts that had been left from the Yadin excavations. There were many small niches in the walls of the cave that had apparently been used for daily life. Pottery and small personal items were found in some of them. People obviously needed places to sleep, the rocks were very hard, and they dug out little areas into the soft dirt of the cave for sleeping and eating in Hall C. These burial niches present a fuller picture of who was in the back chamber of the cave. When we discovered—really rediscovered—the Niche of Skulls in Hall C, which was filled with bones and textiles, we all assumed it was ancient, even though it seemed as fresh as when the people were first buried there. We encountered it on the second day of our excavations, July 4, 2000. At first we were surprised that there were so many artifacts still buried inside. In the second season of our excavations, we had begun to survey the places where Yadin had excavated in 1960–61. One of our prime goals was to reinvestigate the places where Yadin had excavated to see if anything had been left behind and to also reinvestigate the way the cave was excavated. The Niche of Skulls in Hall C was first discovered by Yadin's team on Friday, March 25, 1960, by the same individual who had excavated the bronze artifacts in Hall A, Pinchas Porat (Born: Pinchas Prutzky)! Yadin described it thus:

> On the second day, Friday, 25 March, while most of my team were still busy with the Cave of the Vulture, a group of twelve started for the big cave and for several hours they transferred equipment: lamps, baskets, picks and ropes. Only then did they begin to work. One of the volunteers, a real maverick, Pinchas Prutzky of Kibbutz Lahavot Haviva, broke off from the rest and with a candle in his hand decided to survey the innermost hall on his own. Soon enough he rejoined his colleagues pallid and speechless. This state was caused not so much by the fact that he had crawled into a crevice and could hardly extricate himself from it, but rather from the sight which he faced when he got into that crevice. The next day, on my return from project "Cave of the Vulture." I followed him to his crevice and understood exactly how he must have felt alone there. He led me to the eastern wall of hall C, a couple of meters from the spot where it begins to narrow. I saw there was an opening to a crevice (see the plan of the cave) about half a metre across, between the wall and the adjacent blocks of rock. We crawled along it for two metres, and then the floor began to descend sharply for about a metre, forming a sort of step. Here the passage was most difficult for the height at this point was no more than fifty centimetres, and a largest rock rested on the floor. Only by squeezing and pushing our-

selves with difficulty did we at last manage to get in, and found ourselves in a niche, some eight metres long, and about one and a half
metres high. To the right of the entrance, above a ledge in the wall,
a patch of soot was visible, probably from a lamp that had been
placed there in antiquity. Although I had been warned what to
expect, I was startled at what I saw once I got used to the dim light.
Near the right hand wall lay a heap of skulls, without their jawbones,
placed in several baskets stacked on top of one another. At the far
end of the niche, in the right hand corner there was a separate pile
of bones and jawbones in baskets and wrapped in cloth between
mats. This entire heap had been covered with a large mat. One skull
rolled into a crack. In the middle of the niche on the floor were
remains of a skeleton covered by a colourful rug and other textiles.
Here we found a basket lined in leather, containing the skull and s
of a child wrapped in an almost complete tunic. On the rocks near
the left-hand wall fragments of textiles and tufts of hair were found.
The skulls and bones, with the possible exception of those of the
burial in the floor, all appeared to have been deposited there at the
same time, after having been gathered together, wrapped in mats,
and put into baskets.[99]

Because of the strange arrangement of skulls in one basket, the
niche became known as the Niche of Skulls. It is a mystery that is still
unsolved. According to the analysis which Yadin did with Prof. H.
Nathan from Hebrew University, he concluded that seventeen different people were buried in this niche. Two others were buried in a
niche in the BB passage, and bones were found in other niches. Three
men, eight women, and six children were identified in the Niche of
Skulls. So many women and children, the question is: Where were all
the men and who were these women and children? Of course, it is
clear that this may be part of the story. It is possible that the refugees
who fled to the cave were escaping the middle or end of a war. The
men were fighting. Most of these few people remained to hide out in
the cave. These bones (skulls and some other bones) and the bones of
the Cave of Horrors, located on the other side of Nahal Hever, were
all buried together in an official state funeral on Lag B'Omer in 1982,
the holiday dedicated to the memory of the students of the Rabbi
Akiva, the main rabbinic supporter of Bar Kokhba. These bones were

buried in a state funeral amid much pomp and circumstance. Their significance as political martyrs was very powerful even nineteen centuries after their deaths.

## WERE THESE THE BONES OF BAR KOKHBA FIGHTERS?

The question was: Were these the bones of the Bar Kokhba fighters, as Yadin thought? In addition, if they were Bar Kokhba fighters, they had a very strange burial practice, even given their dire situation as refugees from the Romans. In order for this to have been the burial cave of Bar Kokhba fighters, it must have been in use from the first days of the rebellion, since it requires at least one year to have bones decay from the flesh (more since this cave remarkably preserves the bodies with low humidity and little heat).

During the Greco-Roman period, a custom developed to bury the dead in the ground for a limited time (until the flesh had decayed—perhaps a year), and then the family would transfer their bones into a family cave or crypt. In other cases the body was laid out in its shrouds in a cave for approximately a year, and then the bones were respectfully collected and placed inside an ossuary, a limestone box. But in some cases the bones of more than one person would be placed together in a single ossuary inside a cave. The limestone box again seems to be related to the ongoing concern for ritual purity. It was to limit the possibility that others (especially people from priestly families) would come into direct contact with the bones, even by accident. But this practice also raised a number of very difficult conditions. It assumed that one could afford an ossuary. It also assumed the availability of an artisan to fashion the limestone necessary to create such a box. That was not so easily undertaken during a war. The possibility that the bones in the Cave of Letters were originally laid out in shrouds in the burial niche is obvious. The large number and variety of textiles which surround the bones in the niche raise the possibility that each body was laid out in shrouds at one time and later, collected for future deposit in ossuaries. Yadin felt that the baskets were in place

J. Zias examines bones in the Niche of Skulls. (G. Brubacher/COL Project)

of ossuaries.[100] Ossuaries, however, and the collection of bones in this manner were a practice that ended with the destruction of the Temple in Jerusalem in 70 CE! In general, the bodies would be buried with some grave goods, such as bowls, cooking pots, lamps, etc. Remnants of bowls, cooking pots, etc. were found in the niches.

But the bones in the Niche of Skulls were not cared for in accordance with that custom. One problem still remains regarding the bones. Unlike all other cave burials and finds from this period in which one or two bodies were placed together in a single ossuary, these bones were gathered into very specific categories. The skulls were all together in baskets. In many cases, their jawbones were removed. Yadin mentioned that in one case "a basket was found, lined with leather, in which there were a skull and the bones of a child wrapped in an almost complete tunic."[101] In the rest of the cases "a concentration of skulls was found place in baskets; the jaw-bones were missing from all. The baskets had been stacked one on the other. The bottommost one was torn; on this lay another, round basket containing six skulls. Above this was a flat basket with four skulls."[102]

At the end of the work in the niche, after Joe Zias, our paleo-pathologist, had concluded his work, I realized that the leaving of the bones may not have been an oversight by Yadin. Perhaps this was an attempt by Yadin to tell future excavators that the cave excavation was not finished. I concluded that perhaps this was the way that Yadin was in fact speaking to us from beyond the grave. He could have easily removed all of the bones for analysis and burial. He left them there because in 1960–61—it was just the beginning of the period of serious scientific analysis of bones—he might have been as confused as we were in finding so many bones in such a small location. Yadin concluded: "[A]ll appear to have been deposited at one time, after having been gathered and put into baskets or wrapped in mats—for lack of ossuaries."[103] He even concluded that one of the bodies discovered in the cave was Babatha's. Since her archives were found across from the niche, it seemed reasonable to assume that she might have been buried there as well. If he was right, the dating of her documents is crucial.

# The Life of Babatha

She was apparently born and raised in Maoza, which was near Petra in modern Jordan, and she was quite educated judging from the number of documents and the languages they were written in and the legal maneuvering she was involved in.[104] She was born around 104 CE, because in 124 CE she was already a widow with a young son. Her father owned a date palm orchard, which was deeded to his wife and ultimately his daughter, Babatha. Baba and Babatha were Idumean names not normally used by Jews. Babatha's parents may have included an Idumean, since the name is archaeologically identified with Idumea.[105] Since her son is expressly designated as a Jew by the Roman legal document, it may be that the Romans were not aware of the differences. In fact, the Idumeans were not exactly Jews by choice. In 129 BCE, the territory of Idumea was conquered by John Hyrcanus I. The entire non-Jewish population was forced to convert and males were circumcised. The most famous Idumean was Herod the Great. In the First Revolt, the Idumeans were not full participants in the rebellion. In the end, Idumea, its territory south of the Judean Hill country, and the northern part of the Negev was decimated. It may be that Babatha's parents came to Maoza precisely because of the problems associated with the First Revolt in Idumea and left to avoid similar problems. They apparently had been in Maoza before it became a Roman province. They may have experienced some of the fallout from the Jewish revolt against Rome of 115–117 CE. Perhaps they were deeply entrenched in their lives in the Roman province of Arabia before the Bar Kokhba Rebellion. Babatha seems to have been an only child (or oldest daughter), which created the possibility that she would inherit the control of the family property after the death of her parents.

By 125 CE she was already married to her second husband, Judah, who was originally from Ein Gedi but who had settled in Maoza. Much of the financial issues of their lives revolve around investments in Ein Gedi. It will be these investments that will ultimately bring Babatha to Ein Gedi.

Judah had three productive palm date orchards in Ein Gedi.

Judah had been married to another woman, Miriam, daughter of Beian(os). It is not clear whether Judah lived with Miriam in another household in Ein Gedi or whether he traveled back and forth between Maoza and Ein Gedi with his two wives in two places, but he had been married to her at one point. Polygamy was still permitted in Jewish life, and that explains some of the familial crises which were to come. The Cave of Letters archive of Babatha contains the marriage contract of Judah's daughter, Shelamzion, in 128 CE. Apparently Babatha was then residing in Ein Gedi with her husband. The fact that Judah's daughter's Greek wedding contract is among Babatha's papers indicates she was financially involved in this relationship. In the same year, in February 128 CE, Judah takes a loan from Babatha of three hundred denarii. It is a very telling document,[106] since it tells us that Babatha controlled her own money in their marriage. Instead of a loan (on interest or minimal interest), she allows him to receive it as a deposit which is repayable on demand. A little over a month later, Judah's daughter, Shelamzion, is married to a man in Ein Gedi. The marriage contract contains an impressive dowry of five hundred denarii. Two hundred denarii came from the bride's father. Apparently this is part of the loan/deposit provided by Babatha, the stepmother. Three hundred came from the groom's family. Judah's debts (before his marriage to Babatha) are carried in her marriage contract, showing the type of relationship they enjoyed. We do not know what the relationship was between Shelamzion, Miriam (her biological mother), and Babatha. But it is clear that the fiscal responsibility for Judah's daughter was carried by Babatha even after Judah's untimely death. Judah died around 130 CE, and Babatha seized her husband's property in Ein Gedi as a surety against the debts that she had covered.

The last set of documents found in the Babatha archive in the Cave of Letters revolves around a summons for Babatha to appear in court and depositions by Miriam and Judah's family who want to get back Judah's property. Miriam, Judah's first wife, was a relative of a man named Yehonathan, who is thought to be Bar Kokhba's commander at Ein Gedi. While in the previous documents she appears to be protecting her assets, it would be very difficult in the climate of the Bar Kokhba political regime to protect them if Yehonathan was in charge. If this is the case, the very people who were suing Babatha for return of property would now be in charge of the political situation in the area. She would then have been subject to their whims. Babatha had come to Ein Gedi probably a year before the rebellion broke out to resolve some of the legal problems with the date palm groves, which Miriam and Judah's family were disputing. There is an interesting reference in the summons. In July 131 Barbatha is summoned by Miriam, "an Ein Gedian woman, daughter of Beianos, to accompany her in person before Haterius Nepos, legatus Augusti *pro praetore, wherever his venue may be*, to answer why you seized everything in the house of Judah, son of Eleazar Khthousion, my and your late husband . . . and equally important to attend before the said Nepos until judgement." She was being asked to be present during the proceedings, which meant that she would have to be in Ein Gedi right before the Bar Kokhba Rebellion began. On August 19, 132, she has a receipt for the guardianship of her son in Petra. One of the last documents is a fragmentary summons from late August or early September 132, apparently a continuation of the summons from the year before, which may have dragged Babatha back to the court case with Miriam and Judah's family in Ein Gedi. It is quite possible that she felt compelled to arrive in Ein Gedi or nearby to attend the proceedings in 132 CE, just as the Bar Kokhba Rebellion was about to begin. If this is true, she was caught up in the Bar Kokhba Rebellion quite by accident, and was not a willing participant. Her presence in the Cave of Letters was not by political design or sympathy, nor necessarily because she was pushed out of Maoza for her political sympathies, but because of the legal summons of her husband's family and her apparent devotion to the legal system of the Romans. Since she was ethnically part Idumean, her position may have been slightly less advantaged than that of her Ein Gedi relatives, especially during her legal battles in Ein Gedi. It is quite possible, therefore, that despite Yadin's attempt to make Babatha a political sympathizer and victim of the Bar Kokhba Rebellion, she may not necessarily have been involved at all. She may have been swept up by the events of 132 CE and brought by them to the Cave of Letters by Miriam and Yehonathan's family for her own "protection."

So who was in Hall C with Babatha as the Bar Kokhba Rebellion raged in Judea? Hall C contains the personal items, correspondence, and lives of people who lived in the second century of the common era. They were involved in a war against the Romans that ultimately resulted in one of the greatest disasters of all Jewish history until the Expulsion from Spain in 1492 and the Holocaust in twentieth-century Europe. The people in the Cave of Letters brought the keys to their houses, their beautiful finery, documents of land and property ownership, textiles, and clothes. This shows that they were clearly upper-middle-class Jews who lived a privileged life under Roman rule. Similar to the exiles from Spain in 1492, the rebels thought that they would eventually be able to return to their homes. They brought documents, pieces of paper that meant something in a period of Roman courts and rules. They probably meant little in the context of a rebellion, but the people brought them anyway. They brought only the bare minimum of items and the keys to their homes in Ein Gedi. We do not find their clothes and linens, food stuffs and preparation jars. The mirrors, skeins of yarn, jewelry box, glass plate and jar, and tunics found in the Niche of Skulls with their thick colored bands indicating the high status of the owners all point to an elite group of people. They had not brought their climbing clothes. They left with the clothes they were wearing at the moment that the alarm was sounded to leave. These were not poor refugees. They are wearing the same types of tunics with thick colored bands that one finds in the famous paintings of Rome and its elite of the same period. The personal items and the correspondence found in the cave tell us about a literate people and their upper-middle-class lives in a large and prosperous city such as Ein Gedi. They include the names of individuals who lived in Ein Gedi and who knew and worked with Bar Kokhba. They also include the names of others who figure in the legal documents found there who probably did not make it to the cave. The names Shimon son of Kosiba, Yehonatan son of Beian, Mesabalah son of Shimon, and Eleazar son of Hayyata all appear. Also included are Eleazar son of Eleazar, Eleazar son of Shimon, Eliezer son of Hilkiah, Sapphon son of Shimon, Shimon son of Menahem, Tehinnah son of Shimon, Allimah son of Yehuda, Shimon son of Joseph, Joseph son of

Shimon, Judah son of Joseph, Joseph son of Elazar, and Joseph son of Menashe. Other names are: Eleazar son of Yehudah, Yehonatan son of Mahanayim, Yohanan son of Yeshua, Yeshua son of Yeshua, Yeshua son of Shimon, Shimon the "Clothier," Shammua son of Menahem, Joseph son of Arati, Horon son of Yishmael, Joseph the son of Baba, Joseph the son of Dormenes, Garmillah son of Arahzu, and Menelaus son of Awat-Illah. These names reveal the diverse connections between Roman and Jewish life that had developed and show the interrelations among many people who may have ended up in the cave. Many were related to one another by blood, others by business and sometimes by marriage, but it is difficult to know who made the trek with Babatha. According to these documents, we can see that women were prominent: Miriam daughter of Joseph, Johanna daughter of Makkuta, Miriam the daughter of Beian and Shelamzion her daughter, and Salome Komaise daughter of Levi and Julia Crispina. Babatha was barely thirty years old at the time that she went to the cave and had already lived a full and very active life in what is today Jordan and then later in Ein Gedi. In the cave she may have been accompanied by her second husband's first wife, Miriam, and Miriam's daughter Shelamzion, who was also Babatha's stepdaughter and supported by her during part of her life. At the time she was brought to the Cave of Letters, Babatha was already a widow for the second time. She may have been enjoying a close relationship with another man, Eliezer son of Shemuel, whose papers were also found with Babatha's archive. In short, one finds that this was a closely knit group of perhaps thirty people.

The skulls of seventeen people were discovered in the Niche of Skulls. From this long list of names and correspondents listed above, one wonders whether the seventeen were some of those listed in the correspondence of Babatha or Bar Kosiba. We have only begun the DNA analyses of the bones we found from the niche, but it has already yielded an important piece of information. All of the bones we tested were from different families. They were not related to one another. The choice of bones was based upon a variety of different criteria but there were hundreds of bones in the niche when we got there in 2000. Different sizes of bones were chosen (although all were long bones in order to obtain the most DNA) in the expectation of finding women, men, and children. One of the early facts that emerged, based on the bones we examined, was that they were not related to one another. Whoever they were, they were not just one family of refugees.

We know from some of the Bar Kokhba documents that Bar Kokhba had land at Ein Gedi. Therefore, Ein Gedi would have been turned into a war zone whether the residents sympathized or not. We find in one letter, for example, that one Eleazar son of Hayyata, a wealthy landowner from Ein Gedi, did not cooperate with the Bar Kokhba forces and was punished by confiscation of his land.[107]

If we were to judge solely from the Babatha archive, we would surmise that women in this period were extremely powerful land-owners, fierce fighters for the rights of ownership that they deserved and received. More importantly, if we were to use only her archive, we would infer that she went into the Cave of Letters sometime in late 132 CE and never came out. Her thirty-five documents are precisely dated and range from 94 CE until August/September, 132 CE. If nothing else, her documents tell us how Hellenized many Jews were. She had 6 Nabatean, 3 Aramaic, and 26 Greek documents. The documents tell us how integrated into the Roman legal system Jews in this period were.[108] It appears that uniform, day-to-day, uninterrupted Jewish life in nearby Petra and Maoza, where Babatha was apparently living until the outbreak of the rebellion, continued until 132 CE. Indications from the Babatha archive seem to point to a September date for the beginning of the rebellion. It is possible, however, that the ferment began then, but only later developed into a full rebellion. If this is the case, it would explain why judging how long the rebellion lasted is so problematic. Dates from 2.5 years to 3.5 and even four years are common. It would depend on whether the rebellion broke out around the new Jewish year, which began in September. The end of the rebellion is taken by most to be the ninth day of the Jewish month of Av (July–August), Tisha BeAv of 135, before the new Jewish year in late August 135. The date equivalent to August 132 appears in a document in the Babatha Archive, which shows that the conflict had not yet started. Therefore, some push for a September 132 date for her trip to the Cave of Letters. The September date may also explain other symbolic elements in the rebellion. Much symbolism on Bar Kokhba coins is related to the harvest (palm dates, grapes, etc.) and to the Sukkot holiday, an agricultural pilgrimage holiday when Jews made pilgrimages to the Temple Mount, where the Romans had destroyed the Temple some sixty years earlier. The Lulav and Ethrog (or Etrog), symbols of the Sukkot holiday, also figure on the coins. If the rebellion broke out during that time, pilgrims from around the Jewish world would have swelled the numbers of people who could participate in it, and surely at that time of year they would feel particularly bitter toward the Romans. And if the rebellion started at that time of year, the Lulav and Ethrog may have become symbols of messianic salvation—of a messianic return to the pristine agricultural times before the Temple was destroyed.

The fact that Babatha's documents were found there supports Yadin's suspicion that Babatha had been in the cave, even if she is not one of those people interred in the Cave of Letters. The question is whether we can conclude that she was a political sympathizer of Bar Kokhba or not from the archaeological information presented by the juxtaposition of the niche and the documents. Perhaps she had made the acquaintance of a companion such as Eliezer son of Shemuel,[109] and they were both running away from Bar Kokhba and the madness of the rebellion. Perhaps the entire circle of people Eliezer was involved with, including Eleazar son of Hayyata, whose land had been confiscated by Bar Kokhba, was there to escape the madness of the rebellion. Knowing how wealthy and influential Babatha was, one must wonder whether it was the men who led her there or whether she knew about this cave herself from her many Ein Gedi connections. It is difficult to know; what we do know is that she went to the cave and did not leave with her most precious possessions, the documents.

# Burial Procedure:
# What Does It Tell Us?

One thing we do know is that the treatment of the bones in the niche does not reflect standard Jewish burial procedures, and may tell us a story about a very different group of Hellenized Jews from this period. Yadin's conclusion that the arrangement into baskets of skulls occurred "for lack of ossuaries" is extremely problematic for a number of reasons. The final arrangement into baskets is the problematic part. Who arranged these bones into baskets? A few different possibilities present themselves. First, we are dealing with unusual circumstances. The magnitude of the Bar Kokhba Rebellion may have dictated unusual burial rites. But totally changing the known religious practice does not seem likely for the Bar Kokhba followers. The second possibility is that the gathering of the bones was done by non-Jews or by Jews of the period who did not know proper burial procedures. The third possibility is that the bones were collected by a group of cave dwellers who did not even know the people who were interred there. They separated the bones because it was a simple way to organize the bones of people who were not known and to allow the niche to be used for the laying out of other bodies. This type of burial practice is highly unusual, even anti-Judaic in this period. While it is possible that the cave dwellers did not necessarily observe Jewish law meticulously or were extremely Hellenized in their burial practices, the arranging of skulls together into baskets is highly unusual. This practice of separating the bones into skulls, especially without the jawbones, is found in many Byzantine and early medieval monasteries in the desert, however, and may represent an early antecedent of a later Greek Orthodox practice of burial.[110] The Jewish emphasis on the individual collection and laying out of bones for the future resurrection of the entire body makes the collections of skulls in the woven baskets highly problematic. We began to suspect that this may be another indication that the cave had been used by others before the Bar Kokhba cave dwellers arrived and that the bones may have been collected by the Bar Kokhba cave dwellers at a later point (and as a matter of respect collected into the baskets). These people collected the bones of the unknown occupants of the cave who may originally have been laid out in shrouds. We have now carbon-dated six bones which all are dated to the first and the second centuries. Some of the bodies may indeed have been from the Bar Kokhba Rebellion, while others may have been from the First Rebellion. One body was clearly laid out on a mat when Yadin investigated the niche in 1960, but seventeen skulls were in the basket. Maybe the single body that was laid out was one of the Bar Kokhba fighters and the others, in baskets, from the First Rebellion. Since most of the bones were not laid out but already collected, it suggests two different processes of burial at work. There were many other niches in the cave for potential burial. Why was only one large burial niche chosen? The final pieces were coming together to reveal a full picture of people who were in the cave at different times over a hundred-year period some two thousand years ago.

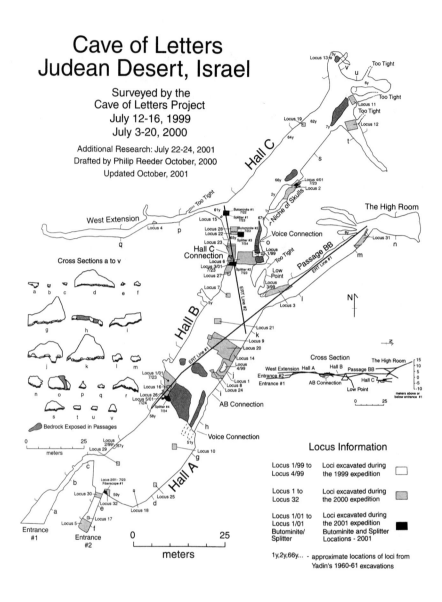

# Cave of Letters
# Judean Desert, Israel

Surveyed by the
Cave of Letters Project
July 12-16, 1999
July 3-20, 2000

Additional Research: July 22-24, 2001
Drafted by Philip Reeder October, 2000
Updated October, 2001

Locus 13

Too Tight
Locus 11
Too Tight
Locus 12
Too Tight

Locus 19

Hall C

Too Tight

The High Room

Niche of Skulls
Locus 4/01
Locus 2

West Extension
Locus 4

Locus 15
Butominite #1 7/22
Splitter #1 7/23
Locus 28
Locus 22
Butominite #2 7/23
Splitter #3 7/24
Locus 23
Hall C Connection
Locus 6
Locus 3/01 7/23
Splitter #2 7/23
Locus 27
Locus 7

Voice Connection

Locus 1/99

Too Tight

Low Point
Locus 3/99

Passage BB

ERT Line #1

Locus 31

Cross Sections a to v

a  b  c  d  e  f

g  h  i

j  k  l  m

n  o  p  q  r

s  t  u  v

Bedrock Exposed in Passages

0        25
meters

Hall B

ERT Line #2

ERT Line #1

Locus 3

N

Locus 21
Locus 9
Locus 20
Locus 14
Locus 4/99
Locus 1
Locus 8
Locus 24

Cross Section
West Extension  Hall A    Hall B    Passage BB
Entrance #2                          Hall C
Entrance #1      AB Connection
                 Low Point

The High Room
15
10
5
0
-5
-10
meters above or
below entrance #1

0        25

Locus 1/01 7/23
Locus 26
Locus 5/01 7/24
Splitter #4 7/24

AB Connection

Voice Connection

Locus 10

Locus 2/99 57y
Locus 29

Locus 51y

c

b

Locus 2/01 - 7/23
Fiberscope #1
Locus 30
Locus 32
59y
Locus 17
Locus 5

a

Entrance #1

Entrance #2

Hall A

Locus 25

Locus 18

0                    25

meters

## Locus Information

| | |
|---|---|
| Locus 1/99 to Locus 4/99 | Loci excavated during the 1999 expedition |
| Locus 1 to Locus 32 | Loci excavated during the 2000 expedition |
| Locus 1/01 to Locus 1/01 Butominite/Splitter | Loci excavated during the 2001 expedition Butominite and Splitter Locations - 2001 |

1y,2y,66y... - approximate locations of loci from
Yadin's 1960-61 excavations

# 10

# Future Secrets of Dead Sea Caves Research

## LEVELS OF OCCUPATION

W e have discovered four levels of use in the Cave of Letters. They are similar to periods of use in many of the Dead Sea Caves. Since these are caves of refuge, they are not full occupation levels. The four levels are:

Level 1—all "modern" materials from the period after Bar Kokh-
ba to the present (135–2004)
Level 2—Second Rebellion period (132–135 CE)
Level 3—First Rebellion period and aftermath (68 CE–132 CE)
Level 4—Chalcolithic period (4500–3200 BCE)

**We start with Level 1:** It is clear to all us who were in the cave in 1999 that illegal (unlicensed) excavations have been going on in the Cave of Letters since 1961. We have found new wiring for some lighting that was used, cigarette boxes and newspapers from different periods, and a host of other telltale signs of occupation. We include ourselves and the excavations of Yadin and Aharoni in level #1, since we too have changed the cave. Most of the illegal excavations include individuals between the excavations of Aharoni and Yadin who entered the cave in search of scrolls. In chapter 8 we reviewed the appearance of some biblical texts from *Nahal Tzeelim* that have finally been traced back to the Cave of Letters after the painstaking efforts of some remarkable researchers. We know that the list of visitors includes local amateur climbers, some cave researchers and geologists, Bedouins, treasure hunters, and thrill seekers who saw the challenge of the climb and the possibility that the cave still contained antiquities as reason enough to risk going there without the benefit of a license and full support staff as we were required to do. I have spoken to some of these people. They were lured to the cave by the myth. In the nineteenth and twentieth centuries the mythology of ancient sites began to develop. Petra, for example, held an allure similar to the Cave of Letters for Israelis throughout the 1950s and 1960s. The Cave of Letters became a place of modern pilgrimage for Israeli climbers with equipment and ability. Medals were actually issued to those brave souls who participated in these excavations. The numbers were small: Fewer than fifty such medals were issued. I have seen them displayed in the homes of those who volunteered for the Aharoni and Yadin excavations. We also have evidence that others have gone to the cave to see for themselves; but very few besides Yadin had produced scientific information that could help us. In this case, we will share with you what we found and what we think still can be found in the cave. It is a part of the secrets of the Cave of Letters. But it's also about how secrets for future research may be attained.

**Level 2** (The Second Rebellion: 132–135 CE) finds are dealt with extensively in three volumes by the Israel Exploration Society. We added to this body of knowledge with coins and our own analysis of elements that were discovered and published by others.

**Level 3** (The First Rebellion until the Second Rebellion: 68–132 CE) is the one that interested us the most. It also was the most problematic. Nine coins have been found in the three excavations of the

Cave of Letters. Aharoni found no coins. Yadin had two coins from the Bar Kokhba period. We found the other seven during our 1999 and 2000 excavations. Technically I could say the coins show a continued use of the cave from the first to the second century. We found the same number of coins from before the Bar Kokhba Rebellion as Bar Kokhba Rebellion coins. Coins are an important part of an argument since they are specific indicators of what people carried often only in specific periods. Coins were and are important propaganda medium because they are handled by everyone and they can carry symbols and inscriptions that often speaker louder and more often than any other vehicle of advertising that was disseminated in those days. Not all coins were legal tender or meaningful after the historical or political events they were meant to commemorate had passed. The symbols and inscriptions, in fact, often rendered them unfit for use in a later period. Of course, in antiquity bronze, silver, and gold coins could be melted down or restruck and used again; they also can be historical benchmarks and kept as collectors' items of an age that had come and gone; but for the most part coins were slides of life as it was lived in a certain time and place, and tell us about the people who used them. Sometimes coins were restruck over other coins for utilitarian reasons, but more often they were restruck to make a political point. For the Jews to strike their coins over the image of the emperor or the Roman Eagle made a statement that often swords and battles could not. The coins in the Cave of Letters, along with other information found in the cave, tell us a story about the life of Jews in this period, and only a few coins can tell us a lot when combined with the other information that we had gained.

Yadin's excavations discovered only one coin inside the cave (and one outside). We discovered one Bar Kokhba–period coin in 1999 and two Bar Kokhba coins in 2000, for a total of four Bar Kokhba coins discovered inside of the cave. The coins from before the Bar Kokhba rebellion (68–112/113 CE) are from a sparkling array of major figures from the first and second century: The Roman emperor Trajan (emperor 98–117 CE), King Rabbel II (king of the Nabateans 70–106 CE), Vespasian (emperor 69–79 CE), and a Jewish-Zealot coin from the First Revolt (68 CE). One could make the argument solely from the coins that the Cave of Letters was continuously in use from 68 to 135 CE.

On one of the early days of the excavations in 2000 we came upon a coin which in retrospect has been called "the smoking gun" for the proof of our hypothesis that the cave had been continuously used by Jerusalem refugees escaping the destruction of the Temple in the First Revolt and others up to and including the Bar Kokhba refugees. On July 11, 2000, in Locus 18, Basket #148, we found a Zealot coin from the second year (68/69 CE) of the First Jewish Rebellion against Rome. The Zealots were the most extreme, most nationalist Jews of the First Revolt against Rome, who minted their own coins in the most difficult moments of the First Rebellion and hoped at every minute that some divine intervention might save them from their inevitable fate. The first-century Jewish historian Josephus Flavius graphically described their horrific and violent end in Jerusalem in his book, the *Jewish Wars*, and then even after Jerusalem fell in 70 CE, the Zealots apparently held out for a number of years. Josephus describes in painstaking detail the attempt by the Zealots to hold out against the Romans, culminating with the Roman siege of the mountaintop fortress of Masada in the Judean desert in 73 CE. This coin in the Cave of Letters is similar to the other coins found at Qumran and Masada, two places where the Zealots found themselves. The Zealot coin found in the Cave of Letters would not be used in the time of the Second Rebellion. It is unusual, since these coins were legal tender only in the short period of the first uprising. These coins were poorly made and immediately lost their value after the rebellion. The effort to melt down Zealot coins would not have been a worthwhile effort, nor were they good candidates for restriking. This Zealot coin is small, less than 3 grams, and made of poor bronze, with an obverse symbol of an *amphora* (a large jar that became a symbol of freedom for Jews) with two handles around an inscription starting on the left which reads "Year Two." (The coins began to be struck in 67 CE.) The coins are struck in paleo-Hebrew. The use of the paleo-Hebrew is an attempt to hearken back to the grand old days of ancient Israelite glory from the First Temple period (before 587 BCE). By the first century CE, the paleo-Hebrew form of Hebrew writing had not been in regular use for hundreds of years! The coin is so poorly made that traces of the *Tof* (X in paleo-Hebrew is a *Tof*) from the other side of

COL
Locus 18
Basket 148
11-07-2000

#25/2000

The Zealot coin. (D. Hadash/COL Project)

the coin are visible on the obverse of the coin. This means that this coin was hastily struck on a poor-quality bronze with poor equipment. This would also mean that this was probably late in year two of the First Rebellion or perhaps it was the end of year two (August 68 CE). It was late in 68 CE that, according to Josephus Flavius, the Jewish historian who accompanied the Romans in the war to chronicle the events, things started to go very, very badly for the Jews in Jerusalem. By this time they had to allow coins with mistakes to be used. This coin is significant for a variety of reasons. While it is true that many other Roman bronze and silver coins were used by the Bar Kokhba rebels both as legal tender and for possible restriking, small antique coins such as those from Rabbel II (70–106 CE) and especially this First Revolt (68 CE) coin would not have been often used or readily available in the time of Bar Kokhba. The small bronze coin of King Rabbel II and the First Revolt coin of the Jews would not have held the symbolic significance that striking over a Roman coin would have held for Bar Kokhba. In addition, the Rabbel and Zealot coins are small enough to make it nearly impossible to restrike any of the denominations commonly in use in the Bar Kokhba currency.

The presence of the First Revolt coin in the Cave of Letters may signal that the cave was used by First Revolt refugees, or it may hint at the significance the First Revolt held for the Second Revolt participants. The symbolism of the First Revolt coin may have made it a relic to the Bar Kokhba refugees; it may have been preserved in the

Cave of Letters for that reason. On the reverse of the Zealot coin is a vine leaf with a small branch and tendril with the inscription: "Freedom of Zion" (*Herut Tzion*) with the *t* of *Herut* being the letter which is on the obverse.[111] The symbolism and the inscriptions of the Bar Kokhba coins parallel those of the First Revolt coins. The date of the Zealot coin found in the Cave of Letters is very significant. The second year of the First Revolt is important because at Qumran we date 68 CE (second year of the revolt) as the time that Vespasian and the Romans passed through Jericho and the Dead Sea area on their way to Jerusalem to destroy the Temple. During the journey they are presumed to have destroyed Qumran. The Cave of Letters would have been a particularly important place of refuge to the Qumranites at that particular moment. The Cave of Letters was close enough to Qumran that it would be an easy journey (and not in the direction of either Jericho or Jerusalem). The Romans occupied Qumran from 68 to 73 (coins and other artifacts verify their occupation there). It was to become one of the staging areas for the final assault on Masada. The use of the Cave of Letters by refugees from Jerusalem and Qumran may have continued nearly uninterrupted from 68 to 113 CE. According to our geologist, Dr. Jack Shroder, there was an earthquake that may have partially sealed the cave (remember that Dr. Jack Shroder had said that Entrance #1 appeared to have been dug out). The Cave of Letters may not have been used after the earthquake of 115 until the Second Revolt, when the cave was again pressed into service. The opening that was partially blocked during the earthquake of 115 was only rediscovered/redug by the refugees in 132 CE and prepared for use at that time.

Another coin adds further information about this period. On July 17, 2000, in Locus 27, Basket #193, a silver tetradrachma Vespasian coin from the year 70/71 struck at Tyre was found. The coin's weight is 14.60 grams with an obverse head of Vespasian right laureate and the inscription of "*Vespasian the King.*" The reverse has a eagle standing on a club head to the left holding a wreath in its beak with a palm branch on the right. It has a border of dots around the outside of the coin. The legend on the reverse is: "*Year 2*" or 70/71 CE.[112] This coin could have been from either the First or the Second

Revolt refugees, many coin specialists told us. This would have been one of the coins that Bar Kokhba might have wanted to purposely restrike with his own images and symbols. The only problem with the theory is that this coin was in a refuge cave, not a place where the hoarded coins were being prepared for restriking. The coin is a fine specimen and could have been legal tender in 132 CE despite its age. It could, however, also be seen as a remnant of the First Revolt use of the cave. It was certainly legal tender in 70 CE when the Zealots would have used the cave.

The other two coins found in our excavations from before the Bar Kokhba rebellion, the Nabatean kingdom coin and the Emperor Trajan coin, might still be in use in this region in 132 CE. The Trajan coin was a beautiful silver coin that would be worthy of being re-struck, but the Nabatean coin was made of bronze and was much less worthy of being restruck. In addition, there is no indication that the people who were in this cave were hoarding coins for restriking. They seem to have been refugees who arrived only with their possessions.

The Bar Kokhba era coins found in the Cave of Letters indicate that it was used at the end of the Second Revolt. A nearly complete set of the Bar Kokhba coinage has been found. The set of coins trace the two-and-a-half through three-and-a-half years of the rebellion and tell us that the refugees who were in the cave were there at the end of the rebellion. On July 17, 2000, in Locus 25, Basket #188, a large Bar Kokhba coin issued in 132/33 with a weight of 10.60 grams was found. It had the traditional wreath decoration tied at the bottom with the palm branch. The legend reads in paleo-Hebrew "Shimon Prince/President of Israel" (*Shimon Nasi Yisrael*) on the obverse. On the reverse it reads "First Year of the Redemption of Israel" (*Shnat echat LeGeulat Yisrael*). The obverse has the distinctive lyre with four strings. There is clear evidence on both sides of overstriking a Roman bronze coin. The bronze coin was in excellent condition, since it was under only one rock layer. On the same day we discovered in Locus 16, in passage AB, a Bar Kokhba coin dated 134/35. It was small, with a weight of 3.30 grams in bronze. It had the palm tree with two bundles of dates and seven branches with a border of dates hanging heavy from its branches, and on the obverse a bunch of grapes. The legend on the obverse is *Shin, Mem, Ayin, Vav,* (final) *Nun.* On the reverse is the name Shimon, and the legend reading around from the right above is: "For the Freedom of Jerusalem" (*LaHerut Yerush[alayim]*).[113] The very simplicity of it, "Shimon as Prince/President of Israel" and a simple message of freedom of Jerusalem (and not all Israel) still in 134–135 CE was used at the end of the rebellion. The last Bar Kokhba coin— without a date—is ascribed to 136 CE, the very end of the rebellion. The name "Shimon" is there, but without the full legend "Prince/ President of Israel." This was the very sad reality that had developed by the end of the rebellion. By not writing a date, they somehow felt that they were putting off the inevitable. The name of Shimon still carried weight and was included on the coin, but without the pomp and circumstance of "President/Prince of Israel." In this cave, like bookends, were two parts of the same epic tale that had begun in 66 CE with the First Revolt of the Jews against the Romans, led to the destruction of the Temple in Jerusalem in 70 CE, and now ended with the failure of the Second Revolt of Bar Kokhba in 136 CE.[114]

In 1999 we discovered two relatively modern coins in the cave. We did not write about this in our reports since they really are not part of the ancient story of the cave. They are, however, certainly a part of the modern epic of the excavations of the Cave of Letters. While surveying in Hall B we discovered a coin from 1959 CE and we knew it had fallen from the pocket of one of the participants in the Yadin excavations. In 2000, in Hall A, after working with metal detectors, we came upon a coin from 1949 CE, which was probably in the pocket of one of the participants in Aharoni's excavations. It, like the 1959 coin, was a reminder of who had been there and when. It continued to remind me that the coins are clues to when people had been in the cave. The coins were more than just a mystery waiting to be solved; they were a key element in the search for a specific type of coin that might tell us conclusively when people were using the cave.

But the coins are only one part of the cumulative evidence we are assembling. In the past two years we have tested forty different items in a variety of ways, and more tests will continue over the next few years. The carbon 14 testing, in particular, has made it possible to say that there was first-century occupation in addition to the second-

Bar Kokhba coin. (COL Project)

century occupation. But who were these first-century occupants of the cave, and were they the ones who brought the bronze hoard with them from Jerusalem or was this a well-known cave used by many different groups in the first and second centuries? When seen together, seven lines of evidence have emerged. I close the book with them for you to consider:

# THE LINES OF EVIDENCE

**1. The archaeological stratigraphy:** Archaeological stratigraphy was where it all began some 150 years ago. The idea that we were able to see geological stratigraphy that paralleled archaeological stratigraphy inside the cave is important. In the cave, since no one was systematically building on top of another layer (as is present in a noncave archaeological context), geological layers often serve as archaeological layers. The roof fall after every geological event provided a consistent layering effect in the cave. We were able to distinguish archaeological layers and artifacts found on one layer were distinguished from other artifacts that were in other geological layers. This "layer cake" format shows itself throughout the Cave of Letters and is also a well-known fact in all archaeology. *The bronze artifacts in Hall A were nearly six feet below* the other geological/archaeological layer of the cave that revealed most of the other finds in Hall B and C. The bronze artifacts were found below a latrinelike area near the entrance to the cave. When we dug down six feet below the Bar Kokhba floor in Hall B we found the oven and the wood that dated to the first century CE. The geomorphological surveys tell us that there are a variety of different layers of occupation in the cave; combined with the archaeological discoveries this tells us that the Cave of Letters has secrets to be uncovered in a layer some six feet below the accumulated roof debris layer.

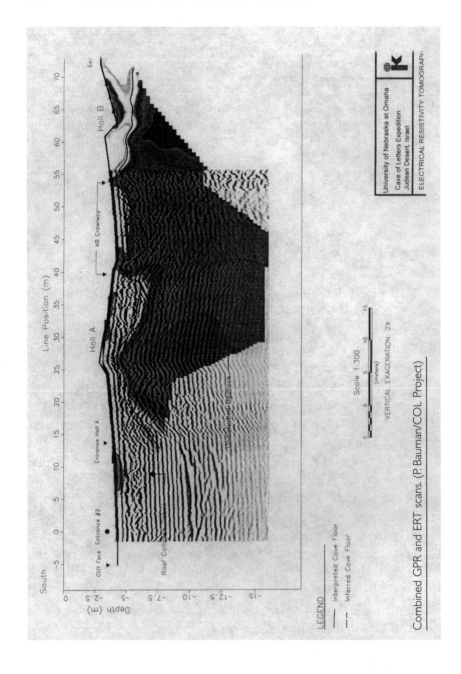

Combined GPR and ERT scans. (P. Bauman/COL Project)

**2. The iconographic comparison:** All archaeology is based upon comparisons of materials from other sites for dating and authenticating. We date architecture, pottery, and other elements by comparison with other dated sites, and a relatively clear time line has been developed that allows us to assess these elements from site to site because we have established comparative models. The *patera* design found in the bronze hoard in the cave of letters has a beautiful Thetis and Achilles that is repeated in other *paterae* from other first-century sites such as Pompeii and Herculaneum. It is also found on the only contemporaneous representation from the Temple of Jerusalem: i.e., the Arch of Titus in Rome. While part of the similarity is that the iconography on the *patera* in the Cave of Letters is of a famous scene from Roman art (it is the equivalent of our George Washington crossing the Delaware in antiquity) and it is represented on the Arch of Titus (which was built after the victories in Judea were complete) on a Jewish artifact, the menorah (Candelabrum), the point is clear. The arch's iconography connects the story of Thetis to the Jewish Temple in the first century. Whether the scene was added to the base of the Jewish Temple artifact (as some think)[115] or was originally part of the menorah's iconography does not matter as much as the fact that this scene directly connects the *patera* of the Cave of Letters to another artifact from the Temple in Jerusalem. It is our contention that the iconography on the *patera* and the arch—of Thetis helping her son Achilles—was a scene that may have been universalized by Second Temple period Judaism (like the later Roman zodiac symbols on synagogue floors and therefore "kosher"). The use of similarly designed bronze incense shovels as ritual objects from a certain time period is much easier. The incense shovels of Bethsaida, Pompeii, and the Cave of Letters are clearly first-century and contemporaneous with the use of the iconography of Thetis both on the arch and elsewhere in the Roman Empire. If the shovels are contemporaneous (Bethsaida/Pompeii/Cave of Letters), and from Temple sites such as Pompeii and the first-century Jewish imperial cult site at Bethsaida, why should we assume that the incense shovel in the cave is anything less?

This is where an understanding of the academic study of religion in the past forty years has changed our understanding of the relationship between Jews and non-Jews (pagans). In the early 1960s, few would have considered the possibility that artifacts with clear Roman mythological/religious scenes on them would have been used by Jews—much less in the Temple of Jerusalem. In the 1950s, in the shadow of the Nazi Holocaust, many scholars of ancient Judaism understood the relationship between Jews and non-Jews as contentious and not conducive to "borrowing" and positive integration in antiquity. Since the 1960s, with the wealth of discoveries of Greco-Roman iconography made at some of the most "Jewish" cities of ancient Israel (Beth Shearim and Sepphoris, for example, site of the Rabbinic Sanhedrins, have Roman zodiac and mythological figures on rabbinic tombs and the synagogue) it has become abundantly clear that the Jews of the Greco-Roman era had found a way of using familiar universal messages by utilizing these common symbols. Some have commented that this trend is a late innovation in Ancient Judaism. These scholars are willing to say that by the third and perhaps fourth century relations were such that Greco-Roman iconography was allowed for the first time in this period. I would argue that such a trend cannot spring up overnight and represents a long period of acculturation. The existence of a first-century text from the caves of the Dead Sea such as scroll 4Q318 (the three-hundred-eighteenth item from Qumran cave 4), which chronicles the details of the mythology of the zodiac, for example, demonstrates that these Greco-Roman symbols had meanings and interpretations that had already been translated into Hebrew and Aramaic in an early period. To think that suddenly, in the third century, Jews "woke up" and decided that it was now permissible to use Roman mythological symbols doesn't make sense. It must have started earlier. And since the Temple in Jerusalem was the model for many of the later synagogues, it stands to reason that these symbols filtered down to the synagogues from a Second-Temple tradition and not that the synogogues suddenly innovated in this later period. In addition, the Herodian Temple in Jerusalem was not the paragon of Jewish ritual that many think. King Herod would have emulated much of the Roman architecture and furnishings of the period to make it meaningful to the Roman authorities. It is not difficult to see that the artifacts that were used in the

Temple may have resembled those used at Roman temple sites—or were gifts from Roman leaders. The Cave of Letters bronze hoard was taken, according to this argument, from the Second Temple and brought to the cave for hiding for future use. The Copper Scroll listing of Temple treasures (taxes and apparently Temple artifacts) in the Cave of Letters as the "Cave of the Column" confirms this fact.

**3. The pottery of the Cave of Letters:** Two elements are clearly first-century and important to our discussion of the occupants. The Herodian oil lamps from the Cave of Letters are the same type as those from Qumran and Masada. Why would Yadin date the oil lamp from Masada as clearly first-century and a lamp from the Cave of Letters to the second century? Herodian oil lamps of the second century are not like the ones from the first century. More importantly, no one carries an oil lamp around for a sixty-year period. Even good ones are too fragile and easily replaceable. The limestone vessel found in the Cave of Letters is very similar to the limestone vessel found two years later by Yadin at Masada. No clear answer was forthcoming short of Yadin thinking that the limestone vessel was still in use two generations after the destruction of the Temple in Jerusalem.

These limestone vessels, however, were very fragile and linked to the purities of Jerusalem when the Temple was standing. In fact it led to assigning limestone vessels found at other archaeological sites throughout Israel to the second century also! In fact, the limestone vessels issue is a very complex one, since these vessels apparently existed in different manifestations at different sites after the destruction of the Temple. Yadin's assignment of them to the second century CE has had a ripple effect in the dating and understanding of many sites. The crucial point for us is that in the 1960s finding a limestone cup that was similar to the ones from Qumran (and then two years later at Masada) should have led Yadin immediately to connect it with the time period of Qumran and Masada in his writings; i.e., the First Revolt. It did not. Yadin's decision to hold that the carved limestone vessels were either made or preserved (as a relic) two generations after the destruction of the Temple in Jerusalem seems to have made to create the false impression that there was no connection at all between the Cave of Letters and the Temple. He seems to have been more interested in playing up the Cave of Letters' connection to the Bar Kokhba Rebellion and its courageous (and tragic) story than having it overshadowed by the connection to the priests, Zealots, and Temple in Jerusalem in the First Revolt as at Masada and Qumran.

**4. Manuscripts in the Cave of Letters:** The discovery (or rather rediscovery) of the existence of the Psalms manuscript in the Cave of Letters (Psalms 7, 8, 10, 11, 14, 15/16, 23, 24, and 29—probably from Hall A) is a crucial finding. It is so unlike any other written piece found in Hall C that it clearly suggests a different group was present in Hall A. The Psalms were the crux of worship in the Temple in Jerusalem and this is the only Judean cave manuscript that preserves these Psalms. It is one of only three Psalms scrolls not found at Qumran; the others having been found at Masada. This knowledge painstakingly gathered over the past forty years would certainly have changed Yadin's mind about the cave, but all he had was a small fragment of Psalm 15/16 to go by. He knew that finding a Psalms fragment (even a small one!) was significant but chose again not to emphasize its importance. The manuscript script is clearly late Herodian and can be located in the first century BCE.[116] Yadin did not know about the manuscript of Deuteronomy or of a fuller Numbers manuscript of the Cave of Letters, but today they all have been ascribed to the Cave of Letters. They all stand out as religious manuscripts, as distinct from all of the secular letters and documents found together in Hall C of the Cave of Letters, and they tell a totally different story about the periods of occupation of the Cave of Letters. As we saw, the biblical manuscripts are similar in many aspects to manuscripts found in the Dead Sea Scrolls at Qumran and at Masada. But it is what makes them different that gives us a clue as to who these manuscripts belonged to. These differences led us to conclude that whoever came to the Cave of Letters was probably not from Qumran. It has already been established that none of the biblical texts found at Masada originated at Qumran because of key differences between the manuscripts. What I will argue is that none of the biblical texts from the Cave of Letters originated at Qumran either, and that they may actually represent either the same tradition as Masada or a totally different tradition. As we noted above, a difference in the Cave of Letters Psalms scroll is the lack of the classic superscription "A Psalm of David" for Psalm 15. At Qumran, Psalms was apparently the most important text, with more copies than any other biblical work and very specific patterns. The Davidic authorship of the Psalms at Qumran was also key. We suspect that the differences point up that the manuscript from the Cave of Letters comes from a different tradition than the Qumran texts. This is one of the ways to explain why the manuscript traditions are different from the Qumran texts. If all ancient Psalms manuscripts have one reading and the Cave of Letters manuscript of Psalms has another reading, only a few possible explanations can apply. One explanation is that it is a simple mistake. But mistakes usually have patterns such as a repetition of a letter or a word causing a copyist to lose his place. But often it is the simpler or shorter text that preserves the original. A longer text is generally an added interpretation or idea from another period or hand. This is the case of a reading in Psalm 15. The Psalm 15 in our Bible is:

1. *"A Psalm of David"*
2. Lord, who shall stay in your tent, who shall dwell in your holy mountain?
3. He who walks with integrity and practices justice, and speaks the truth from his heart.
4. *He who does not commit slander with his tongue,*
5. He who does no wrong to his fellow, and casts no dispersions upon his neighbor.

The text in italics does not appear in the Psalm text fragment from the Cave of Letters and when you examine the text of the Psalm, it is clear that line #4 is really out of place. Line 2 has two parts or comparisons with parallel verbs ("stay"/"dwell"). Line 3 has two parallel verbs ("walks"/"speaks") as does line five, but line 4 adds an extra thought or concept that does not neatly fit lines 3 or 5. It is an addition or interpretation to the text. The fact that it is in Psalms from the Dead Sea Scrolls and our Masoretic (rabbinic) tradition of the Bible means that *the manuscript in the Cave of Letters is a unique tradition*, an original (i.e., early) tradition of text that has not undergone revisions that may have become important in other settings. One can clearly judge that the paleography is from the first century, just as the texts from Masada and Qumran are from the first century. But it is also from another group using this text, presumably not Qumranites or Essenes. We hold that this text of Psalms was from a religious group, possibly priests, that came from the Temple in Jerusalem, and that they brought with them the bronze hoard and hid both the Psalms and the hoard in the cave. They must also be connected with the same individuals who wrote in the Copper Scroll about burying the treasure in the Cave of the Column, and they mention that they placed their copy of the Psalms scroll in the limestone cup that was found nearby! They could be refugees from the First Revolt, which would explain the existence of the Numbers and Deuteronomy scrolls that also came from the Cave of Letters. They represent a totally different group of religious individuals who came to the Cave as refugees under totally different conditions than the people who used Hall C.

Could these texts have just been old texts that the Bar Kokhba rebels were using? Would the inhabitants have been using a manuscript that was almost two hundred years old? Based on ancient standards, of course, they might have been using a manuscript that was almost two centuries old. Do the Bar Kokhba rebels' writings from the rest of the Cave of Letters demonstrate anything like the piety which these manuscripts might suggest? No. In fact, the Bar Kokhba letters suggest well-to-do individuals with fine objects and some Jewish interests. Were they pious readers of an ancient scroll that they brought with them? I do not think so. I do not think that the inhabitants of Hall C used Hall A for anything but bathroom facilities. So who were the people who were using these holy texts?

Had the religious texts that were finally reassigned to the Cave of Letters been found at Masada or any other cave, they would have been said to be first-century religious texts that served as inspirations to a first-century people who had settled there. We have found, time and again, circular reasoning in the understanding of the archaeology of the Cave of Letters. Since the other manuscripts found in Hall C are all from the second century, these religious texts must have been used in the second century as well. If a carved limestone vessel or Herodian-style lamp were found in the Cave of Letters, then limestone vessels and Herodian-style lamps must have been used in the second century. If first-century coins were found in the Cave of Letters, then they must have been in use in the second century. Everything was reinterpreted in light of Yadin's major hypothesis that there were only two archaeological strata in the Cave of Letters—Chalcolithic and Bar Kokhba. Anything that did not fit must be reinterpreted to fit that hypothesis. *I suggest that the Psalms, Numbers, and Deuteronomy manuscripts found in the Cave of Letters better fit a first-century priestly, Essene, or Jerusalemite presence in the cave rather than a second-century Ein Gedi rebel occupation.*

**5. The burials in the Cave of Letters:** All of the elements above help explain the internments found in Hall C. The discovery of bags of skulls separated from the rest of the bones and the state of the burials suggests that there were two different burial periods. The burials of the individuals and the separation of the heads from the bodies suggest that the people who did it were not the same people who laid the bodies out for burial. This process is so different from Jewish practices of the period as to suggest that the people who put these bones in the baskets did not know who they were and were collecting them for later removal or creating more space for their own burials. In any case, these were apparently not the burials of the Bar Kokhba rebels as Yadin thought. Yadin had always assumed that since the refugees arrived in the final period of the revolt, the dead were therefore refugees who came to the cave and died there. The process suggested by the bags of skulls separated from the rest of the bones, however, suggests a long period (since decomposition would need to have taken place before they would be gathered up in bags). Since decomposition is such a slow process in a cave like this (little or no humidity; no soil, bugs, etc. to help the process along), the bag of skulls suggests that the bodies had been laid out many, many years before and only much later collected in these bags for removal. The cave environment preserves all organic matter unusually well. In the tiny cave located just across the Nahal Hever, the Cave of Horrors, the unique climate has yielded "horrific" results. In the 1950s the first excavators there found Second Revolt refugees with skin still intact on the bone! Accordingly, if these were the bones of post–First Revolt refugees who had died in the cave a generation before the Second Revolt and were found by the Second Revolt refugees, then the placing of the skulls together in bags for removal makes much more sense. If, however, the bones are from the Second Revolt refugees, it implies that someone else had come back much later and gathered the skulls into these bags.

**6. The meaning of the coins:** I think the coins demonstrate that the cave was used between the First and Second Rebellions. The 68 CE coin is our "smoking gun." While it is possible that this was a coin for restriking or a relic of significance that was kept for nostalgia's sake, it makes more sense to say that it was brought there by a First Revolt refugee. I do not think it was collected for its poor bronze or dropped by a Bedouin treasure seeker as he rummaged around the cave, as some people have suggested. Nabatean and Trajan coins suggest a post-70 use of the cave. The gap between the 113 CE Emperor Trajan coin and the Bar Kokhba coins in 132 CE implies that there is a gap in the use of the cave until Bar Kokhba dragged these middle-class, well-connected citizens with their beautiful possessions and *keys to their houses(!)* to this cave in the middle of the Judean desert. So I think the second-century CE Cave of Letters may have been the well-known first-century Cave of the Column, which provided the rebels of Bar Kokhba the same relative safety it did to the first-century refugees from Jerusalem who had used it two generations before.

**7. Radiocarbon dating:** Radiocarbon dating was discovered about the same time as the earliest discoveries of the Dead Sea Scrolls. In fact, the entire debate over the dating of the Dead Sea Scrolls was ultimately decided by using this technique in the 1980s and 1990s, after it became more refined. The basic principle of carbon 14 dating is based upon the presence of the carbon 14 isotope in all organic matter such as bones, parchment, and textiles made from animal and vegetable matter. Even though the isotope decays at a precisely measurable rate, the microconditions of any setting can affect the scientific analysis of the data. The caves and the environmental conditions of the Dead Sea are important determining factors in the analysis of the C-14 data. The Cave of Letters is an especially important microenvironment which we paid close attention to so that we could calibrate our C-14 results properly. The conditions of the Cave of Letters and the Dead Sea Caves in general are so unique that the C-14 analysis of

The Zealot coin 68 CE. (COL Project)

items from these caves have become important studies in all Dead Sea Scrolls research. The dating process has brought a new level of certitude for determining the age of certain materials. Linens from the caves were among the first items tested in the late 1940s and early 1950s with this new technique. The dispute over the dates of the Dead Sea Scrolls raged on for years, some scholars insisting that the Scrolls were medieval until this technique was perfected. We had many organic finds from the Cave of Letters. They were found at different archaeological strata, which we could test and associate with dates (albeit a spread of two hundred years is usually found in our work!). **Our conclusion was that although there was a spread of nearly two hundred years for the range of many items, we found that the "true" date of the artifacts tested in the cave was the older extreme and not the average of the age range. This conclusion was reached because of the unique microclimate of the Cave of Letters, and it became increasingly important as we analyzed the results put forward by the C-14 labs.** With such a large variance between the different dates one might ask how we are able to distinguish that the older extreme is more correct than the later extreme and that the date is not the average date in the middle of the extreme. The answer comes also from an experiment that was done on the documents from the Cave of Letters and the Bar Kokhba discoveries from other caves. Its conclusions were important for the dating of the Dead Sea Scrolls but became perfectly transferable for our work.

The unique experiment and theory was built by Magen Broshi, curator emeritus of the Dead Sea Scrolls, and he has written about it in a variety of publications. Broshi figured out how to use the radiocarbon dates for testing documents and artifacts from the Dead Sea Caves because he too was perplexed by the great extremes, that appeared in the results. Because there was no way of knowing whether the earlier range, the later extreme or the middle of the extremes was closest to the correct date, a unique experiment was performed *on dated documents*. None of the dated documents were from the Qumran caves, but three were from Bar Kokhba caves and two were from the Cave of Letters. Here is what was found:[117]

| Scroll | C-14 calibrated date | additional information |
|---|---|---|
| IAA-13433 | 130–321 CE | 56 Hev (Pap Yad in 21—purchase of crop dated September 11, 130) |
| IAA-14987 | 126–234 CE | 5/6 Hev (Pap Yad in 19—deed of gift, dated April 16, 128) |
| IAA-14986 | 144–370 CE | Kefar Bebayou (wadi Murabba' at Cave—house sale, dated to 135) |
| IAA-13415 | 5–80 CE | 4Q258 |
| IAA-13419 | 134–230 CE | 4Q258 |
| IAA-13431 | 72–127 CE | 4Q344 |

In addition, other dated materials from Qumran were tested that were similar to our materials from the Cave of Letters: a linen cloth and a date palm log[118] (these items were dated by other elements in the same locus to 68 CE).[119] In this case, similar to our own wood finds in the Cave of Letters, the wood has a date which approximates the first century CE. Although we might wonder whether the wood was cut at an earlier time and kept around for later use (wood can be hundreds of years old), we learn from the Qumran excavations that the wood that was cut for use is exactly as old as the settlement. Wood was so scarce that if it was cut, it was used almost immediately. The fact that our wood dates to the early first century CE indicates that the wood was probably for use in the oven, which also dates to the first century CE.

The dated Cave of Letters documents, however, were the most dramatic and important evidence for determining dates of undated materials. From their information we have principles for understanding other Dead Sea Scrolls. Magen Broshi, the first curator of the Dead Sea Scrolls, wrote what he had learned from this experiment:[120]

a.   The true dates do fall within or very near the archaeologically established calibrated age ranges. In only one case, the true age is off by ten years.

b.   The true date is not the average of the age range. In the three papyri, the "true" date is in fact the older extreme. Perhaps this has to do with the preservation of the papyrus material.

c.   The age range can be quite broad. In two cases it exceeds two hundred years.

After working on understanding the microclimate of the Cave of Letters, we have concluded that it is a unique environment. Thus, using Broshi's observations, we have a new perspective on the Cave of Letters. Because of the nature of the special microenvironment of the cave, the older extremes for carbon 14 dates preserve the most correct date of *all* materials found there.

Today this is also the conclusion that many of the best scholars have reached concerning much of the materials from the Dead Sea caves that were tested with the radiocarbon method. The use of Accelerator Mass Spectrometry technique required only a small piece (0.5–1.0 mg) of carbon for dating and has overcome the disadvantages of the early radiocarbon dating, which required large amounts of carbon. We found that we could take already existing finds like the rope tied to one of the bronze articles found by Yadin and test them. We discovered that this particular rope had never been treated with harsh chemicals to preserve or clean it. It was never tested by Yadin because Yadin had so much dated material he did not feel it necessary to do very much carbon 14 testing. This was crucial to our investigation. The C-14 dating of the rope connected to the bronze hoard (70–260 CE) is important. The older extreme, 70 CE, is extremely poignant. I had hypothesized that the bronzes were deposited in the Cave of Letters in between the First and Second Rebellion. I never dreamed that we would have confirmation from science that established that the bronzes had been deposited in the cave so close to the time that the Temple in Jerusalem was destroyed!

## USE OF THE CAVE OF LETTERS IN THE FIRST AND SECOND CENTURIES

If we were to prove that some of the artifacts in the Cave of Letters came from the first century and others from the second century, we had to be able to date a variety of artifacts at different archaeological strata. We found, for example, a child's leather sandal at the opening of the Cave of Letters near the spot where we discovered the coin from 68 CE. If we combine these two elements we can get a clearer picture than we can from one isolated coin. The leather sandal was C-14 dated to 80–340 CE, again giving us a clear time line. The child's sandal indicates that it was left there in approximately 80 CE and together with the coin at the opening of the cave suggests that refugees from the First Rebellion sought shelter in the Cave of Letters and perhaps left in a hurry. Sandals were not simple, replaceable items purchased in a store. They were handcrafted to a specific size and foot, and this one the sandal of a child perhaps three or four years old.

The most important carbon dating involves the Niche of Skulls and the oven area. The oven area, the lowest stratigraphically and most untouched area in Hall B, revealed both wood and organic matter from the oven. The oven's date was determined by a piece of organic matter used in the grit of the outside pottery. It is important that it was on the outside and not cooked and carbonized from the inside of the oven. It was removed and tested to 60–340 CE when calibrated. It may indicate that only a short time before the destruction of Jerusalem, the residents were already escaping to the caves, or that it was used by the insurgents in their campaign against the Romans even before the final battles. This would be similar to the Bar Kokhba rebels who used caves and tunnels to store weapons and to plan and launch battles. It also was a place for preparing a backup position in the event of losses in the larger cities. Since the war against the Romans began in 66 CE in Galilee, this might indicate that the cave was prepared only a short time beforehand. The stockpiled wood was not brought from very far away (they are all indigenous woods). But they indicate the difficult task of collecting and preparing for a long siege. The only piece of furniture we discovered was clearly cut down in the early first century and dragged to the cave to be used as a leg of a low table, bed, or chair. It was found at the lowest part of the oven area at the bottom of our excavations in Hall B. It was carved and its early date (calibrated C-14 date: 20 BCE–130 CE) indicates a clear first-century pedigree. The wood around it dates back even earlier. But it would have made this hearth area an important center for the cave occupants in the first century. Many of the personal objects—the comb, other sandal pieces, and palm branch baskets—were all found under the collapsed roof of the AB passage.

The Niche of Skulls is a totally different issue. Not only have we been able to determine that there were two different periods of burial by comparing the contemporary burial customs and the niche's state; the carbon 14 dates indicate that some people from the first century were buried in the niche. Apparently, the second-century occupants discovered the remains when they came to the cave (by this time they probably did not know who these people were but assumed that they were "distant relatives"). There was a gap of eighty to ninety years between the two burials. The first bone sample was dated to 120–390 CE while another sample was dated to 20–250 CE. What this implies is that the people from the second century came to the cave, found the interred remains from the earlier occupation, lovingly collected them in baskets, and ultimately put their own honored dead in the same niche.

| Samples | Calibrated Carbon 14 date |
| --- | --- |
| RTT 3861<br>leather (sandal) | 80–340 CE |
| RTT 3860<br>rope (IAA 286) | 70–260 CE |
| RTT 3726–1.2<br>bone (locus 22) | 50–340 CE |
| RTT 3800<br>bone<br>(niche of skulls) | 120–390 CE |
| RTT 3726–1.1<br>bone<br>(niche of skulls) | 20–250 CE |
| RTT 3726<br>Bone<br>(niche of skulls) | 130–350 CE |
| RTT 3862<br>textile<br>(niche of skulls) | 80–330 CE |
| RTT 3859<br>plant (oven) | 60–340 CE |
| RTT 3916<br>Wood (oven area)<br>(furniture leg) | 20 BCE–130 CE |
| RTT 3917<br>Wood (oven area)<br>Firewood: Christ Thorn,<br>Zisiphus spina christi | 100 BCE–90 CE |
| RTT 3918<br>Wood (oven area)<br>Firewood: White Broom, Retama raetam | 60 BCE–80 CE |

If we take the principles seriously in comparison with our own carbon-dated materials, it means that the older extremes indicate that the materials are from two different time periods within a one-hundred-year period—from the mid–first century through the mid–second century. The conclusions that can be reached from the radio-carbon dates indicate that:

A. The Cave of Letters was most probably used almost continuously as a place of refuge from the First Rebellion and through the Second Rebellion.
B. The bones in the Niche of Skulls were from two different periods of occupation and the bones found there were probably from both periods.
C. The firewood and the oven were for the use of the First Rebellion refugees of the cave. They were probably destroyed in an earthquake between the First Rebellion and the Second Rebellions and covered with roof debris, which precluded the oven's use in the Second Rebellion occupation.
D. The rope around the bronze bowl (RTT 3860-IAA 286) should be dated conclusively to the older extreme, 70 CE. It fits into the theory that this entire group of artifacts was placed in the Cave of Letters in the First Rebellion period. Similar to the oven and firewood, which were buried under a layer of roof debris, they were buried in the entrance of the Cave of Letters. The Second Rebellion refugees probably knew nothing about their existence.

## THE ARGUMENT FOR THE FUTURE

Just as Yadin left us something to ponder in the Niche of Skulls, I think we leave future generations something to work on. In the past archaeologists said that the "stones speak" in much the same way that literary scholars hold that texts "speak." In fact, all of the artifacts may ultimately "speak" in new or unimagined voices in the future. Greater knowledge about the coins of Judea in the period will help us to determine why certain coins are found in certain locations and not in others. The reevaluation of all of the coin finds made in the caves around Judea and Samaria may help us to see if they were in fact the locations mentioned in the Copper Scroll. Now that we understand that the Copper Scroll was not speaking about tons of gold and silver treasure but rather hundreds of pounds of metal treasure that could in fact be measured in coinage and metal objects, we have a different way of evaluating whether or not the treasures of the Copper Scroll have actually been discovered.

Sometimes one small piece of evidence needs to be reevaluated over a long period of time to discover its meaning and significance. One example which stands out in Dead Sea Scroll research was raised by Dr. Adolfo Roitman, curator of the Dead Sea Scrolls, when asked about the changing archaeological conceptualization of Dead Sea research. He pointed out that at the end of the nineteenth century, Prof. Solomon Schechter discovered a manuscript in the Ben Ezra Synagogue of Cairo, Egypt, which he simply called the "Zadokite Document." Although it was found in a medieval Cairo synagogue and it clearly had been recopied in the Middle Ages, Schechter held that this document was actually written much earlier and was from a Jewish sect in Israel from Second Temple times. He based his hypothesis on a form of "Evolution of Ideas" theory. The ideas in this Zadokite Document appeared to be arguments that were not fully understood until a document containing the same information was discovered nearly fifty years later among the Dead Sea Scrolls at Qumran! It means that sometimes we can have a question decided only by unexpected future research and discovery.

## THE SCIENCE OF POTTERY IN THE FUTURE

In our projects at Qumran and the Cave of Letters, we have a team of nearly a dozen researchers in different parts of the world working on the artifacts that we discovered in the Cave of Letters. We will probably complete our research in another decade. Until then, much of what I write is an attempt to explain how discoveries are made. The most ubiquitous find in our excavation were the thousands of pieces of pottery. Although the pottery of the Cave of Letters is very fragmentary (thousands of pieces of different vessels), it may yet yield many new answers in the future. At the present time, although we have thousands of pieces of pottery from different parts of the cave at different stratigraphic levels, it is difficult to assign them to specific periods (first or second century) or even to tell if they were brought from Jerusalem (as we contend some of the scrolls and the bronzes in the cave were brought from Jerusalem), from the settlement of Qumran, or from the settlement of Ein Gedi, where Bar Kokhba and his followers came from. Perhaps in the future we may be able to pinpoint where those things came from. Because most of the pottery was found underneath roof debris, it is extremely fragmentary, and we were unable to do the type of stylistic and restoration studies that most excavations use as evidence for dating a site and establishing the provenance of the pottery. If we had, we would have been able to say more about the pottery. We are, however, part of a new worldwide effort to use science to uncover more about the sources of pottery and the connections between the chemical signatures of the pottery and the pottery itself. We are having our pottery checked (and compared with a database that is being developed of pottery in Israel) using the new technique called *Instrumental Neutron Activation Analysis* (INAA) to learn where the pottery was made. This technique was first applied to archaeological artifacts in the 1950s, but it has been used sparingly because of cost and the requirement to use a particle accelerator or nuclear reactor producing thermal (low-energy) neutrons. It also is a very destructive process in that it requires the researcher to take a small sample of the artifact, (in the case of pottery) reduce it to ground powder, and introduce the sample into the reactor core where the nuclei of the atoms are bombarded with neutrons at a controlled rate. The final result, similar to the C-14 work on organic samples (but this time based upon the gamma rays present in radioactive isotopes as they decay), causes the different trace elements to be detectable because of their different rates of decay. This process allows us to find a "chemical signature" for the pottery and identify its origin by the specific trace elements present in different geographic locations. Since certain types of minerals in certain concentrations appear only in certain locations around Israel (and elsewhere), this process is able to pinpoint the location of origin of the pottery. Neutron activation is extremely sensitive and reveals some seventy-five different naturally occurring elements. Whether the pottery was brought in from Jerusalem, Bethlehem, Jericho, Masada, Ein Gedi, or from any other site for which INAA data exists, we will hopefully be able to match the chemical compositions of the Cave of Letters pottery with the ancient INAA pottery data stored in data banks. This comparison may reveal whether these refugees came from Jerusalem, Ein Gedi, Qumran, or elsewhere. Since Qumran was destroyed in 68 CE, we would also learn something new about who used the Cave of Letters at that time if the connection comes from that direction.

The preliminary results of the pottery analysis were received in time to include in this book. They know that the pottery from the Cave of Letters is *not* from Jerusalem and not from Ein Gedi. Since Yadin held that the bronze artifacts came from Ein Gedi and Bar Kokhba and Babatha had connections in Ein Gedi, it was always assumed that the pottery came with them from Ein Gedi. Now we know that this assumption is not correct. *In fact, our INAA comparison demonstrates that the pottery probably came from Qumran. Since Qumran was destroyed in 68 CE, the pottery we had dug from a variety of locations in the Cave of Letters demonstrates that the coin from 68 CE was not a random find.* Perhaps some of the Jews who left Jerusalem and ended up at Masada in 73 CE may have first hidden from the Romans in the caves in 70–73 CE on their way to Masada. It stands to reason that these Jews must have had stations they used in escaping from Jerusalem with the women, children, food, and goods they brought with them. They did not get to Masada in one day. The caves may have provided them an opportunity to rest, to hide their precious goods, to prepare for the rest of the journey, and to bury their dead. What we found from the first century CE is indicative of a group who also used the Cave of Letters as a refuge during the First Rebellion. The bones in the Niche of Skulls were probably gathered by the Second Rebellion refugees when they came to the cave some fifty-five years later.

How important is this new INAA technique? In the case of the Dead Sea Scrolls it has conclusively resolved the basic question associated with the scrolls; i.e., the connection between the scrolls and the site of Qumran. Prof. Jan Gunneweg of Hebrew University, who has pioneered this work at Qumran, has concluded that the ovoid or cylindrical jars, sometimes called "Scroll Jars," in which the Cave 1 scrolls were found were made at Qumran and not Jerusalem. This understanding has transformed the way that we analyze the data. Where before scholars debated literary references in the scrolls and their connections to the archaeological site of Qumran, this technique resolves the issue in a scientific manner. In the case of the Cave of Letters, we hope that this technique will also resolve the questions raised by the evidence in a scientific manner as well.

## C-14, DNA, NEW TECHNOLOGIES, AND OUR PAST AND FUTURE

Another area that is left for the future will be what the bones in the Cave of Letters will be able to tell us. The bones from the Cave of Letters, in particular, present an area of investigation for the future. The dating of the bones will in the future become better defined as researchers in carbon 14 understand more about the different circumstances surrounding the evaluation of ancient artifacts. The fact that our bones have a $\neq$ factor which is usually over one hundred years makes it difficult to pinpoint the timing of their placement in the cave. In the future, we think that our C-14 results will more specifically tell us when these people died and even more about their lives. The DNA materials taken from the bones will tell us in the future about what these people ate, what diseases they experienced, how they lived (well or ill), and how they died. I was interested in this question for a variety of reasons. I wanted to know how these people died. Did they die of starvation and thirst as we first suspected (and not all but some were buried and laid out by others) or did everyone escape and the bones are only the remains of relatives and friends they brought with them for burial (it was a Jewish custom of the period to bury in caves)? There were three reasons why we suspected starvation and thirst as the cause of death in the case of the bodies that we found:

1. **There are no signs of violence on any of the bodies found in the Cave of Letters.** No holes in skulls, no arrow or sword marks on bones. It is clear that is not the way they died.

2. **It is very difficult to get to the water and food near the Cave of Letters without being seen by the Romans.** That is what the siege is all about. The Romans built a siege camp on top of the hill to wait out the occupants. This is what happened at Masada in 73 CE, only there the Romans did not realize that they had plenty of water from cisterns built into the sides of the cliffs. We did not find cisterns or secret exits here (although we did follow a small tunnel in the west extension for about 60 feet until it became too small for us to get through). The "secret exit" which we suspected was there is where thousands of bats are also found and it is at the end of the western extension in a place that we will not be able to physically enter at the present time. We could not get through it, but we confirmed that there still is air coming in from the outside there. It probably was much larger in antiquity and has constricted because of the same tectonic forces exerted all over the cave. The rebels may have had a secret exit to food and water that enabled them to hold out for many weeks and months. We simply don't know. We have finally figured out a way for them to get to a water supply without being caught but with great difficulty. We have found foodstuffs (dates, olives, pomegranates, etc.) but not many seeds. They could have been saving them for future planting after the war. It was such a small amount of food that we may have the last remnants of their food supply. In the Cave of Horrors, across the way from the Cave of Letters, they found people with skin still intact on the bone (and so horrific and poignant that it is one of the reasons why they called it the Cave of Horrors!) and archaeologists had earlier concluded that they must have died of starvation and dehydration. The people in the Cave of Horrors appear to have died in pain, again without arrows or sword marks, so these people in the Cave of Letters may have suffered a similar fate.

3. There is a single literary reference to the tragic circumstances surrounding the Bar Kokhba Rebellion which is so horrific that

I wanted to see if I could confirm or deny it in the Cave of Letters. It is a single, ambiguous literary reference about the Bar Kokbha Rebellion that is unfortunately imaginable. The literary source parallels other accounts from Josephus and Dio Cassius, first- and second-century writers associated with the First and the Second Rebellions. They both report that the food situation got to the point where cannibalism was necessary.[122] It would have been important to know if things got that bad.

We may ultimately unravel this, but in the meantime we have begun a DNA research project which will extract, sequence, and clone the genetic material in the bones from the Cave of Letters. This will be compared with other DNA from both modern and ancient samples which have been taken, but what is exciting is the prospect that the DNA of those people found in the Cave of Letters may yet reveal their identities to us. There is a new test by which the Y Chromosome can be compared with data banks of DNA—if the DNA was that of a Cohen (Cohen Modal Haplotype—from the priestly stock from Jerusalem). The state of preservation of the bones of the Cave of Letters may help us to understand more about who they were and about our connection to these people. We clearly did not remove all of the artifacts we located in the Cave of Letters with the fiberscope, GPR, and ERT scans. We discovered a variety of other artifacts under the rocks which, despite success with the hydraulic splitter in breaking up the rocks in the summer of 2001, we decided we could not get to them. The argument for the future means that we know that there are other artifacts under the rocks in the Cave of Letters. We know that they might provide answers to our questions, and they may raise new questions. New technologies may yet help us to understand how to safely remove the artifacts so they may be analyzed. We had hoped that the hydraulic splitter would give us access to the artifacts we knew were underneath the rocks during the summer of 2001. We began to break the rocks and I knew immediately that it was not going to provide us with many answers that summer. The hydraulic splitter is a device that Yadin, De Vaux, or Aharoni could only dream about in the 1950s and 1960s. It is small and compact (it weighs 75 pounds, but

96-286/1

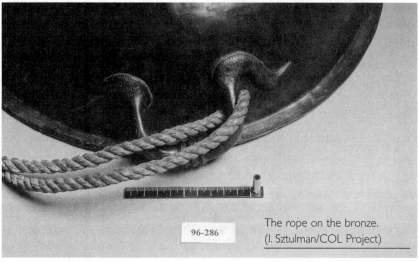

96-286

The rope on the bronze.
(I. Sztulman/COL Project)

at least it could be carried and dragged into the caves), requires only a small amount of work to assemble and disassemble, is mechanical, runs on electrical power, produces no noxious fumes or dust, and yet is as powerful as any jackhammer or demolition equipment. It uses hydraulic power to break rocks. It was effective, perhaps too effective, for it broke rocks weighing three to four tons into smaller, one- to two-ton rocks which were movable but had very sharp edges. I cut myself three or four times moving the rocks as they were being broken up. The limestone rocks were now easier to move, but in the three attempts we made with rocks under which small artifacts (pottery) could be seen, it destroyed everything underneath the now small rock debris. It was clear that if we tried to recover any of the other artifacts, it would destroy anything underneath the rocks as they broke into small pieces. The weight of the stones is enormous, and as they break they fall downward. The sharp edges are liable to cut and shred anything underneath. Perhaps in another forty years, when someone comes to redo our work, they will have a newer technology that will allow them to remove the stones without doing any damage to the artifacts underneath them. I hope it will be in my lifetime.

I save the final secret of the book for the last pages. Most readers will already have picked up the clues to the final secret, others may have to go back to the second chapter ("Origins of a Cave") to read (for nonspecialists) on geology and geography to understand why I save this until the end. I would have avoided reading in detail this "hard science" chapter myself until about ten years ago when I realized that archaeology could be done in a different way and yield better results. I am happy that we learned what we have learned in the Cave of Letters, but it is really the process of excavating in a cave by the Dead Sea that is the most important discovery. First, we discovered that the equipment works in these environments in unexpected ways. We are looking for suggestions from readers concerning what other possible equipment and method of using the equipment might better accomplish this work. The secret I have saved for last is the method of discovery that can be added to help make the process more efficient, more useful, more exacting, or another piece of technology that would make all of the other pieces work together better. This process of discovery which I suggest throughout this book could be repeated

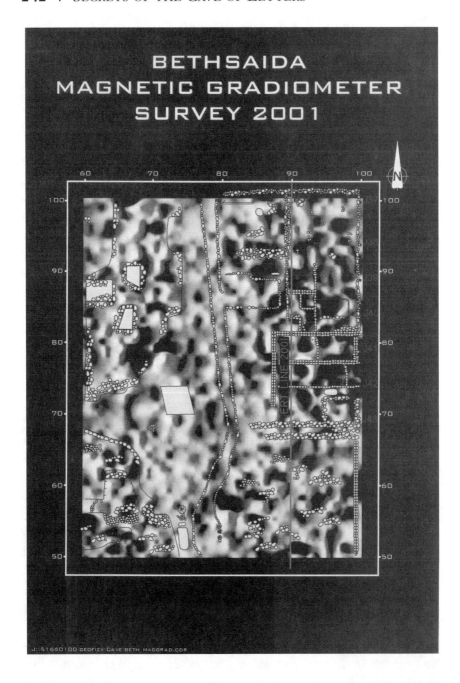

in every one of the caves along the Dead Sea revealing untold treasures. In Project Scroll, conducted by the Israel Antiquities Authority in the 1990s, the conventional method of archaeology was employed in the search of hundreds of caves along the Dead Sea. The exercise did not yield significant fruits. Think if this same exercise had been conducted with a team of specialists like the ones you met in this book! Most important, we now know definitively that most of the caves (remember, there are thousands of caves!) have roof debris on the floor to a depth of 5–6 feet. If a systematic reinvestigation of the caves (even the caves that yielded scrolls!) were done with geophysicists, geologists, geographers, and archaeologists working in tandem with historians, it is clear that new and exciting results would emerge. For the moment our work at the Cave of Letters has stopped and we have moved on to work at Qumran and other sites. We have since moved on with our group to work with other land surveys and excavations at places where major discoveries have been made by serendipity. These sites include places that few people read about, such as Tel Shalem in the Jordan Valley, where the pieces of the largest inscription of a Hadrianic victory arch were discovered in a carrot field, and at Mary's Well (Mary, mother of Jesus) in Nazareth, where an ancient bathhouse was discovered in the basement of a coffee shop. In both places, using the process described in this book, new discoveries may yet emerge. We also are working with future large-scale excavations as well, such as our work at Tel Yavne, an unexplored mound in the middle of the modern city of Yavne that may yet reveal the first-century city of Rabbi Yohanan Ben Zakkai, the enigmatic figure who refounded Judaism after the destruction of the Temple in Jerusalem, and reinvestigating the possible unexcavated areas at a place that is well known for the discoveries there: Bet Shearim. The biggest secret therefore is *the process of discovery* that goes on in many locations around Israel. We may yet return to the Dead Sea, especially as the political situation allows for more secure arrangements in the area. But until then, I am happy with the secrets that we have revealed about the Bar Kokhba caves of the Dead Sea and especially the contribution we have made to the future discoveries in caves along the Dead Sea.

# Notes

1. For more on Bethsaida, read our three volumes: Rami Arav and Richard A. Freund, *Bethsaida: A City by the North Shore of the Sea of Galilee* (Kirksville, MO: Truman State University Press, 1995, 1999, 2004).

2. In an extremely disturbed Hellenistic-early Roman layer of occupation in Area A square G54, locus 152. In the same locus, below and around the find, was found in the preceding days—May 2–6, 1996: Hellenistic cooking pots, casserole bowls, juglets, jars, decorated ware, so-called Galilean bowls, Roman glass, a bow-spouted Herodian lamp, and Eastern Terra Sigillata pottery shards among hundreds of other small finds. This discovery was recorded in *Biblical Archaeology Review* 23, no. 1 (January/February 1997): 32 as a Prize Find.

3. Y. Yadin, *The Finds from the Bar Kokhba Period in the Caves of Letters* (Jerusalem: Israel Exploration Society, 1975), p. 53 (incense shovel number 5, found in locus 57, number 23).

4. R. A. Freund, "The Incense Shovel of Bethsaida and Synagogue Iconography in Late Antiquity," in *Bethsaida: A City by the North Shore of the Sea of Galilee*, vol. 1: 413–59.

5. Yadin, *Finds*, p. 53. Yadin's incense shovel no. 5's handle is 12.3 centimeters long; the overall length of this shovel is thus 23 centimeters. The incense shovel of Bethsaida is 20.5 centimeters in length and 6.7 centimeters in width, and it has a handle which is 11.1 centimeters long.

6. Ibid., pp. 55–57 lists nine incense shovels in Palestine, one in Gaul, three from Pompeii and Herculaneum, and four from Lebanon and Syria (indicating that others are to be found in in the National Museum in Damascus); but this is not a complete list.

7. Ibid., p. 44.

8. Ibid., p. 45.

9. R. A. Freund, "A New Interpretation of the Incense Shovels of the Cave of the Letters," in *The Dead Sea Scrolls: Fifty Years after Their Discovery, 1947–1997, Proceedings of the Jerusalem Congress, July 20–25, 1997*, ed. L. H. Schiffman, E. Tov, and J. C. VanderKam (Jerusalem: Israel Exploration Society, 2000), pp. 644–60.

10. Baruch Safrai, "More Scrolls Lie Buried," *Biblical Archaeology Review* 19, no. 1 (January/February 1993): 51ff.

11. Y. Aharoni, "The Caves of Nahal Hever," *Atiqot: Journal of the Israel Department of Antiquities* (Jerusalem, 1961): 148–57.

12. While I write these words, it is important to note that the Shrine of the Book is undergoing a complete facelift for its fortieth anniversary in 2005, and the Cave of Letters materials have been moved to the Roman archaeology section and are physically disconnected from the story of the Dead Sea Scrolls told in the Shrine of the Book.

13. For a one-volume insight of the contributions of Joseph Aviram to Israeli archaeology, see articles by Amnon Ben-Tor, Seymour Gitin, Alfred Gottschalk, and Hershel Shanks in *The Joseph Aviram Volume of Eretz-Israel: Archaeological, Historical, and Geographical Studies*, vol. 25 (Jerusalem: Israel Exploration Society, 1996), pp. xi–xvi.

14. Yadin, *Finds*, p. 112.

15. Ibid., p. 115n14. "On the basis of our finds, it is now definitely possible—in spite of Kahane's doubts . . . to continue the span of this type [Herodian-type lamps] to the mid-2nd century A.D." These were from the adjacent Cave to the Cave of Letters and the Roman camp, which itself raises other considerations of how long the camp was used. On why the Herodian lamps and the other lamps found in the Cave of Letters should be redated to correspond to the first century CE, see: J. Magness, "The Chronology of Qumran, Ein Feshkha, and Ein El-Ghuweir," in *Mogilany 1995: Papers on the Dead Sea Scrolls*, ed. Z. J. Kapera (Krakow: Enigma Press, 1998), pp. 55–76.

16. Found in "Hall A, two limestone vessels with knife shaved sides." Yadin, *Finds*, p. 115.

17. M. Baillet, J. T. Milik, and R. de Vaux, *Les "Petites Grottes" de Qumran*, vol. 3 of *Discoveries in the Judean Desert of Jordan* (Oxford:

Clarendon, 1962), p. 49; P. Benoît, J. T. Milik, and R. de Vaux, *Les Grottes de Murabba'at*, vol. 2 of *Discoveries in the Judean Desert* (Oxford: Clarendon, 1961); D. Barthélemy and J. T. Milik, *Qumran Cave 1*, vol. 1 of *Discoveries in the Judean Desert* (Oxford: Clarendon, 1955).

18. Yadin, *Finds*, p. 17.

19. Y. Yadin, *Bar Kokhba* (London: Weinfeld and Nicolson, 1978), p. 60.

20. The most recent review is D. H. K. Amiran, E. Arieh, and T. Turcotte, "Earthquakes in Israel and Adjacent Areas: Macroseismic Observations Since 100 B.C.E.," *Israel Exploration Journal* 44, nos. 3–4 (1994): 260. The original article by D. H. K. Amiran is "A Revised Earthquake Catalogue of Palestine," *Israel Exploration Journal* 1 (1950–1951): 225. Also see E. Netzer, ed., "Greater Herodium," *Qedem*, vol. 13 (Jerusalem: Israel Exploration Society, 1981), pp. 28, 134n22.

21. R. G. Boling, *Joshua: A New Translation with Notes and Commentary*, Anchor Bible Series, vol. 6 (New York: Doubleday, 1984), pp. 169–70.

22. Eusebius *Ecclesiastical History* 4.2.

23. Seder Eliahu Rabba und Seder Eliahu Zuta (*Tana DeBe Eliyahu*), 3d ed., ed. M. Ish-Shalom (Jerusalem: Wahrmann, 1969), chap. 28, p. 154.

24. R. Freund, "The Apocalypse of Rabbi Aqiva," in *Studies in Jewish Civilization*, vol. 12: *Millennialism From the Hebrew Bible to the Present*, ed. Leonard J. Greenspoon and Ronald A. Simkins (Omaha: Creighton University Press, 2002), pp. 150–65.

25. *The Life of Flavius Josephus*, trans. William Whiston (Grand Rapids, MI: Kregel Publications, 1978), sec. 38, p. 10.

26. Ibid., p. 354.

27. Flavius Josephus, *War of the Jews*, trans. William Whiston (Grand Rapids, MI: Kregel Publications, 1978), bk. 5, chap. 36.

28. Ibid., pp. 6, 98–99.

29. PT Berachot 14b; P T Sotah 20c; BT Berachot 61b.

30. BT Semahot 8.9: *Treatise Semahot*, ed. M. Higger (New York: Block Publishing, 1931), pp. 154–55.

31. This is found in BT Berachot 61b. "He said to them: All my days I have been troubled by this verse, 'with all thy soul,' [which I interpret,] 'even if He takes thy soul.' I said: When shall I have the opportunity of fulfilling this? Now that I have the opportunity shall I not fulfil it? He prolonged the word *ehad*." Other Akiva martyrdom quotes include: BT Eruvin 21b: "Our Rabbis taught: R. Akiva was once confined in a prison-house and R. Joshua the grits-maker was attending on him. Every day, a certain quantity of water was brought in to him. On one occasion he was met by the prison keeper

who said to him, 'Your water to-day is rather much; do you perhaps require it for undermining the prison?' He poured out a half of it and handed to him the other half. When he came to R. Akiva the latter said to him, 'Joshua, do you not know that I am an old man and my life depends on yours?' When the latter told him all that had happened [R. Akiva] said to him, 'Give me some water to wash my hands.' 'It will not suffice for drinking,' the other complained, 'will it suffice for washing your hands?' 'What can I do,' the former replied: 'when for [neglecting] the words of the Rabbis one deserves death? It is better that I myself should die than that I should transgress against the opinion of my colleagues.' It was related that he tasted nothing until the other had brought him water to wash his hands. When the Sages heard of this incident they remarked: 'If he was so [scrupulous] in his old age how much more must he have been so in his youth; and if he so [behaved] in a prison-house how much more [must he have behaved in such a manner] when not in a prison-house.'"

32. PT Taaniyot 68d: Palestinian Talmud Taaniyot, first printing Venice, 1523 (reprint, Leipzig, 1925).

33. Damascus Document, col. 20.14 ff, *The Dead Sea Scrolls Translated*, 2d ed., ed. F. G. Martinez (Grand Rapids, MI: Eerdmans, 1996), pp. 46–47, and in Cave 1, Qumran, Pesher (Commentary on) Habakkuk, col. 2: 1–3, 5: 9–12, p. 198, for example.

34. *Mechilta DeRabbi Yishmael*, portion *Beshalah*, ed. H. S. Horovitz (Jerusalem: Wahrmann, 1970), chap. 5.

35. *Shir HaShirim Rabbah* (*Song of Songs Midrash*) 32.7, and *Shemot Rabbah* (*Exodus Midrash*), chap. 20. The view of Rabbi Yishmael in *Shir HaShirim Rabbah* 32.7 also states that four oaths were given by the Divine: ". . . one was that they should not rebel against the kingdoms and not calculate the end of days." Midrash Rabbah, two volumes, cited from Vilna: Rom Publishing, 1884–1887.

36. In Tosefta Eruvin, ed. M. S. Zuckermandel (Jerusalem: Wahrmann, 1970), chap. 2 (3 in some manuscripts), law 6, for example, we have a Rabbi Judah ben Tema statement which may be interpreted as Rabbi Judah having indirect contact with the rebels.

37. PT Taaniyot, 68d.

38. Tosefta Menahot 8.23: cited from Vilna: Rom Publishing, 1886–present.

39. BT Taanit 18a lists Rabbi Judah Ben Shammua and his colleagues as being opposed to the decrees of Hadrian. BT Taanit usually cited from Vilna: Rom Publishing, 1886–present.

40. The late-second-century sage Rabbi Yosi ben Yehudah, for example, ruled that one may not make a replica of the Menorah (Candelabrum of the Temple in Jerusalem) out of any metal or even wood (BT Menahot 28b, usually cited from Vilna: Rom Publishing, 1886–present; BT Rosh Hashanah 24a, usually cited from Vilna: Rom Publishing, 1886–present). Another sage of the same period, Abba Shaul, ruled that the use of the Tetragrammaton would be limited in the provinces and synagogue service (even in Jerusalem) from his time onward. Mishnah Sotah 7:6 (*The Mishnah*, ed. and trans. H. Danby [London: Oxford University Press, 1933]), BT Kiddushin 71a (cited from Vilna: Rom Publishing, 1886–present). Only the priests in the future Holy Temple worship would ever be allowed to use the Divine Name again.

41. Mishnah Sotah 8.5 and Tosefta Sotah 7.22.

42. Lamentations Rabbah 2.56, in Midrash Rabbah, 2 vols., cited from Vilna: Rom Publishing, 1884–1887.

43. Ibid., 2.55.

44. Ibid.

45. Yadin, *Bar Kokhba*, p. 128.

46. This is obviously a play on the Rabbi Akiva citation as well. PT Taaniyot 68d. The Apocalypse of Peter, written after the Bar Kokhba Rebellion, uses a similar allusion. Cited in M. Mor, *The Bar Kokhba Revolt: Its Extent and Effect* (Jerusalem: Yad Ben Tzvi, 1991), p. 188n93.

47. Yadin, *Bar Kokhba*, pp. 124–39, 175–81.

48. See R. Freund, "From Kings to Archons: Jewish Political Ethics and Kingship Passages in the LXX," in *Understanding Jewish Ethics*, vol. 1 (New York: Mellen, 1990), pp. 128–43.

49. Bar Kokhba's uncle, Eleazar of Modi'in, may be associated with Eleazar ben Azariah, who was of a priestly family, and therefore Bar Kokhba may also be from a priestly family. The name of one Eleazar as priest is found on some Bar Kokhba coins. E. Mary Smallwood, *The Jews under Roman Rule* (Leiden and New York: Brill, 1981), p. 440nn47–48.

50. Hadrian was known for his restoration projects of cities and temples elsewhere. Dio Cassius (69.10.1) mentions Hadrian's custom of building theaters and holding games in the various cities he visited. He apparently resonstructed a temple of Isis in Rome for the Parthian princes who resided in Rome as hostages—*Corpus Inscriptionum Latinarum*, CIL ed. (Berlin: Mommsen, 1881), 14:2216. On coins of Hadrian are found the following inscriptions: *restitutori Achaiae, restotiori Africani, restitutori orbis terrarum*, etc. [restorer/builder of Greece, of Africa, of the world (i.e., Asia Minor and Syria)]. See: E. Schürer, *A History of the Jewish People in the Time of Jesus*, ed.

N. Glatzer (New York: Schocken Books, 1961), p. 399n68 and especially p. 298 where Schürer states: ". . . he (Hadrian) was a restitutor in all the provinces." Other evidence points to the possibility that Hadrian undertook a restoration project in Jerusalem. The evidence can be divided into different sources:

Epiphanius in *Peri Metron kai Stathmon*, Patrologiae, Series Graeca (PG), vol. 43, ed. Dindorf, pp. 260–61. Vol. 4, pp. 17–18, states that Hadrian specifically wished to restore the city, ". . . but not the Temple."

A source from the third century CE, Menander of Laeodicea, states (in what seems to be a present tense narrative) that "while the largest multitudes are to be found at the festival of the Hebrews living in Syria Palaestina, as they are gathered in very large numbers from most nations . . ." indicating that a form of ceremony connected with the traditional pilgrimages in the time of the Second Temple may have survived beyond the Destruction in the year 70 CE. (This despite the objections of M. Stern who claims that "Menander must have had the period of the Second Temple in mind." For text and commentary see: M. Stern, *Greek and Latin Authors on Jews and Judaism*, vol. 2 [Jerusalem: Israel Academy of Sciences and Humanities, 1980], pp. 413–14.)

But in a Syrian Chronicle from the eighth or ninth century, *Chronicon ad annum Dominum 846 pertinens*, in E. W. Brooks, *Corpus Scriptorum Christianorum Orientalium, Scriptores Syri, Chronica Minora* (Louvain: Imprimerie Orientaliste L. Durbecq, 1955), p. 184, states that in the twelfth year of Hadrian's rule (129) "the Jews were about to build Jerusalem and its Temple. When Caesar appointed Aquila to oversee the work. . . ." Although other early medieval Church materials can be cited to demonstrate that Hadrian was interested in restoring the city of Jerusalem, this is the only source which also implies interest in the rebuilding of the Temple.

Chrysostom, Cedrenus, and Nicephorus Calistus say only that the Jews in the time of Hadrian had rebelled and made an attempt to rebuild the Temple. See: Schürer, *A History of the Jewish People in the Time of Jesus*, p. 294.

For the other sources supporting the view that Hadrian wished to restore the city (but not the Temple) see G. Alon, *Jews in Their Land in the Talmudic Age* (Cambridge: Harvard University Press, 1989), pp. 445–48. There is a large difference of opinion concerning the reading of most of these sources. H. Mantel in "The Causes of the Bar Kokhba Revolt," *Jewish Quarterly Review* 58 (April 1968): 283–84, maintains that "it is extremely unlikely that Bar Kokhba built the Temple, or even an altar" and finds reasons to discount each of the sources mentioned. Finally, he uses an "argument out of silence" stating that if the Temple had been rebuilt and destroyed again it would have been prominently mentioned in rabbinic literature (which it is not). The whole question is in need of reinvestigation in light of the model suggested above. Most historians assume a "conflict" situation between paganism and Judaism and therefore find it unlikely that a Roman emperor would want to restore the Temple.

51. The Epistle of Barnabas, chap. 16.1–5 (in the Codex Sinaiticus) has it as a joint effort: "both they (the Jews) and those they hate . . . will build it" (either the Romans or a Jewish Christian group—see below).

52. Certain evidence does point to the existence of at least a marginally functioning Temple during the rule of Bar Kokhba. The evidence can be classified:

Numismatic evidence: Coins dated to the rule of Bar Kokhba featuring a Temple facade (see: Y. Yadin, *Bar Kokhba* [London: Weidenfeld and Nicolson, 1978], p. 25) provide one piece of information on this subject.

Eusebius in two passages indicates that the Temple was destroyed after the Bar Kokhba Rebellion. First, in his *Theophany* (Syriac), ed. Lee (London, 1842), he states, "The Temples in Jerusalem and on Mount Gerizim were both destroyed in the war of Vespasian and Hadrian" perhaps indicating that the Temple in Jerusalem was functioning during the rule of Bar Kokhba and had to be destroyed (of course the possibility exists that Eusebius is referring to the destructions of the Temple in Jerusalem and on Mount Gerizim separately and respectively here. This understanding is possible inasmuch that no information exists concerning the destruction of the Samaritan Temple on Mount Gerizim during the war of Vespasian.). Also, in *Ecclesiastical History* 4.6.1–4, Eusebius states that the Aelia Capitolina and the "new" Temple (built on the site of the "old" Temple) were built after the war to punish the Jews for the rebellion.

Ariston of Pella (based upon a nineteenth-century discovery of two ancient manuscripts by F. Conybeare), in "The Dialogues of Athanasius and Zachaus and of Timothy and Aquila in Anecdota Oxoniensia, Classical Series, part VIII, ed. F. Conybeare (Oxford, 1898), p. 9. The author proposed that this represents the lost second-century work from which Eusebius drew his description of the Bar Kohkba Rebellion: cited in G. Alon, *Jews in Their Land in the Talmudic Age*, p. 445. One passage states: "When he (Hadrian) arrived at Jerusalem and found the city utterly desolate . . . he took Aquila, a pagan, and entrusted to him the task of rebuilding the city."

Julian, in the *Fragmentum Epistulae*, states (295C): "For as for those who make such a profanation a reproach against us, I mean the prophets of the Jews, what have they to say about their own temple, which was overthrown three times and even now is not being raised up again?" (perhaps indicating the third destruction after the Bar Kohkba Rebellion in the time of Hadrian). This text is cited in Stern, *Greek and Latin Authors on Jews and Judaism*, vol. 2, pp. 552–57, where Stern states: "Two of the destructions of the Temple were carried out by Nebuchadnezzar and Titus respectively. In his reference to the third destruction, Julian seems to have had in mind the desecration of the Temple by Antiochus Epiphanes." This numbering is difficult even according to Stern's terminology. No destruction of the Temple took place during the rule of Antiochus Epiphanes (a "desecration" did take place) while "three destructions" is clearly employed here.

M. Adler (*Jewish Quarterly Review* 5 [1893]: 620 ff) cites this same passage and states: "The 'three' subversions are by Nebuchadnezzar, Herod (in rebuilding Nehemiah's Temple) and by Titus." M. Adler (in the same article) also cites Lardner (*Jewish and Heathen Testimonies*, vol. 4) and states, "(Lardner) counts the final levelling of the Temple site by Hadrian as the third subversion."

Rabbinic sources also provide an interesting support for this information. An extensive literature can be produced from rabbis who lived during this period which speaks about sacrifices, laws of sacrifices and the priesthood, and other rituals related to the Temple. For example, the Mishnah, tractate Midot that deals with the dimensions of the Temple, discussions concerning the priesthood and priestly offerings in Sifre on Numbers, Parashat Korah, sections 116 and 121 (*Siphre d'be Rab*, ed. H. S. Horowitz [Leipzig, 1917; reprint, Jerusalem: Wahrmann, 1966], pp. 133 and 149) deal with these elements as if they are current issues and not theoretical concepts. In regard to sacrifices, mention must be made regarding the Passover sacrifices (Mishnah, Pesahim 7.2; Tosefta Pesahim 10.12; BT Pesahim 115a, 120a, etc.). In the Mishnah of Pesahim 7.2, Rabban Gamliel (who lived during this period) told his servant Tabi, "Go out and roast us the pesah on the grill" (see also the minutiae of the discussion of how and why this could be done in BT Pesahim 74a). Some argue that the Rabban Gamliel mentioned here is Gamliel the Elder, who lived at the time of the Second Temple and is mentioning past history. Additionally, statements like the following found in Exodus Rabbah 61.5 (unless emended) tend to confirm the existence of some form of a Temple. It states: "Rabbi Simeon ben Yohai said, When Hadrian entered the Holy of Holies. . . ."

53. Although Eusebius states that there was "a very big Church of Christ in Jerusalem built by the Jews, until the seige of Hadrian." Cited in A. F. J. Klijn and G. J. Reinink, *Patristic Evidence for Jewish-Christian Sects* (Leiden and New York: Brill, 1973), p. 138.

54. Michael Avi-Yonah in his book, *The Jews Under Roman and Byzantine Rule*, p. 13, states: "Bar Kokhba established his government in Jerusalem and probably resumed the Temple ritual as far as possible." Some historians do not even want to consider the question, so Alon, *Jews in Their Land in the Talmudic Age*, p. 253n1, states, "We shall not here deal with the question which has engaged the attention of some scholars: were there any instances of sacrifices being offered after the Destruction of the Temple?" (in 70 CE).

55. *Roman History*, trans. E. Cary, Loeb Classical Library, Heinemann Ltd. (Cambridge: Harvard University Press, 1925), 8:451.

56. Even until the end of the second century, the legacy of the Second Rebellion was still mythical even from the Roman side. Cornelius Fronto writing to the emperors Marcus Aurelius and Lucius Versus about the Roman losses in the Parthian campaign some two generations after Bar Kokhba, "remember the very great number of Romans slain by the Jews at the time of your grandfather Hadrian, and yet finally, the victory was his." De Bello Parthico, cited in L. Kadman, *The Coins of Aelia Capitolina: Corpus Nummorum Palestinesium*, vol. 1 (Jerusalem: Universitas, 1956), p. 6. Werner Eck, "Der Bar Kochba Aufstand, der kaiserliche Fiscus und die Veteranenversorgung," *SCI* 19 (2000): 139–48; Werner Eck (with H. Cotton) "P. MURABBA'AT 114 und die Anwesenheit römischer Truppen in den Höhlen des Wadi Murabba'at nach dem Bar Kochba Aufstand," *ZPE* 138 (2002): 173–83; "Hadrian, the Bar Kokhba Revolt, and the Epigraphic Transmission, Conference on the Bar Kokhba War, November 11–13, 2001, Princeton, NJ," in *The Bar Kokhba War Reconsidered*.

57. The sources state: Dio Cassius, a "biased (anti-Jewish/pro-Roman)" source states that it was an extensive rebellion. In his *Roman History* 69:12–14 it states: "Fifty of their most important outposts and 985 of their most famous villages were razed to the ground. 580,000 men were slain in the various raids and battles, and the number of those that perished by famine, disease and fire was past finding out."

Rabbinic sources include: Four hundred thousand (BT Gittin 54b, in ed. Vilna: Rom Publishing, 1886–present).

The archaeological finds at Tel Shalem (Salim?) 5 klms from Bet Shean included the largest Hadrianic inscription ever discovered in the eastern empire and a bronze bust of Hadrian found near by. These finds may indicate that the gate of victory with this monumental arch was constructed by Hadrian in the Beth Shean Valley to bolster the Roman troops stationed in the north of the country and to warn the Jews of Galilee about future revolts.

The recent coinage discovery of a Bar Kokhba coin struck over the coin of Aelia Capitolina coins of Hadrian is important. Some contend that Hadrian rebuilt Jerusalem and the Temple Mount and transformed it into a Roman Polis and Temple of Jupiter in his new Aelia Capitolina and this sparked the rebellion. As a result, the Jews all over the realm found this interference to be unacceptable. The Bar Kokhba coin was struck after the Aelia Capitolina declaration and indicates that this was the sequence of events.

Finally, the Babatha texts and presence in the Cave of Letters do not necessarily prove the identification of Babatha with Bar Kokhba, but the larger nature of the rebellion. It had spread to Arabia where she originally resided and she was forced to move as the rebellion was squelched throughout the Roman east.

58. On this issue, see D. Lyon, "Confessions of a Nationalist Archaeologist," in *The Limitations of Archaeological Knowledge*, ed. l'Université de Liège, no. 49 (Liege, 1992), pp. 39–45.

59. M. Mor, *The Bar Kokhba Revolt: Its Extent and Effect* (Jerusalem: Yad Ben Tzvi, 1991), pp. 146–71.

60. W. Eck, "The Bar Kokhba Revolt: The Roman Point of View," *Journal of Roman Studies* 89 (1999): 76–89.

61. Yadin, "The Bar Kokhba Revolt," p. 65. "This was our first encounter—as we learned later—with the remains of Bar-Kokhba's warriors and their families. Tragic as the sight was, and despite the fact that no documents were found, that discovery turned out, with further study to be a mine of information enriching our meager knowledge of clothing, textile and mats in the Roman period."

62. P. Bar Adon, English version of *The Judean Desert Caves: Archaeological Survey, 1961* (Jerusalem: Israel Exploration Society, 1962), p. 216.

63. Ibid., p. 217n36.

64. Bar Adon, "The Cave of the Treasure," p. 199.

65. As we shall see, there is one major find that Yadin did not know about the cave. I think Yadin might have had a different view about the Cave of Letters had he known about the large Psalms scroll and the Numbers and Deuteronomy scrolls that were only recently reassigned to it after masterful comparisons by A. Yardeni and H. Cotton. See chapter 7, "The Cave of the Column and the Cave of Letters."

66. Y. Yadin, "Excavations at Hazor 1968–1969," *Israel Exploration Journal* (*Israel Exploration Journal*) 19, no. 1 (1969): 1–19. Y. Yadin, "Hazor," in *Encyclopedia of Archaeological Excavations in the Holy Land*, ed. M. Avi-Yonah, 2:474–95. Y. Aharoni, "New Aspects of the Israelite Occupation in the North," in *Near Eastern Archaeology in the Twentieth Century*, ed. J. A. Sanders (Garden City, NY: Doubleday, 1970), pp. 254–67.

67. Arad: Y. Aharoni, "Excavations at Tel Arad: Preliminary Report on the Second Season, 1963," *Israel Exploration Journal* 17, no. 4 (1967): 233–49; Y. Yadin, "A Note on the Stratigraphy of Arad," *Israel Exploration Journal* 15 (1965): 180; Y. Aharoni, "Arad: Its Inscriptions and Temple," *Biblical Archaeologist* 31 (1968): 20–32; Y. Yadin, "The Historical Significance of Inscription 88 from Arad," *Israel Exploration Journal* 26 (1976): 9–14. Beer Sheva: Y. Aharoni, *Beer-Sheba I*, Institute of Archaeology Publications 2 (Tel Aviv: Tel Aviv University, 1973); Y. Aharoni, *Beer Sheba: The Excavation of a Biblical City* (New York: n.p., 1973); Y. Yadin, "Beer Sheva: The High Place Destroyed by Josiah," *Bulletin of the American Schools of Oriental Research (BASOR)* 222 (1976): 5–17; Y. Aharoni, "Some Observations on the Recent Article by Y. Yadin," *BASOR* 222 (1977): 67–68. Lachish: Y. Aharoni, *Investigations at Lachish, The Sanctuary and the Residency (Lachish V)* (Tel Aviv: Gateway Publishers, 1975); Y. Yadin, "The Lachish Letters: Originals or Copies and Drafts" in *Recent Archaeology in the Land of Israel*, ed. H. Shanks and B. Mazar (Washington, DC: Biblical Archaeology Society, 1984), pp. 179–86.

68. L. Schiffman, *Reclaiming the Dead Sea Scrolls: The History of Judaism* (Philadelphia: Jewish Publication Society, 1994), and L. Schiffman, *The Background of Christianity: The Lost Library of Qumran* (New York: Doubleday, 1995).

69. Yadin, *Finds*, p. 44.

70. S. Lieberman, *Greek in Jewish Palestine* (New York: Jewish Theological Seminary of America, 1942), p. 1.

71. Cited in Lefkovits, *The Copper Scroll (3Q15)*, p. 8.

72. Ibid.

73. Paul Lapp, "Bedouin Find Papyri Three Centuries Older than Dead Sea Scrolls," *Biblical Archaeology Review* 4, no. 1 (March 1978): 20.

74. D. Barag, "A Note on the Geographical Distribution of Bar Kokhba Coins," *Israel Numismatic Journal* 4 (1980): 30–33 (map on p. 32, fig. 1).

75. For a further detailed study of the terms *Dema* and *Kli Dema*, Lefkovitz, *The Copper Scroll (3Q15)*, pp. 505–45, deals with all of the arguments concerning the terms and their use in different rabbinic literature.

76. M. Lehman, "Where the Temple Tax Was Buried: The Key to Understanding the Copper Scroll," *Biblical Archaeology Review* 19 (1993): 38–43.

77. Lefkovits, *The Copper Scroll (3Q15)*, p. 18n71.

78. *The Documents from the Bar Kokhba Period in the Cave of Letters: Greek Papyri*, ed. Naphtali Lewis (Jerusalem: Israel Exploration Society, 1989), pp. 91–92.

79. Richard E. Friedman, *Who Wrote the Bible?* (San Francisco: Harper and Row, 1997), pp. 89, 150.

80. Lefkovits, *The Copper Scroll (3Q15)*, p. 38n46.

81. Yadin, *Finds*, p. 19.

82. BT Gittin 56a, Tractate Zevachim 54b, Menahot 66b, cited from Vilna: Rom Publishing, 1886–present. Midrash Genesis Rabbah 50.4, Midrash Leviticus Rabbah 34.8, Ruth Rabbah 5.6, Lamentations Rabbah 1.2, Ecclesiastes Rabbah 3.12, among many others. Midrash Rabbah, 2 vols., cited from Vilna: Rom Publishing, 1884–1887.

83. A. Roitman, *A Day at Qumran* (Jerusalem: Israel Museum, 1999), p. 44 photo facing.

84. Y. Yadin, *Masada* (New York: Random House, 1966), pp. 152–53.

85. ". . . [I]mpurity in its origin connected with loathing-reptiles, dead bodies, menses, and other excretions, birds of prey that eat dead bodies, eels, octopus, insects and the like. These are primary sources of impurity and the concept was extended to other objects by analogy and pseudosystematic reasoning." For a complete analysis of the issue see J. Neusner, *The Idea of Purity in Ancient Judaism* (Leiden and New York: Brill, 1973), p. 12.

86. Yadin, *Finds*, p. 115.

87. *The Documents from the Bar Kokhba Period in the Cave of Letters*, ed. Y. Yadin, J. C. Greenfield, A. Yardeni, Baruch Levine, with additional contributions by H. M. Cotton and Joseph Naveh (Jerusalem: Israel Exploration Society, 2002). H. M. Cotton and A. Yardeni, *Aramaic, Hebrew and Greek Documentary Texts from Nahal Hever*, vol. 27, *Discoveries in the Judean Desert* (Oxford: Clarendon Press, 1997). W. Bouzard, "The Psalms Manuscript from the Cave of Letters," in *Dead Sea Discoveries*, vol. 2 (Leiden and New York: Brill, 2004).

88. Nahal Tzeelim, located some five kilometers from Masada, had one part that was in Israel and another part that was not.

89. Lefkovits, *The Copper Scroll (3Q15)*, p. 481. Although it conventionally understood from 1960 onward that the *kk* in the text was to be derived from the word *Kikar* ( = talent of between 21.3–150 kg), herein lay the main problem of the Copper Scroll and one of the reasons why mythic status had been attached to the text: The treasure was thought to be so great. He suggests that the *kk* is in fact *Kesef Karsh* (*Kesef* = money or coinage and not necessarily silver), with *Karsh* being an ancient coinage equal to the weight of ten shekels. Lefkovits suggests that the *kk* is in fact *Kesef Karsh* (*Kesef* = money or coinage and not necessarily silver), with *Karsh* being an ancient coinage equal to the weight of ten shekels. A shekel of this period was thought to be the

Tyrian tetradrachma (at 14.1666 grams to nearly 26 grams depending on the period. For more on this see "Weights and Measures," in *Anchor Bible Dictionary*, ed. D. N. Freedman (New York: Doubleday, 1997), 6:907.

90. Lefkovits, *The Copper Scroll (3Q15)*, p. 488.

91. Ibid., p. 9. From ninety-one tons of precious metals it becomes less than two tons of precious metals.

92. Ibid., p. 471n2.

93. While it is possible that the Bar Kokhba movement cave dwellers buried the bronze artifacts in an attempt to "purify" them, they still would have had to be melted down for possible reuse. There is a Mishnah in Maaser Sheni 5.7 which states that after the destruction of the Temple, metal (coinage) as a replacement for the second tithe which one needed to be dedicated in Temple times (food to be consumed in Jerusalem) could be buried until it was to be used for Temple purposes.

94. The most recent review is D. H. K. Amiran, E. Arieh, and T. Turcotte, "Earthquakes in Israel and Adjacent Areas: Macroseismic Observations since 100 B.C.E.," *Israel Exploration Journal* 44, nos. 3–4 (1994): 260. The original article by D. H. K. Amiran is "A Revised Earthquake Catalogue of Palestine," *Israel Exploration Journal* 1 (1950–1951), p. 225. Also, E. Netzer, ed., "Greater Herodium," in *Qedem*, vol. 13 (Jerusalem: Israel Exploration Society, 1981), pp. 28, 134n22.

95. B. Safrai, "More Scrolls Lie Buried," *Biblical Archaeology Review* 19, no. 1 (January/February, 1993): 50–57.

96. The possibility of a third location in the far end of BB passage also exists, especially if the discovery took place December 12. In the back of the BB passage (before the High Room) there is in fact an area under which one could go. In this area, on July 19, 2000, we located in Locus 31 an entire tunic with part of the belt still intact.

97. B. Rothenberg and Y. Aharoni, *In the Footsteps of Kings and Rebels* [Hebrew] (Tel Aviv: Massadah, 1960), p. 131.

98. RTT 3726-1.2 = bone (locus 22/Safrai #2) calibrated C-14 date 50–340 CE.

99. Yadin, *Bar Kokhba*, pp. 64–65.

100. Yadin, *Finds*, p. 32. Nicolae Roddy, "The Burial Niche of the Cave of Letters," paper delivered at the Society of Biblical Literature International Meeting, Pontifical Biblical Institute and Gregorian Institute, Rome, Italy, July 8–12, 2001; Nicolae Roddy, "The Burials in the Caves of Israel," paper delivered at the Fourth Annual Batchelder Biblical Archaeology Conference at the University of Nebraska at Omaha, Omaha, NE, October 24–26, 2002.

101. Ibid., p. 31.

102. Ibid.

103. Ibid., p. 32.

104. The Babatha Documents are in *Documents from the Bar Kokhba Period I the Cave of Letters, Greek Papyri*, ed. N. Lewis (Jerusalem: Israel Exploration Society, 1989). Also, Hannah Cotton and Ada Yardeni have published all of the texts in the aforementioned texts: see *The Documents from the Bar Kokhba Period in the Cave of Letters*, ed. Y. Yadin et al. (Jerusalem: Israel Exploration Society, 2002). H. M. Cotton and A. Yardeni, *Aramaic, Hebrew, and Greek Documentary Texts from Nahal Hever*, vol. 27, *Discoveries in the Judean Desert* (Oxford: Clarendon Press, 1997).

105. Idumea is a territory in the south of Israel to the north of the Negev.

106. Lewis, *Documents*, p. 71.

107. Yadin, *Bar Kokhba*, p. 128.

108. Another Greek document from the Cave of Letters, a marriage contract for a woman from Maoza and a man from a village near Livias states: "feeding and clothing both her and the children to come in accordance with Greek custom and Greek manners." Lewis, *Documents*, p. 131.

109. H. Eshel, *New Studies on the Bar Kokhba Revolt*, ed. H. Eshel and B. Zissu (Ramat Gan: Bar Ilan University, 2001), p. 105.

110. Y. Hirschfeld, "Spirituality in the Desert," *Biblical Archaeology Review* 21, no. 5 (September/October 1995): 29 with a photograph on p. 33 eerily mindful of how the scene compares to the Cave of Letters.

111. Y. Meshorer, *Ancient Jewish Coinage*, vol. 2, *Herod through the Bar Kokhba Rebellion* (New York: Amphora Books, 1982); Y. Meshorer, "The Coins of Masada," in *Masada*, vol. 1 (Jerusalem: Israel Exploration Society, 1989), p. 102.

112. W. Wruck, *Die Syrische Provinzialpragung von Augustus bis Trajan* (Stuttgart, 1931), pl. 187, no. 83.

113. A. Kindler, "Bar Kokhba Coins" in *The Bar Kokhba Revolt*, ed. A. Oppenheimer (Jerusalem: Zalman Shazar Center, 1980), pp. 165–74; also, *Yidiyot Archaeologiot* 27: 1–93; *Ein Gedi: Archaeological Excavations of 1961–62* (Jerusalem: Israel Exploration Society, 1963).

114. Our thanks for identifications and information to Arieh Kindler. For more information see A. Kindler, *New Studies on the Bar Kokhba Revolt*, ed. H. Eshel and B. Zissu (Ramat Gan: Bar Ilan University, 2001), p. 11.

115. Most recently: R. Hachlili, *The Menorah, the Ancient Seven-armed Candelabrum: Origin, Form and Significance* (Leiden and New York: Brill, 2001), pp. 46 ff.

116. P. Flint, "Biblical Scrolls from Nahal Hever and 'Wadi Seiyal': Introduction," *Miscellaneous Texts from the Judean Desert*, vol. 38, *Discoveries in the Judean Desert* (Oxford: Clarendon Press, 2000) p. 133, dating is on p. 143.

117. A. J. Timothy Jull et al., "Rabdiocarbon Dating of Scrolls and Linen Fragments from the Judean Desert," *Atiqot* (Israel Antiquities Authority, Jerusalem) 28 (1996): 64.

118. G. Bonani et al., "Radiocarbon Dating of the Dead Sea Scrolls," *Atiqot* 20 (1991): 28.

119. F. E. Zeuner, "Notes on Qumran," *Palestine Exploration Quarterly* 92 (1960): 27–28.

120. Magen Broshi, "The New Radiocarbon Dates of the Dead Sea Scrolls and Their Significance," in *The Practical Impact of Science*, ed. S. Pike and S. Gitin (London: Archetype Press, 1999), p. 108.

121. The dates before present (the established date is from the time that C-14 testing began or 1950 CE) are corrected by a number of factors. These are the calibrated dates according to the lab.

122. Lamentations Rabbah, 1.5, a rabbinic Midrash that is interpreting the reported cannibalism in the time of the destruction of the First Temple, relates it directly to the situation present in the time of the Bar Kokhba rebellion. Based upon the words of Lamentations 1.16, paragraph 45, we learn that cannibalism may have existed in the caves. Its setting is particularly chilling given the existence of the "Niche of Skulls" in the Cave of Letters: "Hadrian put up three guards, one at Emmaus, one at Kefr Lekatia, and one at Beth el of Judah. He said 'He who will escape from here will be caught from here, and vice versa.' He would put out the call and say that 'wherever a Jew comes forth, the king wishes to give him an assurance [of safety].' The heralds proclaimed this to them and so captured the Jews. Those who understood [the ruse] did not come out [from their hiding places], but those who did not understand it all gathered in the valley of Beth Rimmon.

"Those Jews who were hidden [in the caves] devoured the flesh of their slain brethren. Every day one of them ventured forth and brought the corpses to them which they ate. One day they said, 'Let one of us go, and if he finds anything let him bring it and we will have something to eat.' On going out he found the slain body of his father which he took and buried and marked the spot. He returned and reported that he had found nothing. They said, 'Let someone else go, and if he find anything let him bring it and we will have something to eat.' When he went out he followed the scent; and on making a search discovered the body [of the man who had been buried]. He brought it to them and they ate it. After they had eaten it, they asked him,

'From whence did you bring this corpse?' He replied, 'From a certain corner.' They then asked, 'What distinguishing mark was over it?' He told them what it was, and the son exclaimed, 'Woe to me! I have eaten the flesh of my father!' This is to fulfil what was said: 'Therefore the fathers shall eat the sons in the midst of you, and the sons will eat their fathers'" (as quoted from the First Temple period episode of Ezekiel 5.10).

# Select Bibliography

Aharoni, Y. "The Archaeological Survey of Masada, 1955–1956." Edited by M. Avi-Yonah, N. Avigad, Y. Aharoni, I. Dunayevsky, and S. Gutman. *Israel Exploration Journal* 7, no. 1 (1957): 1–60.

Allegro, J. M. *The Chosen People: A Study of Jewish History from the Time of the Exile until the Revolt of Bar Kocheba (Sixth Century B.C. to Second Century A.D.).* Garden City, NY: Doubleday, 1972.

———. *The Dead Sea Scrolls: A Reappraisal.* 2d ed. Harmondsworth, England: Penguin, 1977.

———. *The Dead Sea Scrolls and the Christian Myth.* London: Westbridge Books, 1979.

———. *Search in the Desert.* London: W. H. Allen, 1965.

———. *The Treasury of the Copper Scroll: The Opening and Decipherment of the Most Mysterious of the Dead Sea Scrolls, A Unique Inventory of Buried Treasure.* Garden City, NY: Doubleday, 1960.

———. *The Treasury of the Copper Scroll: The Opening and Decipherment of the Most Mysterious of the Dead Sea Scrolls, A Unique Inventory of Buried Treasure.* 2d rev. ed. New York: Doubleday, 1964.

———. "An Unpublished Fragment of Essene Halakha (4Q Ordinances)." *Journal of Semitic Studies* 6 (1961): 71–73, photograph.

Applebaum, S. "The Second Jewish Revolt." *Palestine Exploration Quarterly* 116 (1984): 35–41.

Arav, R., and R. Freund. *Bethsaida: A City by the North Shore of the Sea of Galilee, Bethsaida Excavations Project Reports and Studies, Volume I*. Kirksville, MO: Thomas Jefferson University Press, 1995.

———. *Bethsaida: A City by the North Shore of the Sea of Galilee, Bethsaida Excavations Project Reports and Studies, Volume II*. Kirksville, MO: Truman State University Press, 1999.

———. *A City by the North Shore of the Sea of Galilee, Bethsaida Excavations Project Reports and Studies, Volume III*. Kirksville, MO: Truman State University Press, 2004.

Bauckham, R. J. "Jews and Jewish Christians in the Land of Israel at the Time of the Bar Kokhba War, with Special Reference to the Apocalypse of Peter." In *Tolerance and Intolerance in Early Judaism and Christianity*, edited by G. N. Stanton and G. G. Stroumsa, 38–60. Cambridge: Cambridge University Press, 1998.

———. "The Apocalypse of Peter: A Jewish Christian Apocalypse from the Time of Bar Kokhba." In *The Fate of the Dead*, edited by R. C. Bauckman, 169–58. Studies on the Jewish and Christian Apocalypses, Leiden and New York: Brill, 1998. Originally published in *Apocrypha 5* (1994): 7–111.

Bergler, S. "Jesus, Bar Kochba und das messianische Laubhuttenfest." *Journal for the Study of Judaism in the Persian, Hellenistic, and Roman Period* 29 (1998): 143–91.

Bouzard, Walter C. "The Date of the Psalms Scroll from the Cave of Letters (5/6 HevPs) Reconsidered." *Dead Sea Discoveries* 10, no. 3 (2003): 319–37.

Charlesworth, J. H. *Jesus and the Dead Sea Scrolls*. Anchor Bible Reference Library. New York: Doubleday, 1992.

———. "Reinterpreting John. How the Dead Sea Scrolls Revolutionized Our Understanding of the Gospel of John." *Bible Review* 9 (1993): 19–25, 54.

Cohen, S. J. D. *From the Maccabees to the Mishnah*. Philadelphia: Westminster, 1987.

Cotton, H. M. "The Archive of Salome Komaise Daughter of Levi: Another Archive from the 'Cave of Letters.'" *Zeitschrift für Papyrologie und Epigraphik* 105 (1995): 171–208.

———. "A Cancelled Marriage Contract from the Judaean Desert." *Journal of Roman Studies* 84 (1994): 64–86.

———. "Courtyard(s) in Ein-Gedi: O, Tadub 11, 19, and 20 of the Babatha Archive." *Zeitschrift für Papyrologie und Epigraphik* 112 (1996): 197–201.

———. "Greek Documentary Texts." In *Aramaic, Hebrew, and Greek Documentary Texts from Nahal Hever and Other Sites*, edited by H. M. Cotton and A. Yardeni, 133–279. Oxford: Clarendon Press, 1997.

———. "The Guardianship of Jesus, Son of Babatha: Roman and Local Law in the Province of Arabia." *Journal of Roman Studies* 83 (1993): 94–108.

———. "The Impact of the Documentary Papyri from the Judean Desert on the Study of the Jewish History from 70 to 135 CE." In *Judische Geschichte in hellenistisch-romischer Zeit*, edited by A. Oppenheimer, 221–36. Wege der Forchung: von alten zum neuen Schurer, Munich, 1999.

———. "Land Tenure in the Documents from the Nabataean Kingdon and the Roman Province of Arabia." *Zeitschrift für Papyrologie und Epigraphik* 119: 255–65.

———. "The Language of the Legal and Administrative Documents from the Judean Desert." *Zeitschrift für Papyrologie und Epigraphik* 125: 199, 219–31.

———. "The Rabbis and the Documents." In *Jews in a Graeco-Roman World*, edited by M. Goodman, 167–79. Oxford: Oxford University Press, 1998.

Cotton, H. M., and J. C. Greenfield. "Babatha's Property and the Law of Succession in the Babatha Archive." *Zeitschrift für Papyrologie und Epigraphik* 104: 211–24.

Cross, F. M., Jr. *The Ancient Library of Qumran and Modern Biblical Studies: The Haskell Lecture*, 3d ed. Minneapolis: Fortress, 1995.

———. "Excursus on the Palaeographical Dating of the Copper Document." In *Discoveries in the Judean Desert Discoveries in the Judean Desert of Jordan—III, Les 'Petites Grottes' de Qumran*, edited by M. Bailet, J. T. Milik, R deVaux, with H. W. Baker, 217–21. Oxford: Clarendon, 1962.

———. "The Manuscripts of the Dead Sea Caves." *Biblical Archaeologist* 17 (1954): 2–21 (the first page has a photograph of the two copper rolls in situ).

de Vaux, R. *Archaeology and the Dead Sea Scrolls: The Schweich Lectures of the British Academy*. Oxford: Oxford University Press, 1973.

———. *Discoveries in the Judean Desert II, Les Grottes de Murabba'at*, by P. Benoit, J. T. Milik, R. deVaux, with G. M. Crowfoot and E. Crowfoot. Oxford: Clarendon, 1961.

———. *Discoveries in the Judean Desert of Jordan—III, Les 'Petites Grottes' de Qumran*, by M. Bailet, J. T. Milik, R. deVaux, with H. W. Baker. Oxford: Clarendon, 1962.

———. "Exploration de la region de Qumran (Les Rouleaux de Cuivre)." *Revue Biblique* (Paris) 60 (1953): 557–58.

———. "Manuscrits de Qumran (Le tesor du Rouleau de Cuivre, J. M. Allegro)." *Revue Biblique* (Paris) 68 (1961): 146–47.

———. Preface and introduction to *Discoveries in the Judean Desert III*, edited by M. Bailet, J. T. Milik, R. deVaux, with H. W. Baker, 200–202. Oxford: Clarendon, 1962.

Eck, W. "The Bar Kokhba Revolt: The Roman Point of View." *Journal of Roman Studies* 89 (1999): 76–89.

Eliav, Y. Z. "Hadrian's Actions in the Jerusalem Temple Mount According to Cassius Dio and Xiphilini Manus." *Jewish Studies Quarterly* 4 (1997): 125–44.

Fitzmyer, J. A. *The Dead Sea Scrolls: Major Publications and Tools for Study, with an "Addendum."* Sources for Biblical Study 8. Missoula, MT: Society of Biblical Literature—Scholars Press, 1977 (The Copper Plaque Mentioning Buried Treasure [3Qtreasure, 3Q15]; 1st ed., 1975).

Flint, Peter W. "5/6HevNumbers" and "5/6HevPsalms." In *Miscellaneous Texts from the Judaean Desert*, edited by James R. Charlesworth et al., 137–66. Oxford: Clarendon Press, 2000.

Freund, R. "Jewish-Christian Sects and the Jewish-Christian Debate in the First Four Centuries of the Common Era." In *Jewish Sects, Religious Movements, and Political Parties*, edited by M. Mor, 53–100. Omaha: Creighton University Press, 1993.

———. "Alexander Macedon and Antoninus: Two Greco-Roman Heroes of the Rabbis." In *Jewish Heroes*, edited by M. Mor, 60–100. Omaha: Creighton University Press, 1995.

———. "And the Land Bled Forth Its Produce: Biblical Criticism and Exilic Biblical Images." *Scandinavian Journal of the Old Testament* 13, no. 2 (Fall 1999): 284–97.

———. "The Apocalypse of Rabbi Aqiva." In *Studies in Jewish Civilization*, vol. 12, *Millennialism from the Hebrew Bible to the Present*, edited by Leonard J. Greenspoon and Ronald A. Simkins, 150–65. Omaha: Creighton University Press, 2002.

———. "The Decalogue in Early Judaism and Christianity." In *The Function of Scripture in Early Jewish and Christian Tradition*, edited by Craig A. Evans and James A. Sanders, 126–43. Sheffield: Sheffield Academic Press, 1998.

———. "The Ethics of Abortion in Jewish Hellenism." *Helios* (New Series) 10, no. 2 (Fall 1983): 125–38.

———. "From Kings to Archons." *Scandinavian Journal of the Old Testament* (Summer 1990): 58–72.

———. "Individual vs. Collective Responsibilty: From the Ancient Near

East and the Bible to the Greco-Roman World." *Scandinavian Journal of the Old Testament* 11, no. 2 (Fall 1997): 279–304.

———. "'*Kata Phusin*—According to Nature':The Hellenistic Jewish Bio-Medical Ethics Argument." *Shofar* 7, no. 1 (Fall 1988): 36–48.

———. "Murder, Adultery, and Theft?" *Scandinavian Journal of the Old Testament* (Summer 1989): 72–80.

———. "The Mystery of the Menorah and the Star." In *Nationalism, Zionism, and Ethnic Mobilization of the Jews in 1900 and Beyond*, edited by M. Berkowitz, 125–47. Leiden and New York: Brill, 2004.

———. "The Myth of Jesus in Rabbinic Literature." In *The Seductiveness of Jewish Myth: Challenge or Response*, edited by D. Breslauer, 185–209. Albany: State University of New York Press, 1997.

———. "Naming Names: Some Observations on Anonymous Women Traditions in the Masoretic Text, the Septuagint, and Hellenistic Literature." *Scandinavian Journal of the Old Testament* (Fall 1992): 213–32.

———. "A New Interpretation of the Incense Shovels of the Cave of the Letters." In *The Dead Sea Scrolls: Fifty Years after Their Discovery, 1947–1997, Proceedings of the Jerusalem Congress, July 20–25, 1997*, edited by L. H. Schiffman, E. Tov, and J. C. VanderKam, 644–60. Jerusalem: Israel Exploration Society in cooperation with the Shrine of the Book, Israel Museum, 2000.

———. "Pope Receives Bethsaida Key." *Biblical Archaeology Review* 26, no. 3 (May/June 2000): 60.

———. "Recovering Antiquity: The Convergence of Ancient Literatures and Archaeology in the Search for the Lost City of Bethsaida." In *The Solomon Goldman Lectures*, vol. 7, edited by D. P. Bell, 1–46. Chicago: Spertus Institute of Jewish Studies Press, 1999.

———. "Universal Human Rights in Biblical and Classical Judaism?" *Shofar* 12, no. 2 (Winter 1994): 50–66.

———. "Which Christians, Pagans, and Jews? Varying Responses to Julian's Attempt to Rebuild the Temple in Jerusalem in the Fourth Century CE." *Journal of Religious Studies* 18, no. 2 (Fall 1992): 65–87.

Freund, R., and R. Arav. "The Bethsaida Stele and City Gate Altar." *Biblical Archaeology Review* 24, no. 1 (January/February 1998): 34.

———. "An Incense Shovel from Bethsaida." *Biblical Archaeology Review* 23, no. 1 (January/February 1997): 32.

———. "Return to the Cave of Letters." *Biblical Archaeology Review* 27, no. 1 (2001): 54 ff.

Freund, R., H. M. Jol, J. F. Shroder Jr., and P. Reeder. "A GPR Archaeological Expedition at the Cave of Letters, Israel: An Eighth International Conference on Ground Penetrating Radar," edited by D. A. Noon, G. F. Stickley, and D. Longstaff. *SPIE* 4084 (2001): 882–86.

Freund, R., J. F. Schroder Jr., and R. Arav. "Bethsaida Rediscovered!" *Biblical Archaeology Review* 26, no. 1 (January/February 2000): 44 ff.

Goodenough, E. R. *Jewish Symbols in the Greco-Roman Period.* 13 vols. New York: Pantheon, 1953–1968.

———. "The Menorah among Jews of the Roman World." *Hebrew Union College Annual* 23 (1950–51): 449–92.

Goodman, M. "Babatha's Story." *Journal of Roman Studies* 81 (1991): 169–75.

Hachlili, R. *Ancient Jewish Art and Archaeology in the Land of Israel.* Leiden and New York: Brill, 1988.

———, ed. *Ancient Synagogues in Israel. Third–Seventh Century CE.* BAR International Series 499. Oxford: Oxford University Press, 1989.

———. "The Niche and Ark in Ancient Synagogues." *Bulletin of the American Schools of Oriental Research* 223 (1976): 45–53.

———. "The Zodiac in Ancient Jewish Art: Representation and Significance." *Bulletin of the American Schools of Oriental Research* 228 (1977): 61–77.

Harkabi, Y. *Bar Kokhba Syndrome, Risk and Realism in International Politics.* Chappaqua, NY: Rossel Books 1983.

Isaac, B. "Cassius Dio on the Revolt of Bar Kokhba." In *The Near East under Roman Rule, Selected Papers,* 211–19. Originally published in *Scripta Classica Israelica* 7 (1983/84): 68–76.

———. "Judaea after 70." In *The Near East under Roman Rule: Selected Papers,* 112–21. Originally published in *Journal of Jewish Studies* 35 (1984): 44–50.

———. "Judea in the Early Years of Hadrian's Reign." In *The Near East under Roman Rule: Selected Papers,* 182–97. Originally published in *Latomus* 28 (1979): 54–66.

———, ed. *The Near East under Roman Rule: Selected Papers.* Leiden and New York: Brill, 1998.

———. "Roman Colonis in Judaea, the Foundation of Aelia Capitolina."

Isaac, B., and A. Oppenheimer. "The Revolt of Bar Kokhba: Ideology and Modern Scholarship." In *The Near East under Roman Rule: Selected Papers,* 200–56. Originally published in *Journal of Jewish Studies* 36 (1985): 33–60.

Jol, H. M., M. Broshi, H. Eshel, R. A. Freund, J. F. Shroder Jr., P. Reeder, and R. Dubay. "GPR Investigations at Qumran, Israel: Site of the Dead

Sea Scrolls Discovery. Ninth International Conference on Ground Penetrating Radar," edited by S. K. Koppenjan and H. Lee, April 29–May 2, Santa Barbara, California. *Proceedings of SPIE* 4758 (2002): 91–95.

Kon, M. "The Menorah of the Arch of Titus." *PEW* 82 (1950): 25–30.

Laperrousaz, E-M. "L'etabblissement de Qoumran pres de la mer Morte: forteresse ou couvent? (avec evocation du 'Rouleau de cuivre,' 3Q15)." *EL* 20 (1989): 118–23.

———. "Methodologie et datation des manuscrits de lay Mer Morte: Le Rouleau du cuivre, 3Q15." *New Qumran Text und Studies: Proceedings of the First Meeting of the International Organization for Qumran Studies, Paris, 1992. Vol. 15. Studies on the Texts of the Desert of Judah*, edited by George J. Brooke and Florentino Garcia Martinez, 233–39. Leiden and New York: Brill, 1994.

———. *Qoumran, L'etablissment essenien des bords de la Mer Morte. Histoire et archeologie du suite*. Paris: Picard, 1976.

Lehmann, M. *Essays and Journeys* (Hebrew). Jerusalem: Mossad Harav Kook, 1982.

———. "Identification of the Copper Scroll Based on Its Technical Terms." *Revue de Qumran* (1964): 97–105.

———. "A New Interpretation of the Term 'Shadmoth.'" *VT* 3 (1953): 361–71.

———. "Where the Temple Tax Was Buried: The Key to Understanding the Copper Scroll." *Biblical Archaeology Review* 19 (1993): 38–43.

Levine, Baruch Abraham. "Jews and Nabateans in the Nahal Hever Archive." In *The Dead Sea Scrolls: Fifty Years after Their Discovery*, 836–51.

Lewis, Naphtali. *The Documents from the Bar Kokhba Period in the Cave of Letters—Greek Papyri*. Vol. 2. *Judean Desert Studies*. Jerusalem: Israel Exploration Society, Hebrew University of Jerusalem, Shrine of the Book, 1989.

Lieberman, Saul. "The Importance of the Bar-Kokhba Letters for Jewish History and Literature." In *Texts and Studies*, 208–209. New York: Ktav, 1974.

Marks, R. G. "Dangerous Hero: Rabbinic Attitudes toward Legendary Warriors." *Hebrew Union College Annual* 54 (1983): 181–94.

McCarter, P. K., Jr. "The Copper Scroll Treasure as an Accumulation of Religious Offerings." *Methods of Investigation of the Dead Sea Scrolls and the Khirbet Qumran Site: Present Realities and Future Prospects*, edited by Michael Owen Wise, Norman Golb, John J. Collins, and Dennis G. Pardee. *Annals of the New York Academy of Sciences* 722 (1994): 133–48.

―――. "The Mysterious Copper Scroll: Clues to Hidden Temple Treasure?" *Bible Review* 8 (1992): 34–41, 63–64.

―――. "The Mystery of the Copper Scroll." In *Understanding the Dead Sea Scrolls: A Reader from the Biblical Archaeology Review*, edited by Hershel Shanks, 227–41, 309. New York: Random House, 1992.

―――. *Nabataean Coins.* Vol. 3. *Qedem.* Jerusalem: Institute of Archeology, Hebrew University of Jerusalem, 1975. Distributed by the Israel Exploration Society.

Meshorer, Y. "A Coin Hoard of the Bar-Kokhba's Time." *Israel Museum News* 4 (1985): 43–50.

Mildenberg, L. "The Bar Kokhba War in the Light of the Coins and Documents Finds 1947–1982." *Israel Numismatic Journal* 8 (1984–85): 27–32.

―――. *The Coinage of the Bar Kokhba War,* Typos 6. Aarau, Frankfurt a.M., Salzburg: Sauerlander, 1984.

―――. "Rebel Coinage in the Roman Empire." In *Greece and Rome in Eretz Israel, Collected Essays*, edited by A. Kasher, U. Rappaport, and G. Fuks, 62–74. Jerusalem: Yad Izhak Ben-Zvi, 1990.

Mor, M. "The Bar-Kokhba Revolt and Non-Jewish Participants." *Journal of Jewish Studies* 36 (1985): 200–209.

―――. "The Samaritans and the Bar-Kokhba Revolt." In *The Samaritans*, edited by A. D. Crown, 19–31. Tubingen: Mohr, 1989.

Pixner, B. "Copper Scroll (3Q15)." *Anchor Bible Dictionary*, vol. 1, edited by David Noel Freedman, 1133a–34a. New York: Doubleday, 1992.

―――. "Das Essenquartier in Jerusalem und dessen Einfluss auf die Urkirche." *Das herilige Land* 113 (1981): 3–14.

―――. "An Essene Quarter on Mount Zion?" In *Studia Hierosolymitana, Part 1: Archaelogical Studies*, 245–84. Collectio Maior 22. Studium Biblicum Franciscanum, Jerusalem: Franciscan Printing, 1976.

―――. "Unravelling the Copper Scroll Code: A Study of the Topography of 3Q15." *Revue de Qumran* (1983): 323–61, plans i–iv.

Rabello, A. M. "The Ban on Circumcision as a Cause of the Bar Kokhba's Rebellion." *Israel Law Review* 29 (1955): 176–214.

Reinhartz, A. "Rabbinic Perceptions of Simeon Bar Kosiba." *Journal for the Study of Judaism in the Persian, Hellenistic, and Roman Period* 20 (1985): 171–94.

Schäfer, P. "Bar Kokhba Revolt and Circumcision: Historical Evidence and Modern Apologetics." In *Judische Geschichte in hellenistisch-romischer Zeit*, edited by A. Oppenheimer, 119–32. Wege der Forschung: von alten zum neuen Schurer, 1999.

Schechter, S. *Fragments of a Zadokite Work.* Documents of Jewish Sectaries 1.

From Hebrew Manuscript in the Cairo Genizah Collection, University Library, Cambridge, and with an English translation, introduction, and notes. Edited by Joseph A. Fitzmyer. New York: Ktav, 1970.

Schwartz, D. R. "On Barnabas and Bar-Kokhba." *Studies in the Jewish Background of Christianity*, 147–53. Tubingen: Mohr, 1992.

Sperber, D. "Between Jerusalem and Rome: The History of the Base of the Menorah as Depicted on the Arch of Titus." In *In the Light of the Menorah, Story of a Symbol*, edited by Y. Israeli, 50–53. Israel Museum Catalogue, no. 425. Jerusalem: Israeli Museum, 1969.

———. "The History of the Menorah." *Journal of Jewish Studies* 16 (1965): 135–39.

Wirgin, W. "The Menorah as Symbol of Afterlife." *Israel Exploration Journal* (Jerusalem) 14: 102–104.

———. "The Menorah as Symbol of Judaism." *Israel Exploration Journal* (Jerusalem) 12 (1962): 140–42.

———. "On the Shape of the Foot of the Menorah." *Israel Exploration Journal* (Jerusalem) 7 (1961): 151–53.

Wolters, Albert M. "Apocalyptic and the Copper Scroll." *Journal of Near Eastern Studies* 49 (1990): 145–54.

———. "The Copper Scroll." In *The Dead Sea Scrolls after Fifty Years: A Comprehensive Assessment*, vol. 1, edited by Peter W. Flint and James C. VanderKam, 302–23. Leiden and New York: Brill, 1998.

———. *The Copper Scroll: Overview, Text, and Translation*. Sheffield: Sheffield Academic Press, 1996.

———. "The *Copper Scroll* and the Vocabulary of Mishnaic Hebrew." *Revue de Qumran* 14 (1990): 483–95.

———. "The Fifth Cache of the Copper Scroll: 'The Plastered Cistern of Manos.'" *Revue de Qumran* 13 (1988): 167–76.

———. "History and the Copper Scroll." *Annals of the New York Academy of Sciences* 722 (1994): 285–98.

———. "The Last Treasure of the Copper Scroll." *Journal of Biblical Literature* 107 (1988): 419–29.

———. "Literary Analysis and the Copper Scroll." In *Interestamental Essays in Honour of Jozef Tadeusz Milik*, edited by J. Zdislaw, 239–52. Kapera, Krakow: Enigma, 1992.

———. "Notes on the Copper Scroll (3Q15)." *Revue de Qumran* 12 (1987): 589–96.

———. "The Shekinah in the Copper Scroll; A New Reading of 3Q15 12.10." In *The Scrolls and the Scriptures: Quman Fifty Years After*, edited by Stanley

E. Porter and Craig A. Evans, 382–92. *Journal for the Study of the Pseude-pigrapha*, Supplement Series 26. London: Roehampton Institute, 1997.

Yadin, Y. *Bar Kokhba*. London: Weidenfeld and Nicholson, 1971.

———. "Expedition D." *Israel Exploration Journal* (Jerusalem) 11 (1961): 36–52.

———. "Expedition D—The Cave of the Letters." *Israel Exploration Journal* (Jerusalem) 12 (1962): 227–57.

———.*The Finds from the Bar Kokhba Period in the Cave of Letters*. Vol. 1. *Judean Desert Studies*. Jerusalem: Israel Exploration Society, 1963.

Yadin, Y., and J. C. Greenfield. "Aramaic and Nabatean Signatures and Sub-scriptions." In *The Documents from the Bar Kokhba Period in the Cave of Letters—Greek Papyri*, by Naphtali Lewis, 135–49. Vol. 2. *Judean Desert Studies*. Jerusalem: Israel Exploration Society, Hebrew University of Jerusalem, Shrine of the Book, 1989.

Yadin, Y., J. C. Greenfield, and A. Yardeni. "Babatha's Ketubba." *Israel Exploration Journal* (Jerusalem) 44 (1994): 75–101.

———. "A Deed of Gift in Aramaic Found in Hahal Hever: Papyrus Yadin 7" (Hebrew). In *Yosef Aviram Volume*, edited by David Ussishkin et al., 383–403. Jerusalem: Israel Exploration Society, 1996.

Yadin, Y., and J. Naveh. *Masada: The Yigael Yadin Excavations, 1963–1965: Final Reports. Volume 1: The Aramaic and Hebrew Ostraca and Jar Inscriptions*. Jerusalem: Israel Exploration Society, 1989.

Yarden, L. *The Spoils of Jerusalem on the Arch of Titus: A Re-investigation*. Stockholm: Svenska Institutet i Rom, 1991.

———. *The Tree of Light: A Study of the Menorah*. London: East and West Library, 1971.

Yardeni, A. *The Book of Hebrew Script: History, Paleography, Script Styles. Calligraphy and Design*. Jerusalem: Carta, 1991.

———. "The Decipherment and Restoration of Legal Texts from the Judaean Desert: A Reexamination of *Papyrus Starcky* (P. Yadin 36)." *Scripta Classica Israelica* 20 (2001): 121–37.

———. "A Deed of Sale from the Judaean Desert: Nahal-Se'elim 9" (Hebrew). *Tarbiz* 63 (1994): 299–320.

———. *The Nahal Se'elim Document*. Beer-Sheva: Ben Gurion University of the Negev Press; Jerusalem: Israel Exploration Society, 1995.

———. "Notes on Two Unpublished Nabataean Deeds from Nahal Hever." In *The Dead Sea Scrolls: Fifty Years after Their Discovery*, 862–74.

———. *Textbook of Aramaic, Hebrew, and Nabataean Texts for the Judaean Desert* (Hebrew). Jerusalem: Hebrew University, Ben-Zion Dinur Center for Research in Jewish History, 2000.

———. "Two Being One? A Deed of Sale from Wadi Murabbat'at" (Hebrew). In *Frank Moore Cross Volume*, edited by B. Levine, P. King, J. Naveh, and E. Stern, 64–70. Jerusalem: Israel Exploration Society, 1999.

Yardeni, A., and J. C. Greenfield. "A Receipt for a Ketubba: Nahal Se'elim 13" (Hebrew). In *The Jews in the Hellenistic-Roman World: Studies in Memory of Menahem Stern*, edited by Isaiah M. Gafni, Aharon Oppenheimer, and Daniel R. Schwartz, 197–208. Jerusalem: Zalman Shazar Center for Jewish History, Historical Society of Israel, 1996.

Zeitlin, Solomon. "The Dead Sea Scrolls: 1. The Lamech Scroll—A Medieval Midrash. 2. The Copper Scrolls. 3. Was Kando the Owner of the Scrolls?" *Jewish Quarterly Review* (New Series) 47 (1956/57): 245–68.

# Index

273